Understanding
Michigan
Black Bear

Understanding Michigan Black Bear

2nd Edition

The Truth About
Bears and Bear Hunting

Richard P. Smith

Smith Publications

Understanding
Michigan Black Bear
2nd Edition
The Truth about Bears and Bear Hunting

by Richard P. Smith

Published by:
> **Smith Publications**
> Lucy & Richard Smith
> 814 Clark St.
> Marquette, MI 49855

Copyright © 1999 by Richard P. Smith
Second Edition
First Printing 1999
Printed in the United States of America

All photos by the author unless otherwise credited
Cover photo by Richard P. Smith
Cover design by Robert Howard
Book production, research & design by Lucy Smith
Interior layout by Sans Serif, Inc., Saline, MI

Library of Congress Cataloging in Publication Data
Smith, Richard P.
Understanding Michigan Black Bear: The Truth about Bears and Bear Hunting / by Richard P. Smith.—2nd ed.
Bears and Bear hunting—Michigan
QL737.C27 S6 1999   599.74′446Sm
ISBN 0-9617407-9-5 Softcover

For Terry DeBruyn
who is the Bear Biologist
I would have liked to have been!

Contents

Acknowledgments

First and foremost, I want to thank those people who were/are interested in banning bear hunting in Michigan for the encouragement and motivation to write this book. Without their help, this book probably would not have been published. The list includes Jim and Beverly Rogers, founders of SPORT; Matt Reid, Marty Williams and Charles Jonkel with the Montana based Great Bear Foundation; Heidi Prescott, National Director for The Fund For Animals, which is based in New York City; Gary Tiscornia, Executive Director of the Michigan Humane Society and Tom Beck with the Colorado Fish and Game Department's Wildlife Division.

I'm even more grateful to the DNR wildlife biologists and researchers who have allowed me to spend time with them in the field, answered my many questions, responded to requests for information about bears and bear hunting and have been helpful in other ways. The list includes Larry Visser, Elaine Carlson, Tim Reis, George Burgoyne, John Hendrickson, Jim Hammill, Doug Wagner, Mike Koss, Rob Aho, Richard Shellenbarger, John Ozoga, Bob Doepker, Ralph Bailey, Dick Aartila, Gary Boushelle, Karl Hosford, John Stuht, Sandra Schultz, El Harger, Karen Noyce, Dave Garshelis, Bruce Kohn and Gary Alt. Thanks also to U.S. Forest Service biologists and employees Lynn Rogers, Pat Berringer, Don Elsing, Kevin Doran, Dick Anderson, Bryan Barnett, Ken Wilson and Gary Olson.

Some conservation officers and other DNR employees provided assistance, too, and those that come to mind are Leo Erickson, Bernie Morgan, John Bezotte, Mike Holmes, Ron Stiebe, Veterinarian Steve Schmitt and Mike Pollard. I want to thank a number of people for their kind assistance in helping me photograph black bears. They include Bruce and Craig Smith, Terry DeBruyn, Jim Haveman, Dave Raikko, Bruce and Jason Dupras, Jim Butler, Buck LeVasseur and my wife Lucy. My apologies to anyone who I have neglected to mention. I also want to thank the late Ken Lowe, Tim Reis and Terry DeBruyn for taking the time to review and comment on prepublication drafts of the first edition of this book.

Special recognition are due Terry DeBruyn for his unswerving dedication to bears and bear research inspite of countless challenges encountered along the way, not the least of which has been funding; Kay Richey for doing a tremendously efficient and speedy job typesetting and laying out the first edition of this book; wife and business partner Lucy for doing many of the tasks necessary to make this book a reality as well as plenty of other things that make my job easier and more efficient.

Foreword

The black bear (*Ursus americanus*) historically ranged over the entire state of Michigan. Now, it is largely confined to portions of the northern Lower Peninsula and the Upper Peninsula. Bears do not fare well in areas of concentrated human activity, as evidenced by their extirpation from the southern half of the Lower Peninsula.

For most people (myself included) the sight of a black bear in the wilds of Michigan is a pinnacle outdoor experience. Somehow, one's sense of awareness seems heightened and people who experience it are often able to recall vividly the colors and smells of the wild associated with the event. There is a great deal of intrinsic worth in just knowing that black bears roam free in much of Michigan's forests. This knowledge adds immeasurably to the outdoor experience.

As critical an issue as our ability to manage black bears is, it should not be (for hunters and non-hunters alike) our top priority. The real problem facing black bears in Michigan is not an annual harvest. But, rather it is the insidious loss of habitat and the continued encroachment of humans into what was formerly bear habitat and the fragmentation of that habitat by roads and human development. Preservation of large tracts of roadless land and minimizing forest fragmentation by leaving travel corridors is needed to help ensure the future of bears in the state of Michigan.

Richard P. Smith's book *Understanding Michigan Black Bear explains all you* need to know about bears in Michigan, including the role of the hunter in the management of these animals, in a practical and authoritative way. Richard's interest in the biology of the black bear has taken him across all of North America to interview and spend time in the field with biologists. His role as a hunter and photographer has added depth to his understanding of these animals. Regardless of how you feel about hunting, this book is a must read if you are genuinely concerned with the presence of a viable bear population in Michigan.

Terry D. DeBruyn
BEAR RESEARCHER

Introduction

If you want to learn about Michigan bears, including how to avoid problems with the animals, and/or bear hunting, this is the book for you. The text tells you all you want to know about the animals and their management. The pages that follow have a tremendous amount of information and I bet what's written on them will answer most of your questions. After reading this book, you are certain to be more knowledgeable about the animals than you were before because there's some information in this book that I don't think has been published elsewhere.

A full 10 chapters, more than any other section, are devoted to what has been learned about Michigan bears through research. Several of those chapters discuss special bruins that have played valuable roles in helping us understand bears in general. One of those chapters is devoted to a pair of orphaned cubs my wife and I helped raise and return to the wild. Another chapter is devoted to how orphaned cubs are dealt with today.

The four chapters that make up section two may be the most important in the book. They are about nuisance bears and those that have attacked people. There's plenty of advice about how to avoid problems from either type of animal.

If you want to learn how or where to hunt bears in Michigan, this book probably isn't what you are looking for. If, however, you want to better understand the hunting of bears in the state, why it's done and what impact it has had and does have on the animals, you should find what you are looking for in section three. The fourth and last section discusses efforts to ban bear hunting and what's behind them.

When I started bear hunting with bait back in 1967, it never occurred to me that some day I would feel compelled to explain the method to all of the residents of the state, so they could understand the valuable role the technique plays in managing Michigan's bears, to make sure it continues to serve in that capacity into the future. There was no way I could, of course, because the method was new to me back then, too, and I knew little about it. Baiting was not an important consideration in terms of bear hunting at that time anyway because few hunters did it and the same is true for hunting with hounds.

Bear hunting itself wasn't even popular back then and managing black bears was practically unheard of. I had no way of knowing how things would change over the course of more than 30 years. Today, however, I'm well aware of how bear hunting and management have evolved since 1967 because I've paid careful attention. It was easy because I was interested and involved.

Most of the changes have been for the better and recognition of the value of black bears has been largely responsible for that. That's great. The more people that appreciate bears, the better. Even today, however, I have a hard time understanding why everyone in the state (actually, only Michigan voters) should learn about bear hunting in order to preserve it.

The Michigan Department of Natural Resources (DNR) is responsible for setting bear hunting regulations and managing black bears. The appropriate personnel in that agency understand the role that baiting and hounding play and that these methods in no way threaten bears in the state. If anything, the techniques have a positive influence on the way they are presently regulated. Most other bear hunters also understand this and that's the way it should be.

It will become obvious after reading this book that both the DNR and bear hunters have taken steps to close or limit bear hunting in various parts of the state when warranted. There are more restrictions on bear hunting today than there have ever been due to cooperative efforts of the state agency and sportsmen. The reason for this is they share concern for the resource.

The majority of the state's residents trust the DNR to properly manage bears and bear hunting, which they have done. Beyond that, many of them don't care. What's more, most residents are not affected one way or another regardless of how bears are managed because Michigan's bears live in the northern two-thirds of the state and most of the people call the southern part of the state home.

For these reasons and more, it's not fair that residents of Detroit, Grand Rapids or Lansing; some of whom will never set foot in the state's bear habitat nor want to, had a chance to have as much influence on the future of bear hunting as myself or a DNR wildlife biologist who are informed about the subject. Fair or not, that's what happened. A state law that was probably adopted with little or no thought about implications for wildlife management, allows any issue to be placed on the statewide ballot during an election, as long as enough signatures are obtained from residents supporting it.

Despite the fact the placement of bear hunting on the state ballot may not have been fair, it provided a unique opportunity to educate state residents about bear hunting and management. Fortunately, an educational campaign designed to take advantage of that opportunity proved successful. Many of the voters who went to the polls in 1996 knew what they were voting about.

I hope to continue that educational effort with this book. It's must reading for anyone who plans to spend time in Michigan's bear country, whether for hiking, camping, fishing or hunting. Of course, you don't have to visit bear country to learn about the animals. The words on the pages that follow will help take you there.

Section
1

Research

(Left) Ear-tagged black bear on Drummond Island lifts its head as it recovers from drug.

Chapter 1

A Bear's Year

Most Michigan black bears begin life in the normally dark to semi-dark interior of a den during January. Cubs average about 12 ounces in weight when born, but large ones may weigh as much as a pound. The newborns are basically hairless, with their eyes closed. The tiny bears' hair grows quickly after birth and their eyes open after about six weeks.

As many as five cubs may be born to an exceptionally healthy, adult female bear. One year I photographed a large female with five cubs on a Menominee County farm. Although females with five cubs aren't often seen, the birth of four cubs to Michigan females is not unusual. During a recent winter, for example, Department of Natural Resources (DNR) wildlife biologists documented the presence of denned females with four cubs each in Alger, Dickinson and Menominee Counties in the Upper Peninsula (U.P.); Wexford and Montmorency Counties in the northern Lower Peninsula. The average number of cubs born to adult females is between two and three.

Winter may seem an odd time for such helpless creatures to be born and it is, compared to other mammals in the state, but it is something the animals are well adapted for. Inspite of the harsh weather common during Michigan winters, most cubs manage to stay warm and thrive on a rich diet of milk provided by their mothers. The temperature inside maternal bear dens might be a little warmer than outside, but the mother bear is the real heater. Cubs stay warm by clinging to their mothers during the first weeks of life. As their hair grows, it provides enough insulation to help keep them warm, too.

Timing of cub births is one of a number of unique aspects of the black bears' life history that you will learn about in this chapter. Many features of their life cycle are fascinating because they are so different from most other animals. Females with cubs,

Most Michigan bears are born in dens during January and they average less than a pound in weight. Their eyes are closed at birth and they generally open after six weeks.

for instance, are the only Michigan mammals that nurse their young for about three months without eating.

For this reason, the fall diet of pregnant females is extremely important. They not only have to accumulate enough fat to sustain themselves during their winter sleep, they have to store enough food to feed their cubs during the same interval. The layers of fat on a female's body are converted to milk to feed her young as well as producing enough energy to keep her going.

Research has shown that some pregnant females that don't reach weights of at least 150 to 160 pounds by the time they enter dens, may not produce cubs at all. This is why delayed implantation is such an important part of the reproductive cycle of black bears. Fertilized eggs don't implant in the uterus until females enter dens, even though they were bred months earlier. Implantation may not occur in females that have not gained enough weight, which increases their chances of survival. Reproduction will be discussed in more detail later on.

Females with cubs may lose as much as 35 percent of their weight over the winter and that's why it's important for them to put on as much weight as possible before winter arrives. A female that enters a den weighing 300 pounds during fall, for example, will probably weigh in the neighborhood of 195 pounds when she leaves it with her cubs the following spring. Pregnant females weighing in at 200 pounds, will drop down to 130 pounds by spring and 175 pounders will only end up weighing about 113 pounds.

It's no wonder that females with a fall weight of 150 pounds seldom produce cubs. If they did, their spring weight would be less than 100 pounds. Winter weight loss among bears that don't have cubs to feed is closer to 20 percent.

Pregnant females usually select the most protected den sites such as rock caves, hollow trees, stumps and logs, beaver houses, cavities under the root systems of fallen trees and brushpiles. They will dig dens in the ground under stumps, vacant buildings and in other locations. Not all bears seek protection from the elements in enclosed dens though. Some build nests on the top of the ground, lining them with grass, leaves and bark and others simply curl up under a fallen tree where their thick layer of fat and long coat insulates them from the weather.

The physiology of black bears is such that it isn't necessary for them to urinate or defecate during their long winter sleep. Something that they do get rid of while denned though are their foot pads. The calloused outer layer of the pads are shed, leaving them with soft new pads to break in when spring arrives.

Most Michigan bears leave their dens sometime during April, although, in parts of the southern U.P. and the L.P., they may vacate winter quarters as early as March. As a rule, bears still have some fat left by spring that will help carry them through a month or more of lean pickings until enough food is available for them to start gaining weight again. Healthy males normally have the most fat left by spring, which will play a vital role in preparing them for the breeding season that encompasses late spring and early summer (late May through early July).

Males and females without young are normally the first to leave dens and females with cubs are last. Even when females with cubs leave dens, they don't normally travel far because the youngsters aren't capable of covering much ground at first. Cub weights vary dramatically by the time they leave the den, but those that weigh at least five pounds have a good chance of making it. Cubs from large litters usually average smaller than singles or twins because available milk is divided among more mouths.

Mother bears nurse their young during most of their first year of life. Young

Female black bear in a hole between fallen trees selected as a den.

bruins normally begin eating solids during May when they are about five months old. The amount of solids they eat gradually increases and dependency on milk decreases. Studies done in Michigan years ago determined that cubs as young as six months old can make it on their own if they lose their mothers. The youngsters instinctively know what foods to eat and to seek out a den for winter sleep.

Under normal circumstances, cubs spend about 1 1/2 years with their mothers before separating. They den together during the cubs' second winter and remain together until late May or June of the following year when the adult females are ready to breed again. Because cubs usually spend more than a year with their mothers, adult females only breed every other year, as a rule.

Production of milk (lactation) when females have cubs, prevents them from coming into heat. A female may breed two years in a row if she loses her cubs or becomes separated from them for a period of days. Once nursing and milk production stops, a female may come into breeding condition, if this happens before July.

There are a number of factors that can result in cub loss. Young have been known to drown in dens that become flooded or can be claimed by other accidents. Females

Female black bear nursing a pair of cubs. Young bears suckle during most of their first year of life, but they begin eating solids by May and milk from their mothers becomes a less important part of their diet by fall.

with cubs that are harassed in their dens or disturbed by logging, mining or development, sometimes abandon their young. A deer habitat improvement project in Ontonagon County one winter, led to the accidental loss of a trio of cubs.

A DNR bulldozer operator was knocking trees down to serve as browse for deer when the den the cubs were in was disrupted. The mother bear abandoned the site and the newborns died. All three cubs were males that were between two and three weeks old and weighed 28 to 32 ounces when they died.

Although the loss of those cubs was unfortunate, they were put to the best use possible. They became part of a bear exhibit prepared by the Science Museum of Minnesota in St. Paul. Mounts of the cubs were used in the re-creation of a den scene. The mount of a 19-year-old adult female was placed with the cubs.

Predators such as wolves, coyotes, bobcats and other bears also prey on cubs. After a female with cubs leaves the den in the spring, cubs often wander away from their mothers for short periods of time, either getting out ahead of her or straggling behind, and that's when cubs are most vulnerable to predators.

A young bear's greatest test of survival, in many ways, comes when it separates from its mother at the age of 1 1/2. It will be on its own for the first time and can still be taken by predators, if it isn't careful. Yearlings are especially vulnerable to getting into trouble because they often travel long distances in unfamiliar territory, especially males, and are accident prone.

Young males typically disperse from their mothers' home range to establish a territory of their own and sometimes cover more than 100 miles before settling down. This prevents inbreeding. Some males disperse as yearlings and others don't make a big move until they are two years old.

Yearling females are normally permitted to claim part of their mothers' territory as their own, but a portion of their range is also outside the area occupied by their mothers. Since young females spend more time in areas they know and don't travel as far as males, they have a better chance of survival. When it's time for yearlings to separate from their mothers, they don't often do so willingly. Females normally have to drive them away.

It's no fun to watch a female black bear that is ready to sever ties with her offspring, as I have on a number of occasions. The yearlings seldom understand the need to separate from their mothers, therefore, the female frequently has to resort to drastic measures to get the message across. They chase their young repeatedly, using aggressive sounds in the process, and sometimes end up hitting or biting the young bears.

After repeated abuse, the yearlings eventually reach a point when they realize it's in their best interest to stay away from mom. That's actually why the female turns on her youngsters. She's ready to seek the company of males again to prepare for having another family and adult male bears can and will kill cubs and yearlings, if they get the chance.

Bear Researcher Terry DeBruyn of Chassell said a habituated female that he followed in Alger County for a number of years separated from two sets of yearlings at close to the same time during late May of 1992 and 1994. But he also documented something that may not have been observed before. Each of those two years after the female had successfully mated, one of her male yearlings tried to rejoin her. Then the mother bear's aggressiveness toward her offspring was repeated, sometimes over a period of days, until the youngster was finally driven off.

As adult females approach breeding condition, they are pursued relentlessly by males. Mating takes place when the time is right. A female may mate with more than one male over a period of two or three days. Under those circumstances, cubs from the same litter may have different fathers.

Once females are bred, fertilized eggs begin developing, but they only go as far as the blastocyst stage before development stops. Blastocysts remain in the uterus, but do not implant and develop further until females enter dens during October or November. This is what is referred to as delayed implantation. In most mammals, fertilized eggs implant in the uterus soon afterward to continue development.

Breeding is the most important role adult male black bears play in the population during the course of a year and this function occupies much of their time from late May into July. It isn't unusual for the breeding territory of males to cover 100 square miles or more and those areas are established to encompass the home ranges of as many females as possible. Before breeding actually begins, males travel widely, marking their territories by leaving their scent on saplings and trees.

A female with a pair of yearlings. The mother will separate from the yearlings when they are about 1 1/2 years old.

Bears scent mark in a number of ways. While walking, they frequently straddle saplings and their scent is deposited as they rub against them. Males will also grasp a sapling or clump of small stems in their mouths and turn so they are pulled tight over their back and rub against them.

To mark large trees, males stand on their hind legs, with their back against a tree and rub against the trunk. They sometimes turn their head and bite pieces of bark from the tree while rubbing against it. When evergreen trees that are five to 10 feet high are marked, bears sometimes bend the top of the tree over a shoulder with a front paw while rubbing against it. The tops of these trees may be broken by this behavior. Bear hair can frequently be found on the trunks of trees marked by the animals.

Females scent mark in much the same way males do, but they don't normally do as much of it. Scent marking enables bears of both sexes to determine where each other are, which is important during breeding season. Females often travel widely in search of males when they are ready to breed, increasing their chances of finding a suitable mate. When an adult male crosses the scent trail of a female in heat, he will follow the scent until finding her. It's not unusual for a number of males to be following the same female. The largest and/or most aggressive male usually does most of the mating.

Delta County Sheriff's Deputies Brian Lauscher of Gladstone and Ed Oswald of Bark River had an unusual experience with a male bear intent on breeding one June. They responded to a location near Hyde where an adult female weighing 175 pounds had been killed attempting to cross a highway. Lauscher said they heard noise in the

The black bear breeding season is from late May into July.
Females may mate with more than one male.

ditch near the dead bear that they thought might have been made by cubs, so they investigated.

The animal ran off ahead of them and they thought it sounded big enough to care for itself and they were right, as they later found out. While dragging the carcass of the dead bear off the highway, a 350 pound male came out of the woods to find out what was happening with his prospective mate. It left grudgingly, but later returned and dragged the dead female 120 yards into the woods.

The female was apparently killed as it was being chased by the male. The breeding season was underway and the female was probably in heat. By September of that year the Delta County Sheriff's Department had handled eight bear vehicle accidents, according to Sergeant Gary Ballweg of Kipling.

Once mating season is over, males spend the rest of the year looking for food to regain weight they've lost and to prepare for winter. Pregnant females do the same thing, putting on as much weight as possible so they will have enough fat to sustain themselves and their cubs over the winter. Most weight gain is during late summer and fall and that's why annual production of soft and hard mast (berries, fruits and nuts) is so important to bears. The failure of major natural foods can cause problems for bears and people.

If natural foods are scarce, bears seek out whatever they can to replace their normal diet. Agricultural crops such as corn, oats and other grains are attractive and so are commercial bee hives, bird feeders, pet food left outside, people food in backpacks and campgrounds as well as discarded human food in garbage cans. Domestic livestock may even be targeted by bears when other foods are scarce. The potential for conflicts between bears and man are very high during years when natural food production is low.

Bears are normally the losers when this happens because many of them are killed by people who view the animals as threats to their safety or livelihood. Hungry bruins can be dangerous, but they seldom are. However, there's no doubt they are a threat to the livelihood of farmers and beekeepers. The animals can do a lot of damage in grain fields and to bee hives.

Fortunately, bait put in the woods by hunters, photographers and people interested in watching wildlife can help reduce bear/human conflicts during years when natural food is scarce. Bears benefit from this supplemental food source by putting on weight that will help them during the course of the winter. For pregnant females, access to bait may determine whether or not they will have cubs. The same food source may prevent cubs and yearlings from starving.

When natural foods are scarce in some areas, but abundant in others, bears from miles around will concentrate in the locations that have food. Bruins will keep traveling until they find a source of food. Trips of 40 miles or more aren't unusual.

Hard mast such as acorns, beech and hazel nuts are some of the most important fall foods for bears. Wild cherries and apples can also be an important part of the fall diet of bruins. Berries they depend on for nourishment during summer and early fall months are wild strawberries, blueberries, raspberries, thimbleberries, buckthorn berries, Juneberry or sugar plums, blackberries and dogwood berries. Ants are high on the black bear's list of preferred foods during the summer, too, and research indicates bruins may rely heavily on insects when berries are scarce.

Other insects bears depend on for food are bees and hornets. When bears rip into an ant colony, bee hive or hornets nest they are most frequently after the larval insects rather than the adults in addition to any honey that might be available, because they have more protein. Bears also eat adult insects. Snow fleas are eaten by bruins, too, usually during early spring when these tiny insects gather in large masses.

Vegetation also makes up a large part of a black bear's diet during spring and summer and they will dine on plants in the fall, too. Grasses are among the first food bears eat in the spring. Other items their diet includes are leaves, clover, dandelions, goatsbeard, cattails, aster, water plantain, swamp thistle, sweet cicely, calla, jack-in-the-pulpit, hawkweed, sarsaparilla and much more.

They prey on fawns plus moose and elk calves that they encounter during the spring and will scavenge the carcasses of car-killed deer. Bruins love beaver and catch some themselves, but also eat carcasses discarded by trappers after the pelts are removed. Bird's eggs and young birds found in nests are on the black bear's menu, too. If food is abundant, bears prosper.

Males attain larger sizes than females. Peak fall weights for females are probably between 300 to 350 pounds. The heaviest males on record for Michigan have weighed more than 600 pounds. It's not unusual for older males to weigh 500 pounds before they enter dens. The heaviest black bear recorded for the state had a dressed weight of 650 pounds. It was shot in Iron County during November of 1950 by the late Herb Mitchell of South Haven. He shot the big bruin in its den during gun deer season after following its tracks in the snow. The animal would have had a live weight between 715 and 740 pounds.

(Right) An adult male stands on his hind legs to mark a tree by rubbing his back against it. Males will sometimes leave bite marks in the bark at head height. "Bear trees" like this will frequently have bear hair on the trunk.

The late Evelyn and Arthur Lindahl stand next to an Iron County black bear weighing 650 pounds dressed that Herb Mitchell of South Haven shot during November of 1950. (photo courtesy Warren Groth)

The oldest bear on record for Michigan is a male that was 35 3/4 years old that was shot in Iron County with the aid of hounds by Steve Kolbach during the fall of 1987. The old male had a dressed weight of 380 pounds. There are numerous records of both males and females exceeding 20 years of age in the state. During one season, for example, six of the bears bagged by hunters were between 25 and 28 years of age. Two males were 28, a female was 27 and the remaining three oldtimers, two of which were females, were 25. Since the oldest bears are often the toughest for hunters to get, there's probably a higher proportion of old animals in the population than kill figures indicate.

Most Michigan bears begin their long winter sleep during late October or November, but some may not seek a den until December. The majority of bears in the U.P. are normally in dens by mid-November. When natural foods are abundant, bears tend to den later than normal to take advantage of the bumper crop. When foods are scarce, they may den earlier than normal as a means of conserving the energy they already have stored. Pregnant females and those with yearlings are often the first to enter dens and males are among the last to begin their winter slumber.

Information gathered by Bear Researcher Terry DeBruyn indicates that pregnant females may prepare and select den sites during summer months, which is the first clue that den selection is far from a haphazard process. He has watched an adult female he is able to walk with dig a number of dens during the summer. The animals probably choose the best location when it's time to den. If disturbed from one den, they probably don't waste much time going to an alternate.

Sometime during the winter, the life cycle of a new batch of bears begins when cubs are born.

Black bear feeding on acorns, an important fall food for bruins.

Terry DeBruyn removes a cub that's less than six weeks old from a den.

Chapter 2

Winter Den Work

One of the best ways to monitor the well being of Michigan's black bear population is to examine the animals while they are in winter dens and wildlife biologists have been doing so on an annual basis since 1987. Studies that have been underway since 1986 in various parts of the state, which involve live trapping and radio collaring bruins, have enabled researchers to locate collared bears in their dens.

The eastern U.P.'s Drummond Island was the focal point of an intensive bear study until 1993. Around the time the island study ended, another project coordinated by DNR Wildlife Biologist Doug Wagner in Crystal Falls, began in the southern U.P. Another research project that was begun in Alger County during 1990 was concluded in 1999. Some bruins in the northern Lower Peninsula have been fitted with radio collars for a number of years, but efforts to expand research in that region got underway during 1993 and that work continues.

Since the health of Michigan's bear population hinges on cub production and survival, the most valuable information is gathered from the dens of adult females. Cubs are born during the winter, usually in January. Cubs that survive their first year of life also den with their mothers the following winter.

So by checking the dens of mature females fitted with radio collars, biologists are able to determine how many cubs are being produced and how many survive. Due to the fact that cubs spend more than a year with their mothers, most female black bears of cub-bearing age give birth every other year. Den checks of young females enable biologists to determine at what age they mature.

Researchers determine the ages of all collared bears by pulling a small premolar tooth at the time the animals are captured. Premolars are located behind canine teeth and they are removed for aging because bears don't need or use them for feeding. Cross sections of those teeth show rings or annuli for each year of a bear's life.

Examining the dens of female black bears with newborn cubs and yearlings may sound like hazardous duty, but it isn't. DNR Bear Researcher Dr. Larry Visser, who works out of the Houghton Lake Research Station, has been involved in hundreds of

A radio collared female that had three cubs when checked in its den. The adult and cubs were returned to their den soon after this photograph was taken.

den visits and he remains alive and well, having suffered no bear inflicted injuries. So does DNR Wildlife Biologist Doug Wagner. The same is true for DNR Veterinarian Steve Schmitt and Elaine Carlson, who have assisted Visser, and bear biologist Dr. Terry DeBruyn, who spent 10 years studying bears in the U.P.

Most den checks are conducted during February and March when newborn cubs are large enough to be handled safely. The weather is usually warm enough then that bruins can be removed from dens for examination without causing any problems. Nonetheless, bears are laid on mats and covered with coats while outside the den, when they aren't being examined.

The hardest part of checking bear dens is often getting to them. Some of the sites are in remote locations or thick swamps that require lengthy snowmobile rides or hikes on snowshoes to reach. Dens are located by following signals from radio collars worn by bruins.

Occasionally, the denned bears are hard to find once the site is reached. One winter I was with Visser and DeBruyn when it took them over an hour to locate a small bear that had denned under a fallen tree. The tree was large and so much snow had accumulated around it that they had to excavate several holes to finally locate the animal. Digging and sawing to remove snow, limbs and branches that are in the way is frequently required to remove bears from dens as well as to reach them.

Larry told me about two dens on Drummond Island that thwarted his efforts to reach the sleeping bears. One was a massive brushpile and the other was a rock cave that had a long, narrow entrance with a 90 degree turn that was impossible for a person to get through. Brushpiles and cavities created by fallen trees are frequently selected as den sites by female bears. They also use excavated dens, caves, hollow trees, beaver houses and will even make ground nests lined with bark, grass and leaves, which are usually located in thick cover.

Researchers try to approach dens as quietly as possible to avoid disturbing bears. Females with newborn cubs are sometimes awake or sleeping lightly. Young bears and males can be light sleepers, too. A few bruins are so alert in dens that they run off when approached, especially in the northern Lower Peninsula where winters tend to be milder than the U.P., but most remain in dens even if they are awake. Those that are sleeping sometimes wake up when injected with a muscle relaxant.

During the first week of February 1999, for instance, Visser had an exciting experience with a large adult male black bear that was in a ground nest. He said the animal was sound asleep in the open as he approached and he was able to sneak up close enough to inject it with a dose of drug from six feet away. After injecting it, the bear lifted its head, so he thought he should give it another dose of drug.

Anxious to immobilize the big bruin as quickly as possible, Larry bent the needle when he attempted to make a second injection and ended up not getting any more drug in the animal. About that time, the bear decided to leave the nest and started right toward Larry. He said he made a lot of noise and tried to look as intimidating as possible. It apparently worked because the bruin turned and went the other way, but the bear ended up running down the packed snowshoe trail that Larry and his assistants made while approaching the sleeping bruin. As the drug started to take effect, the bear left the trail and went down a short distance away.

Larry said he's glad it was one of those deals that was over quickly. He commented that there wasn't time to get worried or scared until after it was over. He added that he was standing on a packed trail the bear had made when gathering materials for its nest and that's why the animal started to go that way. The bear's weight was estimated at 400 pounds, but it could have been heavier. It proved to be too heavy to weigh. Larry said the bruin looked awful big stretched out on the snow where it fell.

Once a denned bear is located, often with the aid of a flashlight, the animal is injected with a drug from a syringe on the end of a pole referred to as a jab stick. The dosage is based on the animal's weight. The muscle relaxant usually takes effect in five to 10 minutes. Most bears are asleep when drugged and the drug prevents them from waking up when handled. The drug is essential to put down animals that are awake.

In dens occupied by a female and yearlings, the adult is usually injected first, followed by her offspring. That was the procedure DeBruyn used one March in a den containing an adult with one yearling. Terry had to remove the female from the den with the help of Visser and U. S. Forest Service Wildlife Biologist Kevin Doran from Munising. He then had to go in the large den to drug the yearling.

Once that was done, Terry turned his attention to processing the female. When his back was turned, the yearling climbed out of the den and tried to run away. I was standing off to the side taking photos and saw the yearling emerge, calling it to Terry's attention. He reacted fast enough to cut the young bear off before it got far, then covered it with Kevin's coat until the drug took effect. Even if DeBruyn hadn't acted as swiftly as he did, the bruin wouldn't have gotten far in the deep snow before the drug took effect.

Visser said he once had an undrugged yearling leave a Drummond Island den in deep, fluffy snow. DNR Wildlife Biologist John Hendrickson from Marquette was in attendance that day. Hendrickson grabbed the floundering yearling by the hair on its

Poles like the one Terry DeBruyn is putting in the snow with a syringe on the end, are referred to as "jab sticks" and are used to inject immobilizing drugs into denned bears. Larry Visser has a second dose ready in case it's needed.

back and tossed it back toward the den entrance. Realizing it was safer in the den than the deep snow, the yearling re-entered the den, where it was drugged.

A yearling escaped from DeBruyn for the first time during den checks in March of 1995. The drugged adult blocked access to the yearling, so the adult had to be removed from the den before Terry could drug the yearling. While its mother was being moved, the yearling climbed out the top of the den and took off. The snow was deep and fluffy, but the den was in a thick cedar swamp and the yearling got enough of a head start on Terry that he was unable to catch it. The yearling probably rejoined its mother in the den after the people left.

When a female has three yearlings, as a number of DeBruyn's collared animals have had, a den can get crowded. Due to the confusion created by crowded conditions in one such den and the fact that he had to inject a couple of the yearlings more than once, Terry thought he had drugged all of the yearlings, but it turned out he missed one of them, a female. The three yearlings, two of which were males, were curled up together in the den, making it difficult to determine which body parts belonged to who, at times. The males required a couple of injections of muscle relaxant apiece to put them under, but when it came time to drug the third yearling, DeBruyn began wondering if he might have already injected it in the confusion. Rather than risk giving one of the bears too much drug, he decided to remove them all from the den.

As it turned out, the yearling female hadn't gotten a dose of muscle relaxant. She yawned lazily when carried from the den, but otherwise showed little indication she hadn't been drugged. Before she was weighed and measured, however, Larry Visser noticed that the female was more alert than her brothers.

She was given an injection at the time to make sure she didn't wake up. The year old animal weighed 47 pounds compared to weights of 52 and 57 pounds for her brothers.

"When we were handling her, she probably thought it was her brothers pushing and shoving her," DeBruyn said. "She was probably used to that and that's probably why she didn't wake up even though she wasn't drugged."

One of the more pleasant aspects of den checks involving females with newborn cubs is keeping the cubs warm while their mother is weighed, measured and examined. The best way to do that is to tuck them inside a volunteer's coat. It's usually not difficult to find volunteers for the task because bear cubs are cute and cuddly.

Cubs are also weighed and, in most cases, ear tagged, before being returned to the den with their mothers. Yearlings are usually fitted with ear tags and radio collars before going back in dens. New collars are sometimes put on bruins that were previously collared, too, to insure that the animals can be tracked for another year and to adjust the size of collars to allow for growth from one year to the next. When the Drummond Island and Alger County studies ended, collars were removed from study bears during den checks.

The DNR is able to gather valuable information about bear growth rates, longevity and dispersal from cubs that are ear tagged during winter den checks. One such cub that was bagged by a hunter two years later exhibited exceptional growth. Steve Tasson from Ishpeming shot the 2 3/4-year-old male that had a dressed weight of 300 pounds on September 27th in south Marquette County. The bruin's live weight would have been in the neighborhood of 350 pounds, which is exceptional for an animal of that age. It averaged a weight gain of more than 100 pounds for each year of its life.

When that bear was marked as a cub, it was one of two males in a litter of four that were all tagged in the den with their mother by DNR employees Doug Wagner and Monica Joseph out of the Crystal Falls office on March 8, 1995. Their den was in Dickinson County. The adult female was so large, she wasn't weighed.

Her genetics for large size were obviously passed on to her young. Even at the time the cub was tagged, it was big, tipping the scales at 8.25 pounds. Most cubs weigh less than six pounds at that time of year after being born during January.

One of the two females from the litter was killed by a car as it attempted to cross a road on July 22, 1995. Since there's no record of the second female being killed, it's thought to still be alive.

The second male from the litter dispersed to the south from its mother's home range when 1 3/4-years-old, according to DNR records, and was killed by a hunter near Crivitz, Wisconsin during the fall of 1996. That male was also big for a yearling, having a dressed weight of 142 pounds.

The male that Tasson killed dispersed to the north. It ended up about 40 miles from where it had been tagged.

As part of the process of monitoring the health of denned bears, blood samples, temperatures and heart rates are usually taken and their teeth examined for wear or damage. Sometime during the winter, yearlings lose their milk teeth, which are replaced by canines. Foot pads are also checked to determine how shedding is progressing. To keep study bears healthy, they are usually given a dose of antibiotics.

Although denned bears aren't normally aggressive or pose a threat to people that stumble upon them, an encounter with a denned bear can prove fatal for dogs, if they get too close, as one Marquette County rabbit hunter found out. After having his best rabbit dog killed by a bear, the hunter warns others who are afield with dogs during the winter to make an effort to keep dogs away from bear dens. Preventing the interaction between bears and dogs during the winter is beneficial for both animals. Bruins that feel threatened can easily kill a dog, which is what happened in this case.

Bears that are chased from dens by dogs use valuable energy that can reduce their chances of survival, especially if they are not able to reden quickly in a spot that offers them adequate protection from disturbance. In cases where females with newborn cubs are involved, the cubs could die if abandoned by their mothers.

Bears are so numerous in the U.P. now that the odds of stumbling across a denned bruin have increased. It's not unusual for bears to den in habitat where rabbits are found. The bear that killed the rabbit dog was a female with at least two yearlings that were spending the winter under a large blowdown in a swamp.

The dog owner wasn't hunting at the time his dog found the bear den. He was simply out for a walk to exercise his dogs. He had three dogs with him when they smelled the bears and started barking. The den entrance was only marked by a breathing hole.

His best dog started digging in the snow to uncover the den. The snow gave way under the dog and he fell in the den. Fortunately, the other two dogs managed to avoid a similar fate.

If the bruins had been sleeping, the barking woke them up. After the dog fell in the den, there was a brief commotion, during which one yearling bear left the den, then all was quiet. The hunter estimated the yearling's weight at 60 pounds.

The dog's owner is sure the adult female killed his companion quickly. After things were quiet for a while, he heard bones breaking, which he thought was the bear crushing the dog's skull.

The female then appeared at the den entrance and called to the yearling that left. The frantic hunter was only 10 yards away at that point, doing his best to keep his two remaining dogs away from the bear. He had one of them by the tail and the other one was between his legs. He said the bear had his missing dog's blood on her face.

Understandably upset, he hollered, "Get back in there you son of a bitch," and she did. The yearling then returned to the den and the hunter left with his two dogs in tow.

The man said he has never shot a bear and doesn't intend to, unless one comes at him. He said he doesn't blame the bear for what happened, but he's not happy about losing his best dog either. He hopes that relating his story might help prevent the same thing from happening to someone else.

Anyone who finds a denned black bear should contact a local DNR wildlife biologist such as Doug Wagner at Crystal Falls or Larry Visser at Houghton Lake. The telephone number at the Crystal Falls DNR office is 906-875-6622 and the number for Houghton Lake is 517-422-6572. There is a possibility researchers may want to collar the animal for study. If a denned bear is a female with newborn cubs, disturbance should be kept to a minimum. Females have been known to abandon their cubs if disturbed.

However, normal human activity near a lone bear that's denned is seldom a problem. Josh Bennett from Marquette, who was 13 years old at the time, got a chance to find that out during the fall of 1995 when a bruin selected a hollow stump a matter of feet from his Marquette County tree stand to spend the winter in. It was the first week

(Right) Melissa Sterling keeps a cub warm in her coat while the young bear's mother is being weighed and measured.

Larry Visser attaches ear tags to a cub before it's returned to a den with its mother and any siblings. The tags help biologists identify the animals if they turn up later.

of November when Josh first noticed the bruin curled up in the stump near his perch. His first reaction upon detecting the bear's presence was normal for someone interested in seeing deer.

He was concerned that the bear would keep deer away. However, he had already moved his stand earlier that fall when a large tree blew down nearby. He didn't want to move again, if he didn't have to, so he continued hunting from the same spot to find out what happened.

As it turned out, the sleeping bear's presence didn't have any noticeable impact on whitetails that visited his stand nor did Josh's presence impact the bear. In fact, he

*Josh (with flashlight) and Stuart Bennett look at a sleeping bear
that denned in a hollow stump near a tree stand Josh
hunted deer from with bow and arrow.*

managed to arrow his first buck from that stand during mid-December. The accomplishment was extra special because his father (Stuart) was perched nearby and captured the event with a video camera.

One of the 6-pointer's antlers fell off when it ran after Josh shot it. The second antler came off while father and son were handling the carcass. Nonetheless, the boy was understandably happy about bagging his first buck from such a unique stand.

The Bennetts checked on the sleeping bear periodically and it ended up spending the entire winter in the hollow stump. The activity around the den during hunting season didn't disturb the animal.

Chapter 3

A Tale of Two Cubs

I had been approached by bears at open pit dumps before, but not like a young male did on the evening of July 30, 1988. The bruin acted like he knew me. As far as I knew, I had never seen the bear before, but the 150-pounder walked right up to me as though he wanted to say, "Hello," and shake my hand. Actually, it appeared as though the bear wanted to play.

I always carry a five to six-foot long walking stick that doubles as a club with me when photographing and watching bears and I used the pole to keep the animal its length away by putting the end of it against his chest. Playfully biting and pawing at the club kept the bruin occupied and seemed to satisfy it. The bear seemed perfectly comfortable close to me and Craig, a cousin of mine who was also there, and that seemed strange.

It wasn't until later that evening as Craig and I discussed the bear's behavior and what might be responsible for it, that I realized I might know that bear afterall. My wife Lucy and I had helped raise a pair of orphaned cubs two years earlier and had returned them to the wild within 20 miles of where that dump was. We put radio collars on them before they were released in the hopes of monitoring their progress, but the collars weren't tight enough and both bears slipped out of their collars soon after they were on their own.

One of the cubs was a male and the other a female. It would have been easy for the male we handled to cover the distance from where it was released to the dump during those two years. In fact, young males often wander widely before establishing a territory of their own. In addition, when open pit dumps were common in the U.P., bears often came from miles around to feed at them during summer months. A jaunt of 20 miles for such a smorgasbord is nothing to a bear.

Lucy and I always wondered if the bears we released had survived. There was a

(Left) Male bear that may be one of the cubs Lucy and I helped raise, feeding on wild cherries.

37

possibility that the male had and he was the friendly animal that tried to interact with me that evening during July. Craig and I returned to the dump the following evening and the same bear was there. It acted as friendly as it had the day before. Craig, by the way, also had contact with the bear when it was a cub, if it was the same animal, and it could have recognized him, too.

To test my theory about the animal being the cub my wife and I helped raise, I let the bear get closer than the day before. I extended the back of a hand toward the bruin to let him smell it like I often do when meeting an unfamiliar dog. I did this twice and both times the bear's nose touched the back of my hand. The second time, the bruin started to lift his upper lip as though he was about to playfully bite my hand like dogs often do.

Not willing to trust the bear that much and as a means of discouraging the attempt, I said, "No," firmly and pulled my hand away. When Lucy and I had the cubs, we frequently used that word when they were doing something they weren't supposed to, much the same way a dog would be trained to understand such a command. The bear appeared to understand and made no attempt to do anything else.

There's no way to know for sure, but I feel strongly that bear was one of the two cubs my wife and I raised. I don't know any other way to explain its behavior. It's a good feeling knowing that at least one of the animals adapted to the wild and survived after having been raised by people for part of its first year of life. We can only hope the female did as well and it may have.

When I first saw the cubs on April 16, 1986 I would have never guessed that Lucy and I would end up playing an important role in their lives. Buck LeVasseur, who produces a weekly outdoor television show called Discovering for WLUC-TV in Negaunee, got a call from U.S. Forest Service Wildlife Biologist Don Elsing, who is now retired, about a bear den with cubs. Buck made arrangements with Don to photograph the den on that day and asked if I wanted to come along and I did.

Forest Service employees Bryan Barnett and Ken Wilson found the den near Thunder Lake in Schoolcraft County during early March in a stand of red pine trees while marking trees to be cut. There was plenty of snow on the ground at the time and there was only a round hole in the snow to mark the location of the den. The sound of cubs attracted their attention to the spot. A number of people had visited the den to see it since then and the mother had been observed outside the den a couple of times.

Barnett and Wilson took Buck and I to the den on the morning of April 16th. The female was asleep at the den entrance at the time. Because it was windy, we tried to sneak in position to photograph the animal, but she heard us and went in the den, which was a hole in the ground. We waited for a while to see if the female would come out in the open again. When she didn't, we left and returned the next morning.

We met Forest Service employee Gary Olson, who went to the den with us. We heard cubs calling as we approached the den. There were three cubs outside the den and there was no sign of their mother. We thought the female had left the cubs temporarily and would be back, but that wasn't the case. She had abandoned them due to too much human disturbance.

Buck checked the den again on the 18th and the mother hadn't returned. He only saw two cubs. He said they appeared weak and dehydrated. The third cub had wandered off and/or had been taken by a predator. Concerned about the survival of the remaining cubs, I discussed the situation with former DNR Wildlife Biologist Dick Aartila from Escanaba. We agreed that the best thing to do would be to feed the remaining cubs and leave them in the den for the time being, on the chance the female might return.

Lucy and I went to the den that evening with a pair of baby bottles and formula to put in them. The cubs nursed readily. After returning the cubs to the den, we covered the entrance before leaving to prevent the cubs from wandering off like their sibling had. If the female returned, she would be able to easily uncover the entrance.

After we returned home that evening, we got permission from Don Elsing to take the cubs home with us to care for them if the female had not returned by the following day. There was still no sign of the cubs' mother by April 19th, so Lucy and I became their foster parents. We were originally only supposed to have the cubs for a couple of days until they could be transferred to someone else, but we ended up keeping them for almost a month.

The cubs were small when we got them and I regret not having weighed them. I think they might have weighed less than five pounds, but they grew fast on baby formula. I spoke to a number of people who had experience raising bear cubs after we obtained the wildlife babies to make sure we fed them the right thing. Some used a 50/50 mixture of Carnation evaporated milk and water, others used baby formula and still others preferred a formula called Vet-A-Lac that is commonly used at zoos and is available from veterinarians.

The baby formula worked fine. One of the people I spoke to recommended using nipples designed for premature babies on the bottles and they worked well until the cubs got bigger, then Lucy switched to regular nipples. We fed the cubs every three or four hours at first and they only ate an ounce or two of formula at a time, but food consumption rapidly increased. It didn't take long before we realized the importance of wearing gloves during feedings to protect our hands from the cubs' sharp claws. When done feeding from the bottle, the male enjoyed sucking the skin on Lucy's neck.

We kept the cubs in a cage in our basement where it was dark and they slept most of the time between feedings. We took them outside as often as possible. Since the plan was to return the cubs to the wild when they were big enough, we figured it was important to give them some exposure to what would be their natural environment in the future. Letting them run would also give them valuable exercise to help develop their muscles.

We took them for their first walk on April 22nd. The cubs were not yet coordinated enough to run well, stumbling and tripping frequently, but it didn't take many field trips for them to improve. The female was the larger of the two at the time and she climbed a tree above head level that day, managing to return to the ground on her own. The climbing ability of both bears quickly improved, too.

The cubs did a lot of playing and wrestling during time in the field, which is typical behavior for young bears. They also showed good instincts for searching out food, sampling leaves and other types of vegetation that they encountered, which I was pleased to see.

Karen and Bob Stowe of Marquette took over care of the cubs on May 14th. The young bears had grown too big for the cage we had for them by then and they needed more room. The Stowes kept the cubs in their sauna, putting tree trunks inside for the bears to climb.

By May 28th, the cubs were sucking down a full bottle of formula and starting to eat solids. We visited the Stowes that day to see the cubs and find out how they were doing. Karen said she was mixing oatmeal and dog food with their formula and they were lapping up apple sauce. She added that the young bears learned how to turn the shower on in the sauna, making it necessary to cut the water supply off to the shower to prevent it from happening repeatedly.

Lucy Smith with cubs abandoned by their mother as a result of too much disturbance by humans. The den entrance is visible in the right corner.

On June 6th, the cubs made another move to a cage at Marquette's Presque Isle Park. A small zoo used to be operated there and the cubs were one of the attractions that summer. Lucy and I visited the bears in their cage as often as possible, bringing natural foods with us to feed the animals, so they would recognize them when they encountered them in the wild.

The cubs were returned to the wild on September 23rd. Lucy and I put radio collars on them that morning and we thought they were tight enough that the bears would not be able to get them off, but we were obviously wrong. We didn't have access to ear tags at the time, but figured they would be available by the time we checked them in their dens during the upcoming winter and could put them on then. Unfortunately, we never got another chance to mark the bears for identification.

Both cubs were in excellent shape when we released them. By then the male was larger than his sister. He probably weighed around 75 pounds and she was around 50. We figured they had enough accumulated fat to help them survive the winter. Based on previous research done in Michigan, we knew they would instinctively seek out a den or dens on their own. There was no way of knowing whether the two would stay together.

We took the cubs to a remote location for release where we figured their chances of interacting with people would be minimized. They followed us into the woods like they had when they were much smaller and had a hard time walking. After hiking about a mile, we decided it was time to leave them and that was the hard part. In order to discourage them from following us further, I had to scare them and I did that by running at them and hollering.

Mother bears do much the same thing when they separate from their yearlings and it worked. We knew it was important to turn on the cubs to increase their chances of becoming independent. Although it was in their best interest, it was still tough to do, especially for Lucy. She shed some tears as we left the cubs behind on the way out of the woods.

It was a real disappointment when we learned later that the cubs had lost their collars near where we had left them. DNR Wildlife Biologist John Hendrickson and his wife Carol went with Lucy and I to check on the cubs and John located both collars with telemetry equipment. At that point, we figured we would never know the fate of the two bears. However, by the following spring I found out what had happened to the female.

She ended up at the rural Baraga County residence of Marshall and Carolyn Kuivinen during the first week of October. The small bear was "very, very friendly," and "really liked kids," according to Mrs. Kuivinen. The Kuivinens thought the cub's mother had been killed, so they started feeding it.

Although the bear was never restrained in any way, it remained in the vicinity of the Kuivinen's home throughout the winter and they named it Bonzo. An empty tool shed filled with straw became the bear's den. The bruin didn't sleep throughout the winter in its manmade den like most bears do, only remaining inactive for a day or two at a time, according to Mrs. Kuivinen, because food was constantly available.

She said Bonzo and a dog they owned "got to be very good buddies." The two used to play together until the dog was killed by a car on a nearby highway.

The bear was also very smart, learning how to open doors with its front paws while standing on its hind legs. It was that trick that got Bonzo in trouble during March of 1987. The Kuivinen's neighbor went into her basement to do her laundry one day and the bear was waiting for her at the bottom of the steps.

The female was picked up by a DNR conservation officer on March 20th and relocated to a remote portion of Baraga County. Unfortunately, I didn't learn about this

Cubs wearing radio collars at the time they were released.

until after the bear had already been returned to the wild. I would have liked to put the radio collar back on her before that happened. That was the last we heard about the female.

We had no idea what happened to the male until I saw what I think was him during July of 1988. I encountered that same bear every summer for the next five years, photographing him on a number of occasions each year and his behavior was always the same. He not only acted like he knew me. He trusted me.

The last time I saw him was July of 1993. I only saw him once that summer. He was getting to be a big bear by then. He obviously avoided most other people to stay alive that long, but I think he made a mistake that summer by appearing before the wrong person and was killed.

There are other possibilities, of course. The bear could have been hit by a vehicle as he crossed a road or been live trapped and relocated. However, I think he was experienced enough to avoid those fates. Regardless of what happened to him, he lived longer than most bears in the wild and I like to think Lucy and I helped make that possible.

(Left) The two cubs during one of the first walks we took them on in the woods. We wanted to introduce them to surroundings similar to what they would be living in when they were returned to the wild.

Chapter 4

One-Of-A-Kind Black Bear

A black bear born in Michigan during January of 1989 was one of the most valuable and unique representatives of its species in North America for a number of years. The animal used to live in the wild like others of its kind, yet it was tolerant of humans. In fact, the bear liked contact with people, not only being around them, but being touched and petted, too.

That is what made the bruin unique. Because of the animal's affinity for people, its temperature and heart rate could be taken at practically any time, and rapid eye movement could be monitored as it slept, which made it valuable in terms of learning more about the physiology of wild black bears. The fact that this bear didn't have a "normal" upbringing is responsible for it becoming such a rare individual.

The bruin was one of two cubs born in the northern Lower Peninsula's Missaukee County near Lake City to a female that had constructed a ground nest for the winter rather than seeking shelter in an enclosed den. The young female and her brother were about two months old when the bear family was discovered by hikers. Word spread about the mother and cubs, resulting in daily disturbance by people who wanted to see and photograph the bears.

Some of the visitors made noises and poked the mother to get her to look up or move so the cubs could be seen. The harassment became too much for the adult female and she eventually abandoned the cubs. The day after the mother left her cubs, a conservation officer followed her tracks in the snow. The tracks led steadily away and he turned back after trailing her more than a mile.

The officer then rescued the cubs in the hopes a new home could be found for them. There were two options. They could either be put in a zoo or placed with a foster mother. Wild females with cubs will frequently adopt an orphan when they are still in the den. Wildlife biologists have discovered that bear mothers don't begin

(Left) The female cub that was born in Michigan and abandoned by its mother due to human disturbance, was placed with a foster mother in Minnesota.

distinguishing one cub from another until after they leave their winter den. They accept any cub in the den with them as their own.

Once mother and cubs leave the den, the adult soon knows the identity of her off-spring and is more likely to reject or kill an orphan.

Putting the cubs with foster mothers was the preferred alternative, so they could be returned to the wild. In this case, it also proved necessary because no zoo in the upper midwest could be located that was willing to raise the cubs. The problem was finding suitable foster mothers.

An extra cub can sometimes overburden a foster mother, reducing the amount of milk available for each baby bear, which can threaten the survival of all of the cubs. Healthy black bears are known to have as many as five cubs in a litter, but litters of one to three are more common. Females with one or two cubs of their own are the best can-didates for foster mothers because they are more likely to be able to handle an extra youngster.

Due to an ongoing bear research project underway on Drummond Island, a num-ber of females with cubs were fitted with radio collars and the locations of their dens were known. However, one of the objectives of the research being conducted on the is-land was to determine natural cub production and survival. There was a possibility that putting the orphans with foster mothers on the island would impact the results of that study, so those females were rejected as foster parents.

Females with cubs that were wearing radio collars were also available in Wiscon-sin and Minnesota as a result of bear research underway in those states. Both cubs ended up being flown to northeast Minnesota where former U.S. Forest Service Bear Biologist Dr. Lynn Rogers selected a foster mother for each of them. Due to a bumper crop of hazel nuts the previous fall, Rogers' collared females were unusually fit to adopt cubs. Another advantage of sending the Michigan bears to Minnesota was fe-males with cubs were still in dens in Rogers' former study area near the Forest Ser-vice's North Central Experiment Station at Ely.

Before being transferred to Rogers, Wisconsin DNR Bear Biologist Bruce Kohn attempted to place the male cub with a mother in his study area that had already left her den, and she rejected it.

During the weeks that elapsed from the time the cubs were abandoned until Rogers got them, they had become imprinted on people. They had been bottle fed and cared for by Joe and Barb Rogers with the Wildlife Recovery Association near Mid-land, while they awaited adoption. An attempt was made to isolate the cubs from peo-ple as much as possible, but eliminating all contact was impossible. They were aban-doned at a critical stage in their lives when bonding with their mothers normally would have taken place.

The male cub, which weighed nine pounds at the time, was placed with a 17-year-old female weighing 175 pounds that had two cubs of her own. The young male clung to Rogers' neck as he steered a snowmobile toward its new home in the Su-perior National Forest. Following is Rogers' account of the adoption.

"I stopped 100 yards from the den and the cub followed close behind as I walked toward the surface nest similar to the one the cub had been born in. This nest was in a thickly wooded spruce lowland next to the dark upturned roots of a windfall. The mother was sitting upright in the nest, sideways to me, watching with an uninterested, lethargic look.

"Ten yards away, I picked up the cub and gently tossed him halfway to the den. He yelped as he plopped on the snow, and the mother suddenly leaped from the nest, bounded over the windfall, and tried to gather the cub to her, grunting with concern. The terrified cub screamed, turned on his back and fought her with all four feet. She turned away and the cub scampered back to me. The mother then moved off and I put the cub in the nest with the female's two cubs, but he was afraid of them, too, making threatening gurgling sounds.

"I watched through the trees as the cub left the nest and climbed a tree. The mother returned, checked her cubs, then climbed the tree, again grunting her concern for the orphan. The next day I returned to find the cub up a different tree, the mother's tracks under the tree, and the female with her cubs at a tree 75 feet away, patiently waiting for the new cub to join them. When the cub saw me, he descended the tree and tried to climb my pant leg.

"I pushed the reluctant cub back to the mother. She ran to him. He squalled and ran back to me. I gently tossed him past the mother. He screamed, unable to get to me without going past the solicitous mother. I hurried away before he could get around her. When I returned the following day, the mother was standing guard under a tree with three cubs in it!"

Response of the female cub, which weighed about the same as her brother, to its foster mother was similar to her brother's. She was placed with a four-year-old that had one cub. The adult female was unique in her own right. Although she had spent her entire life in the wild, she was habituated to humans, meaning she learned to tolerate the presence of people nearby as she went about her normal daily activities. Rogers is responsible for pioneering the habituation of black bears for study purposes, which has been a major breakthrough in gathering intimate details about the animals' behavior, food selection and much more.

Adoption of the female cub from Michigan by this bruin played a major role in the development of the youngster as a one-of-a-kind representative of her species. The problem was not getting the mother bear to accept the new cub, but vice versa. The presence of a guest with Rogers when this adoption took place added an interesting twist to the proceedings.

"After being pushed toward the mother bear, the cub ran back and climbed the pant leg of Ugo, a visiting Italian who spoke very little English. His look at me was priceless as the mother carefully pealed the clinging cub off his pant leg with her mouth. The cub soon gave up and accepted the strange mother."

Once the cub accepted its new mother, it easily adapted to living in the wild, but the bond with people remained intact. As part of the ongoing study of the Michigan bear's foster mother, Rogers and his assistants periodically visited the family to check on their progress and behavior, sometimes following them for 24 hours. This helped maintain the young bear's interaction with people and was partly responsible for development into such a unique individual that was equally comfortable among bears and people.

While interaction between the young female and people was maintained, the opposite approach was used with the male to see if that might make a difference. He and his new family went undisturbed. The female that had adopted the male cub was checked in her den the following winter.

Only one yearling was with the foster parent. It was a male, but so were the other two cubs that the Michigan bear was placed with. Since the orphan wasn't marked, it is impossible to know which animal survived. There is a good probability that the animal was the one from Michigan, however, because he was twice as big as his step brothers at the time he was adopted.

One of the objectives of the adoptions of the Michigan orphans by wild mothers was to determine if cubs that have developed an attraction for people can be successfully returned to the wild. The answer to that question is obviously, "Yes." The long term benefits of doing so in this case were tremendous in terms of furthering our understanding of black bears.

The one-of-a-kind female separated from her foster mother and step sister on May 26, 1990, according to Rogers. He said the adult was approaching another breeding cycle and she actively chased her daughters away, which were a year and a half old at the time. The bear biologist explained that's normally how and why family breakup occurs among black bears. He added that the timing of family breakup varies, but it occurs most often during June in northern Minnesota.

Both yearling females established their own territories within a portion of their mother's home range, which is usually what happens. While mother bears give up a portion of their territory to their daughters, male offspring disperse and eventually establish a home range of their own in a new area. The Michigan female's territory included the North Central Experiment Station where Rogers used to work, making it easier for he and his assistants to monitor the animal's activity.

I visited Rogers during early September of 1990, both to see how the female was doing and to learn more about his research. My arrival was timed to coincide with the opening of Minnesota's bear season on September 1. Since the study area was not closed to hunting, Rogers had enlisted the help of volunteers to follow each of the three bears that were habituated to people. The volunteers gathered information about the bears' behavior as well as reducing the chances one of the valuable bears would be shot.

By September 1, the 1 3/4-year-old female from Michigan weighed 125 pounds, almost tripling the 43 pounds she weighed during spring. Handouts of food she got at the research lab were largely responsible for her unusual weight gain. Her sister had lived on a natural diet all summer and she only weighed 84 pounds, which is more in line with the normal weight of yearling female black bear.

I spent part of one day following the female from Michigan and it was a treat to be able to walk with such an animal and observe its behavior. Spending time with the bear made it easy to understand how valuable this animal and the two others like it were in furthering man's understanding of black bears. Information was gathered by walking with these bruins that would be impossible to obtain any other way.

The unique bear that got its start in Michigan mated with a wild male during the spring of 1991 at the age of two and gave birth to three cubs in January of 1992 as she turned three years old. When Rogers' research ended in June of that year, there was concern that the female's willingness to trust and seek contact with people might lead to problems. The only way to eliminate potential conflicts was to remove her and her cubs from the wild. A zoo known as Grandfather Mountain, which is along the Blue Ridge Parkway near Linville, North Carolina was considered the best home for the bear family.

"I've been all across this country looking at bear programs and the captive habitat at Grandfather Mountain is the best I've seen," Rogers said after the bears were relocated to North Carolina. "There are a number of cherry trees with loads of fruit

(Right) Dr. Lynn Rogers from Ely, Minnesota with the one-of-a-kind bear when she was 1 3/4 years old and weighed 125 pounds.

developing, and the one-acre enclosure is rich in jewel weed, which is one of her favorite foods in the wild. It is planted with red clover, which is what the Forest Service plants for bears in Minnesota, and it has some black berries and strawberries, too.

"I selected Grandfather, also, because the bears get a good balanced diet. Mildred (the mountain's mascot) is one of the oldest captive bears I know of at age 26, which is a good recommendation in itself. And the staff shows real concern for the bears. For example, they will spread the food out in a number of locations around the enclosure so that the bears can forage for their food more like they would in the wild.

"During her 3 1/2 years, this bear has provided information that will help the whole species forever," Rogers continued. "Now she will be involved in public education as part of the interpretive program here at Grandfather, doing about as well with her life as possible in the way of educating mankind about her species."

The well traveled adult female that got her start in Michigan is still at Grandfather Mountain.

Although the story about the two bear cubs orphaned in Missaukee County has basically a happy ending, it is important to remember that a unique set of circumstances made this possible. It is not always possible to find homes for orphaned cubs, either in zoos or the wild. Females with cubs that are encountered in dens are better left alone. If they are disturbed, there is a chance the mother will abandon her cubs. Cubs that remain with their natural mothers have the best chance of survival.

Never pick up cubs that appear to be abandoned because, in most cases, they aren't. Denned females may leave their cubs if startled or disturbed, but they will frequently return after people have left the area. The same thing often happens if a female with small cubs encounters humans after they've left the den. An example of that occurred in north Marquette County on March 28th one year.

Gary Herriman and a partner were cutting firewood in an area that had been logged when they heard the cries of bear cubs. There were three of them and their mother had been scared off by the mens' presence. Unsure what to do, Herriman contacted Bear Researcher Terry DeBruyn, who lived in Marquette at the time, and he returned to the scene with them. By the time they got back to the area, the mother was with the cubs.

Cubs taken from dens may not survive. Robert LaFleur from Alpena illegally removed three cubs from a den one winter. Two of them died of starvation and the same thing might have happened to the third if it hadn't been turned over to a veterinarian. LaFleur was ticketed, fined and lost his hunting privileges.

The surviving cub was transferred to a rehabilitation center in Oregon after being cared for by Dave Siegrist for a while.

(Right) Unique female with two of her three cubs soon after they arrived at Grandfather Mountain in North Carolina. She's looking up at the third cub that is in tree above the other two. (Photo courtesy of Hugh Morton)

Chapter **5**

Dealing With Orphaned Cubs

Prior to 1993, when Michigan black bear cubs were orphaned in the wild, they were often shipped out of state where they were placed in rehabilitation centers that would return them to the wild or put them with wild foster mothers. That's what happened when a cub born in Iron County during January of 1992 was separated from its mother. It was shipped to Pennsylvania after it was abandoned by its birth mother in the den.

The mother bear didn't abandon the cub willingly. She was chased away by a dog, according to DNR Wildlife Biologist Doug Wagner at Crystal Falls, who cared for the cub for 2 1/2 weeks before it left the state.

The expectant female selected a hollowed out area under a blowdown as her den during the fall of 1991 and the site wasn't far from a house. The home owner's dog found the den during late winter after the cub was born. Most cubs are born during January.

The dog's barking outside the den on at least two occasions forced the mother bear to leave its cub. Conservation Officer Jim Bowerman from Iron River retrieved the cub when its mother didn't return after two days and turned it over to Wagner.

Wagner kept the cub, which weighed about eight pounds, in his basement while trying to locate a foster mother with cubs of her own. Mother bears that are still in dens will readily accept orphaned cubs put with them. Once females with cubs have left their dens they are less likely to accept orphans because they are usually able to identify their offspring by then.

However, Pennsylvania Bear Biologist Gary Alt developed a technique that increases the chances that female bears will adopt orphans after they've left their dens. He discovered that Vicks Vaporub will temporarily block a mother bear's sense of

(Left) DNR Wildlife Biologist Doug Wagner started collaring adult females in the U.P. during 1993 to serve as foster mothers for orphaned cubs so the orphans could remain in Michigan rather than being shipped to another state.

smell. So when an orphaned cub smeared with the substance is introduced to a foster mother, she can't tell it's not one of her own and usually accepts it.

Radio collared female bears with cubs are often chased up a tree and then the treated orphan is sent up a tree to join them. A number of radio collared females with cubs were present in Michigan at the time the Iron County cub was abandoned, both in the U.P. and the northern L.P. where studies were underway, but DNR researchers decided they didn't want to try to place the orphaned cub with one of them. Gary Alt from Pennsylvania then agreed to take the orphan.

On the day the cub arrived, Alt and his wife introduced it to a female with two cubs of her own. It was raining heavily and they encountered the family of bears in a ground nest at close range. The U.P. cub, which had already been descented with Vicks, was sent off to join them there.

The main reason Michigan researchers did not want to try to place the orphaned cub with one of the radio collared study animals in the state is they were concerned it would affect the results of their research. Cub production and survival was one aspect of the studies. Adding cubs to existing litters would obviously have an impact on those findings. An orphaned cub might reduce the chances of survival of a female's own off-spring, for example.

Starting in 1993, Doug Wagner took steps to insure a supply of foster mothers would be available in the state when cubs were orphaned in the future. Experience with the cub that was shipped to Pennsylvania served as incentive for him to start work on such a program. Wagner started fitting female bears in Iron, Dickinson and Menominee Counties with radio collars for the express purpose of placing orphaned cubs with them, if and when the need arose.

At the same time Doug was insuring a potential supply of foster mothers, he monitored cub production and survival of the collared animals. Since that information had not been gathered from the southern U.P. before, the effort served a dual purpose. It's valuable to gather data on bears from various parts of the state so results can be compared.

Placing orphaned cubs with wild foster mothers is obviously the best course of action, when possible. It gives the young bears a second chance for a normal life in the wild. There's no better way for a cub to learn how to survive in the wild than from an adult female that has done it. However, orphaned cubs that can't be placed with foster mothers, can still be successfully returned to the wild. More on that later.

Doug got his first chance to place an orphaned cub with a foster mother during 1996. He got an orphan weighing 2 pounds, 12 ounces from the Lower Peninsula. On March 1 he put that cub in a den with a female that had three cubs of her own. All of the cubs were ear-tagged for later identification.

Since cubs normally den with their mother during the second winter, Wagner figured he would find out if the fostering worked when checking the collared female in her den during 1997. Unfortunately, it didn't work out that way. The mother bear had three yearlings with her in the den, but they had all lost their ear tags, so it was impossible to determine if the orphan had survived. One cub had been lost during the course of a year, but it was impossible to tell which one it was.

During 1997, three orphaned cubs needed foster mothers. The cubs were from the same litter and Doug got them on February 17, 1997. Their mother was four years old and was part of bear research underway in the northern Lower Peninsula. The adult female died of respiratory failure after being drugged in the den so she could be

*DNR Wildlife Biologist Doug Wagner fits a new radio collar on an
adult female black bear that may serve as a foster mother to an orphaned cub
in the future. (DNR photo by Dave Kenyon)*

Orphaned cubs are ear-tagged for identification before being placed with a foster mother so their survival can be checked the following year. Unfortunately, cubs sometimes lose their tags, making it impossible to determine if orphans survived.

examined. Her death was a freak accident. Hundreds of bruins have been handled in a similar fashion with no problems.

Each of the orphans were placed with adult females in the U.P. that had three cubs of their own and would be able to handle one more infant. Litters of four aren't unusual and as many as five cubs have been born to some females. Two of the orphaned cubs went to separate dens in Menominee County and the third was placed in a den near Kenton. This time, Doug was able to determine his efforts paid off.

The orphan that was put in the den near Kenton weighed four pounds and was placed there on the same day Wagner got the triplets. One year later, on February 17, 1998, the orphan was still with its foster mother in their new den. It weighed 50 pounds then.

There was at least partial success with one of the other orphans that weighed 4 1/2 pounds when it was placed in a Menominee County den with a female and her triplets on February 28, 1997. The adult female slipped out of her radio collar before leaving the den. However, Doug saw her 100 yards from the den during April and she had all four cubs with her.

The results are unknown on the third orphan put with a Menominee County foster mother on February 24, 1997. The orphan weighed four pounds at the time. Like the situation Doug encountered on the orphan placed with a foster mother during 1996, all of the yearlings that were with the female the following year had lost their ear tags. Three out of the four cubs had survived to become yearlings. One female yearling was missing, but it was impossible to determine if it was the orphan or the one the adult had given birth to.

Other bear research in Michigan has determined that cub mortality isn't unusual. Loss of cubs tends to be higher among large litters, but females that only have one or two cubs sometimes lose cubs, too. Cub survival is usually highest among older, more experienced mothers like those orphans are placed with, but veteran mothers sometimes also lose cubs to predation and accidents.

A foster mother that Doug placed an orphan with after she left her den during 1998, for example, had triplets when she was checked in the den, but when Wagner caught up to her on June 8, she only had one cub with her. The orphan weighed 11 pounds and Doug had already smeared it with Vicks when the adult female and her remaining cub were treed. The orphan was then placed on the tree the other two were in and it climbed up to join them.

Doug said the two cubs were together in the tree for three hours before he left. He saw the same female on June 11 and she still had two cubs with her. Wagner thought they were the same two cubs that had been in the tree with her on the 8th. The adult female was shot during the 1998 hunting season, so a den check during 1999 to determine if the two cubs survived was impossible.

Work that Wagner has done with cubs that are orphaned during the fall confirms that they have an excellent chance of survival. He found that they don't have to be taught to seek a winter den. They do it instinctively.

A pair of cubs that Doug got during September of 1995 are perfect examples. They were orphaned when their mother was killed after being hit by a vehicle as she attempted to cross Highway U.S. 41 in the city limits of Marquette. The cubs climbed a nearby tree where they were tranquilized and transferred to Wagner.

The male and female cubs weighed 47 and 59 pounds respectively when Wagner got them on September 13th. He released them in Iron County on the 18th after fitting them with radio collars and ear tags.

Doug said he thought the cubs would stay together, but they separated, leaving the area where they were released. The signal from the female's collar was eventually located west of Amasa toward the end of September. The bruin remained in a small area for about 10 days and the wildlife biologist thought she might den there, but she ended up moving south of Alpha before denning.

The male cub denned near Iron River. He weighed 113 pounds on December 6, 1995. His radio collar was removed at that time. Ear tags remained intact and there's been no report of that bruin having been taken by a hunter.

The orphaned female weighed 53 pounds when checked in her den on February 1, 1996. Her weight had gone up to 77 pounds when checked on March 16, 1997 and 120 by February 12, 1998. She was killed by a hunter on September 25, 1998 at the age of 3 3/4.

The third orphaned cub that Wagner collared during the fall of '95 was a 95 pound male that was caught in a leghold trap near Felch on October 24th. He tranquilized the bruin to release it from the trap and to fit it with a collar. At the time, the wildlife biologist didn't know the cub was an orphan. He thought it would rejoin its mother after being released from the trap and they would den together.

However, when he checked the bear in its den on January 25th, it was alone. Wagner said it dug a hole under a downed cedar tree for its winter sleep. The bruin's weight was down to 77 pounds when checked in its den, but that was normal weight loss. Bears always lose weight in winter dens.

Besides the three cubs orphaned during the fall, Wagner has also monitored three bears that were collared and released as yearlings after having been cared for by

A pair of cubs that were orphaned in the fall when their mother was killed by a car, did fine on their own. After being fitted with radio collars by Wagner, they gained weight normally, denned on their own and adapted to living in the wild.

humans. Two of them were in the biologist's care for about a month and a half before being released. He got both yearling females during early March, a time when most bears are still denned.

One captured in Ontonagon County on March 4, 1995, only weighed 17 pounds. It had traveled 3 1/2 miles from its original den site where it was disturbed by a logging operation. The second one was from Dickinson County and it weighed 47 pounds, but had 22 porcupine quills in its face and chest, which were removed. That yearling was found in a Norway resident's garage on March 6, 1995. Both bruins gained 60 pounds before they were released on April 21st.

Wagner said the larger of the two females, which was 107 pounds when it was returned to the wild, was located near Covington during the summer of 1996 and then contact was lost with its collar. The smaller female that weighed 77 pounds when released, ended up denning north of Lake Michigamme, according to Wagner. She survived until the fall of 1997 when she was shot by a hunter in Baraga County.

The third yearling was located as an orphaned cub in a tree near the Hermansville Post Office and turned over to Delta County Wildlife Rehabilitator Sheral Cantrell during 1994. She cared for the young bear until January of 1995, trying to minimize its contact with people, so it could be returned to the wild. Then Wagner took the year-old animal weighing 85 pounds, to a den site in northeast Iron County that had formerly been occupied by another bear, putting a collar on it and a blue tag in its left ear.

Wagner said the yearling stayed in the den all winter, but when it left the den during the spring of 1995, it managed to get rid of its collar. This bear was taken by a

One orphaned cub was cared for by wildlife rehabilitator Sheral Cantrell
until winter and then placed in a den as a yearling weighing 85 pounds.
Despite the fact the bear had been fed by humans for months,
it didn't become a nuisance, surviving primarily on natural foods.

hunter in Gogebic County 90 miles west of the den it had been placed in, on September 20, 1997 when she was three years old. She was identified from her ear tag. She weighed 157 pounds when killed.

One of the most encouraging findings from those three yearlings, according to Wagner, is that despite the contact those bears had with people and the food they provided, the animals avoided people and stayed out of trouble since they were released.

The results also indicate that orphaned cubs can be successfully returned to the wild. Wagner hopes to keep between eight and 12 adult female black bears fitted with radio collars on an annual basis to serve as foster mothers. He said that's the optimum number that will insure some of them will have cubs during any given year.

Sandra Schultz with drugged female bear that she live-trapped and ear-tagged on Drummond Island while working for the DNR.

Chapter 6

The Drummond Island Story

Drummond Island, a 125-square-mile chunk of real estate at the eastern end of the Upper Peninsula along the lower St. Marys River, proved to be a perfect place for resumption of major bear research in Michigan during 1986. The island was closed to bear hunting starting in 1983 due to concern about the population there. Twelve bruins were known to have been taken by hunters on the island during 1982 and bear hunting pressure had also been high during preceding years.

The closure gave DNR researchers the opportunity to study an unhunted population and determine how many animals there were before reopening the island to bear hunting, so the impacts of hunting could be assessed. The island situation was considered ideal for research because the water surrounding it was thought to be a barrier to movement of bears to and from the island. Biologists found out otherwise during the study, but there was probably less change in the population due to bears coming and going than there would have been on the mainland.

The bear population estimate determined for Drummond also enabled the DNR to test the validity of a bait station index to bear abundance that had been started in 1984. The island was one of the locations in the state where the index was tried. The index is conducted by placing baits at random locations along survey routes. After a specified period of time, the number of baits visited by bears is determined.

An estimate of bear numbers can be made based on the number of baits visited. High visitation would reflect a high bear population and low visitation would mean the opposite. An increase in visitation over a period of years, which is what happened on Drummond, would indicate an increasing population and a decline would suggest fewer bears are present. Only 10 percent of the island's bait stations were visited by bears during 1984, but it increased to 38 percent in 1985 and 50 percent during 1986 when the intensive bear study was started there.

On the mainland, visitation rates also increased during the bait station index, especially since the permit system started in 1990. Current estimates put the bear population in Michigan at a minimum of 15,500 animals.

Another plus for basing a bear research project on the island is the DNR had a building there that would serve as headquarters. The fact that public property was abundant on Drummond was another reason for doing bear work there. University of Wisconsin Graduate Student Sandra Schultz was hired to trap bears during the first two years because of her previous experience with capturing bears for research purposes in Wisconsin. DNR Researchers Larry Visser and Elaine Carlson, who were based at the Houghton Lake Wildlife Research Station at the time, played major roles in the study and were assisted by many other DNR employees and volunteers.

Live traps and snares were used to capture and mark as many bears as possible during the summer of 1986. Both culvert and barrel type live traps were used to catch bears on the island. The major difference between the two types of traps is the barrel variety are slightly smaller and much lighter, enabling researchers to carry them for placement in locations where it would be difficult to put culvert traps. Culvert traps are mounted on wheels and are towed to trap sites with vehicles.

Besides portability, the two types of live traps are basically the same. They have trigger mechanisms toward the rear and sliding trap doors at the front. Bait is attached to triggers and when bears pull on the bait once inside, doors fall, trapping animals inside.

Snares used to catch black bears are simply loops of heavy-duty, spring-loaded cable, with one end fastened to trees, that are thrown over a bear's foot once triggered and lock in place when a bear tries to run away. The devices are normally set in the ground near bait and are sprung when bruins step on them, but the rocky soil on Drummond made it difficult to set snares properly. Researchers experimented with snares set in PVC pipes the first summer that accounted for the capture of two bears.

Once caught, bears were injected with a drug to immobilize them, so they could be marked for later identification. A syringe fitted on the end of an aluminum pole called a jab stick was used to administer muscle relaxant to captured bears. The amount of drug used to immobilize the animals varied based on the animals' weight.

At the same time bears were tagged, biological information was obtained from each animal. A small premolar tooth was removed from bruins so their ages could be determined, for example. Body measurements, weights and blood samples were also taken. After processing of an animal was complete, an antidote was administered to speed up recovery from the muscle relaxant and bruins returned to the wild wearing ear tags. Colored streamers were applied with tags to the ears of all males. Streamer color varied, depending upon where the animal was caught on the island.

A total of 23 bears were marked on Drummond during 1986, 12 of which were females. The oldest bear captured was an 18-year-old male, but bruins that were 16 and 17 years old were also trapped. One of the yearling males that was tagged and fitted with orange streamers, was seen swimming to the mainland on August 25 by a fisherman. The animal was sighted again the next day further west near Caribou Lake.

On September 10th, opening day of bear season on the mainland, the young male was killed by a hunter near Cedarville. Where that bruin ended up was 33 miles west of where it was ear-tagged and 20 miles west of DeTour Village. While the main intent of the Drummond Island study was to estimate bear numbers, the project provided other interesting information about the animals' movements, as the above example illustrates.

Trapping and tagging bears continued on the island during 1987 and 1988. A new dimension was added to the study in 1987 with the placement of radio collars on some of the animals. A percentage of both males and females were fitted with collars. All of the animals that were handled got ear tags. By the time trapping was completed for the year in 1987, 45 bears had been tagged and 26 were wearing collars.

The total number of bears handled went up to 78 in 1988, according to Elaine Carlson. She said about 50 bruins were wearing radio collars by that fall when the island was reopened to bear hunting. Yearlings handled during den checks were collared as well as animals trapped during the summer. Eleven yearlings were collared in dens during March of 1988, for example, and 13 newborn cubs were counted.

By 1988 bear numbers were high on the island, too high for some residents. Nuisance complaints were common and that's why a hunt was planned. To protect the island's bears from possible overharvest during the hunt, a decision was made to limit hunting pressure through a permit system. A total of 70 permits were issued in a random drawing for two hunts, with 30 permits for the first one starting September 10 and 40 for the second starting September 24. Experimentation with permit bear hunts and how they should be regulated began on Drummond and helped set the stage for the statewide permit system started in 1990.

A minimum harvest quota of 12 bears was established for each of the two island hunts in 1988. The season would close at the end of the day on which bear number 12 was registered. All hunters were required to register animals they bagged by 11:00 a.m. on the day after making a kill. The taking of more than 12 bruins was possible under this system, but not enough to exceed the maximum quota of 20 established for each hunt.

Larry Visser estimated there were 80 to 100 black bears on Drummond prior to the first bear hunt there in five years. He said about 80 of the animals were 1 3/4 years old or older and he guessed there might be 10 cubs. At least five bears that would have been legal to hunters were known to have died on the island prior to the first hunt. Three adult females are thought to have been killed by other bears, a yearling female was shot illegally and another yearling female was hit by a car.

The adult females that were killed by other bears were five, seven and 13 years old, according to Elaine Carlson. She said the 5-year-old had cubs and the other two had yearlings. The female with cubs was killed and partially eaten by another bear, probably an adult male. It's unknown whether that female's cubs survived. Carlson said that six of 13 cubs handled in dens on Drummond the previous winter were known to have died.

There's an excellent chance that all of the females were killed while trying to protect their young. However, competition for food and space might have also played a role. Adult females will kill each other in territorial disputes. With approximately 100 bears on the island, they may have reached a saturation point. The findings about bears killing each other on the island indicate that cannibalism and predation among bears might be highest in an unhunted population.

Besides the five documented bear deaths on the island before the first hunt, two males were also known to have left the island. An adult male swam to Ontario's Cockburn Island and a yearling male swam to the mainland. Visser said the yearling was bagged by a hunter near Hessel on September 10. Another young male swam to Ontario's St. Joseph Island during 1987 and was killed there a year later.

Only 25 of the 30 permit holders registered for the island's first hunt in 1988

During the study, a number of bears left Drummond by swimming to the mainland or one of the nearby islands that are part of Ontario.

starting on September 10. That season was only open for three days. Ten bears were killed on opening day, one on the second and two on the third for a total kill of 13. Bear number 12 was registered on September 12 and one more bruin was tagged by the end of that day.

Thirty-one out of 40 hunters showed up for the second hunt starting on September 24. Despite the fact there were more hunters in the field during that session and still plenty of bears left, only nine were registered during the full seven days of hunting. Results from the second hunt indicate that bears are less vulnerable to hunters after a week of hunting.

Seven of the nine bears taken on the second hunt were wearing radio collars and two were unmarked. This compares with seven collared animals, two with ear tags and four unmarked that were registered on the first hunt. That information, along with reports of other bears seen by hunters, helped the DNR fine tune their population estimate for the island.

Hunters who used hounds registered a total of four bears, two during each hunt, and the remainder were tagged by those hunting over bait. Bow hunters accounted for three bears on Drummond during 1988, taking two of those during the first hunt. One of the archers, Harold Lover from Montrose who participated in the first hunt, accounted for the largest bear collected from the island that fall. He shot a 5 3/4-year-old male that weighed 295 pounds in the round and 240 pounds dressed. That bear was live trapped and weighed during early July and it tipped the scales at 190 pounds then.

The heaviest bear registered on the second hunt was a 3 3/4 year-old female that had a dressed weight of 200 pounds. That same bear had a live weight of 115 pounds during the summer. A dressed weight of 65 pounds was recorded for the smallest bear taken during both hunts. It was a yearling female that only weighed 27 pounds when checked in its den the previous winter.

One 7-day hunt starting September 22 was held on Drummond during 1989 and 30 permit holders harvested 15 bears for a 50 percent rate of success. Visser estimated 60 bruins that were at least yearlings were on the island that fall. There were 33 collared bears present before the hunt and eight of those taken by hunters had collars.

All 15 of the bears killed by hunters during 1989 were taken over bait. There were hunters using hounds that year, but windy, wet conditions during the hunt negatively affected their success.

When the Drummond Island bear study was started, it was only supposed to last two years. However, the need for more information was soon recognized and the life of the project was extended a number of times. Intensive research continued for at least seven years. Most radio collars were removed from Island bears during 1992 and '93. When the statewide permit system was started in 1990, Drummond was recognized as a separate bear management unit and it remains that way today. One of the most important lessons learned from research on the island is that bear hunting with bait and dogs can be effectively managed under a permit system while maintaining a healthy bear population. In fact, bear numbers continued to increase on Drummond after hunting resumed.

During den work conducted on the island in the first months of 1991, a total of 21 cubs were handled, including three sets of triplets. A pair of yearlings with one of the adult females wearing a radio collar that Larry Visser examined that winter were the smallest he had ever seen. The adult only weighed 105 pounds. The smallest yearling tipped the scales at 20 pounds and its sibling weighed 25 pounds. The smallest yearling died the following spring.

Extreme competition for food among the island's bears might have been responsible for the small size of that female and her yearlings. Visser said more than 100 bears were on Drummond by 1991. He added that the desired population level was 60 animals. The harvest goal for hunters on the island that fall was 19 bears, but they fell short of that tally, perhaps because of the timing of the hunt.

Experimentation with the timing of hunts and hunting pressure on success continued on the island. In 1991, for example, a 7-day hunt was conducted from October 8-14. Fifty-one permits were issued for that season, but only 47 permittees actually hunted.

The kill was the same as it had been during 1989 with fewer hunters. A total of 15 bears were registered by hunters in 1991 for a 32 percent rate of success. The harvest was comprised of eight males and seven females and only three of the females were adults (at least 4 years old). Four of the males weighed in excess of 300 pounds.

The biggest bruin weighed 573 pounds in the round. Another went 480 pounds, a third had a live weight of 420 pounds and the fourth big male had a dressed weight of 295 pounds. All four adult males were taken with the aid of hounds. Six of the 15 bear taken by hunters on the island during 1991 were fitted with radio collars.

The Drummond Island Bear Project uncovered many important details about bruins that will prove valuable in future management of the animals across the state, some of which has already been mentioned. It was also determined that the island population includes a lot of mature females, for example. For that reason, the harvest on Drummond always included a high proportion of females. So the rate of removal of females wasn't hurting the population, as is sometimes suspected when the kill includes a significant number of females. High female harvests were to be expected in view of the

*Elaine Carlson and Larry Visser process a collared bear on Drummond Island
with the help of DNR Veterinarian Steve Schmitt and
former Wildlife Division Chief Karl Hosford during den work.*

number present and the same situation may exist in other areas where more than normal numbers of females are taken by hunters.

Based on den checks, the average age at which Drummond's females first produce cubs is 4.6. The average litter size among adult females is 2.1. Interestingly, it was determined that most cubs are born on odd numbered years and cub survival was the lowest during even numbered years when the fewest cubs were born. The lowest cub survival rate on the island of 49 percent occurred during 1990 and the highest survival rate of 95 percent was documented in 1991. Male cubs had a lower survival rate than females, which might partially explain the high number of females in the population.

Data obtained on Drummond will be compared with information gathered elsewhere in the U.P. and the L.P. to get an even better handle on what's happening with Michigan black bears. Although limited research will continue on the island in the future, the last of the collared bears were removed during the fall of 1993. Bear hunting success remained high on Drummond that fall due to the presence of plenty of animals. Due to lower than expected harvests the previous two years, a harvest goal of 24 bears was set for 1993 and that's how many bears were bagged.

Two of those 24 were the last ones on the island still wearing radio collars. Visser removed most of the collars from island bears during den visits the previous two winters, however, there was one male he was unable to retrieve a collar from because it always ran when approached. Island resident Pat Kelly shot that bear during the hunt. The 6-year-old male weighed 450 pounds. A female with a nonfunctioning transmitter in its collar, which Visser had been unable to locate, was also bagged. Visser added that six women participated in the 1993 Drummond Island bear hunt and they all filled their tags by the end of the second day of the season.

A male bear that was born on Drummond during 1989 was killed about 100 miles away in Ontario during the spring of 1997. The bruin was handled as a cub on the island, according to Visser, and then fitted with a radio collar in 1990 when it was a year old. Larry said the bear left the United States in June of 1991 at the age of 2 1/2, swimming from Drummond to nearby Cockburn Island, which is in Canada. The bruin denned on Cockburn and the radio collar that allowed researchers to monitor its movements was removed during February of 1992 while it was denned.

But the bear retained its identifying ear tags. Over the years since the collar was removed, the animal continued moving eastward. It swam from Cockburn to Manitoulin Island, which stretches many miles in an east/west direction.

The animal ended up at the far northeast end of Manitoulin south of the town of Little Current by the spring of '97. The 8-year-old male had an estimated weight of 275 to 300 pounds when it was killed, indicating it was healthy.

Visser added that some bears move from Ontario into Michigan, too. During the study on Drummond, he found that some adult males that were residents of Cockburn Island would swim to Drummond during the breeding season and then return to Ontario. Some of those animals could have been born on Drummond, too, though.

The number of harvest tags issued for the island was constant from 1992 to 1995 at 38, but the number of bears taken each year varied, which clearly shows factors other than hunting pressure and methods affect harvest. There were 14 bruins registered during 1992 and 16 in 1994 compared with the 24 taken in 1993 and 18 during '95. Factors such as natural food availability, number of bears present, timing of the

67

Larry Visser weighs a collared bear bagged by a hunter on Drummond Island during 1988. The island was closed to bear hunting from 1983 through 1987.

hunt, weather conditions and experience level of permittees have as much impact on bear harvest as the hunting methods used and perhaps more so in some cases. The bottom line is that research on Drummond Island clearly shows that the use of bait and hounds for bear hunting does not hurt the population.

Due to the fact the harvest goal for the island was exceeded during 1995 and '96 and public acceptance of bears has increased there during recent years, the harvest goal was reduced for 1999 along with a corresponding reduction in hunting permits. Visser said 13 bears were known to have died on Drummond of nonhunting mortality over a 5-year period. Five of them were killed by other bears, four were car kills and three were illegal kills.

An adult female bear licks a paw injured by a male while protecting her cubs from him. The male bit off three of the female's toes. Five adult females were killed by other bears on Drummond Island during a 5-year period.

SUMMARY OF DRUMMOND ISLAND HUNTS			
Year	Permits Issued	Harvest Goal	Harvest
1988	70	24	22
1989	30	11	15
1990	30	15	11
1991	51	19	15
1992	38	17	14
1993	38	24	24
1994	38	14	16
1995	38	14	18
1996	30	15	19
1997	31	15	15
1998	29	15	7
1999	14	7	

Marking as many bear as possible in any given area is the best way to determine population levels, but it's time consuming and expensive to trap and tag them like this one.

Chapter 7

How Many Bears Are There?

The best way to determine how many bears there are anywhere is to mount an intensive trapping effort to capture and visibly mark as many of them as possible. It's generally impossible to catch all of the bears in a given area, even when the most sophisticated methods are used. However, over a period of time during which many bears have been marked, it's possible to determine the proportion of marked versus unmarked bruins in the population through sightings, recaptures and hunter harvest, to come up with a fairly accurate estimate of the number of bears present.

That very thing was begun on Drummond Island in 1986, with intensive research continuing there through 1992. The total number of bears handled had reached 78 by 1988, according to DNR Wildlife Technician Elaine Carlson, who played an important role in the island study. DNR Bear Biologist Dr. Larry Visser, who headed up the island research, estimated there were 80 to 100 black bears on Drummond during the summer of 1988. He said about 80 of the animals were 1 3/4 years old or older and he estimated there might be 10 cubs.

The figure of approximately 100 bears on the island was as accurate as possible since a high percentage of the population had been handled during the intensive study. At that level, there was approximately one bear per square mile, which is extremely abundant for black bears anywhere. However, from all indications, Drummond's bear population was even higher in 1991.

Due to the time, cost and other limitations involved in an intensive trapping and tagging effort on a statewide basis, alternative census techniques have evolved to determine approximately how many bears we have in Michigan. One of the methods developed by Visser still involves marking as many bears as possible, but an antibiotic mixed with bait does the marking. Since bears only have to eat treated food to be marked, it's easier, cheaper and more efficient to mark large numbers of animals.

The antibiotic used to mark bears is tetracycline. After it is eaten, the antibiotic is deposited in bones and teeth, leaving stains. In teeth, the tetracycline mark is permanent.

A bait station index is the second method used to estimate bear numbers in parts of

Michigan. This technique involves the placement of baits spaced about a mile apart in predetermined areas. The baits, consisting of sardines or bacon, are then checked after 7 to 14 days to determine how many of them were taken by bears. The baits are hung high enough in trees so that bears have to climb the trees to reach them. The claw marks bruins leave in trees are obvious clues about what took the bait.

Cameras have been used to monitor what type of animal took baits in some areas. The cameras have also been valuable in determining the number of marked versus unmarked bears taking the baits. Raccoons and fishers are the most common nontarget animals that take baits besides bears.

The primary function of the bait station index is to help biologists determine whether bears are increasing or decreasing. Visser said the bait station index is most effective for monitoring bear populations in small areas like Drummond Island and in locations where animals are spread out like they are across the northern Lower Peninsula. He said the biomarker method (tetracycline), on the other hand, is most effective where bears are abundant over a large area like they are on the U.P. mainland.

There was and is an excellent correlation between the bait station index on Drummond Island and the increase of bear numbers to high levels. The first year the index was tried on the island, which was 1984, only 10 percent of the baits were taken by bears. The visitation rate went up to 38 percent in 1985 and hit 50 percent by 1986. Every year since then, the percentage of baits taken by bears on the island during the index have either exceeded 50 percent or were close to 50 percent.

In fact, bear numbers appear to have been highest on Drummond, according to the index, from 1992 through 1994. Bait station visitation rates exceeded 60 percent each of those years. As a result of the high bear population on the island then, hunter success was exceptionally high, which helped reduce the population to a more acceptable level.

Hunters registered 24 bears on the island during 1993 and 15 for 1994. By 1995 the number of baits taken by bruins was close to 50 percent again. So the island's bear population is still high and it should remain that way under current management practices that include hunting with bait and dogs under a permit system.

Tetracycline marking studies were conducted in the U.P. independently of bait station index surveys from 1989 through 1993. A total of 600 tetracycline laced baits, consisting of capsules wrapped in bacon, were used per year. Instead of baits being spaced at one mile intervals, they were spaced at a rate of a maximum of one for every 25 square miles to reduce the chances of a bear eating more than one bait. Baits were hung high enough in trees that bears couldn't reach them from the ground.

Treated baits were hung for two weeks (only one week in 1989) and then sites were examined to determine how many had been taken by bears. Those that hadn't been eaten at the end of that time, were removed. The fact that an increasing number of baits were taken by bears each year of the study corresponds to a steady increase in U.P. bear numbers since 1989.

Only 88 tetracycline baits were eaten by bears during 1989, for instance, compared to 246 in 1993. There were 196 baits consumed by bruins during 1990, 175 in 1991 and 236 for 1992. The availability of competing food sources such as fruits,

(Left) A black bear stands on its hind legs to grab a bait that is part of the DNR's bait station index. The index gives an indication of whether bears are increasing or decreasing based on the number of baits visited by bears. The number of bruins in the U.P. were also estimated by putting tetracycline in baits, so they would be marked with stained teeth.

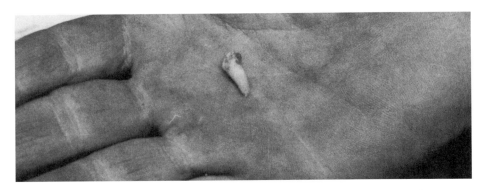

*Cross sections of small premolar teeth like this one are examined under a
microscope to determine how old the animals were that they came from
and to check for tetracycline stains.*

berries and farm crops, can impact the number of baits taken by bears from one year to
the next. That's probably why slightly fewer baits were eaten by bears during 1991
than 1990. Natural foods were abundant during 1991.

To determine the number of marked versus unmarked bears in the population,
teeth from bruins bagged by hunters were examined. This was already being done anyway to gather information about the ages of bears harvested by hunters. By counting
the rings or annuli in stained cross sections of small premolar teeth, it is possible to determine how old bears are. All hunters who shoot bears in Michigan are required to
register the animals with the state and most successful hunters provide a tooth from
their kills during registration.

Tetracycline stains show up as a fluorescent yellow color when examined. Distinct
lines appear for each time a bear has eaten tetracycline, whether during the same year
or successive years, so it's possible to correct for bears that have been marked more
than once. Those correction factors are considered along with the number of baits
eaten, the number of teeth that are marked and those that are unmarked; to calculate
population estimates.

Since Tetracycline marking studies began during 1989, the teeth from 7,250
Michigan bears had been examined for stains through 1997. A total of 414 of them
were marked.

Visser said the resulting estimates represent a minimum figure for the number of
bears present in the U.P. He said a big part of the reason for that is bears that take tetracycline baits are more likely to be harvested than those that don't, especially the year
they were marked. Visser added that population estimates from tetracycline marking
become more accurate as more data is gathered from marked animals during succeed-
ing years. He feels that four years of data from each year of marking, for example, provides a more accurate estimate of bear numbers than calculations from just the first
year after bears are marked.

Based on Visser's calculations, he estimates that the U.P. bear population increased by three to four percent per year during the period 1989 through 1995. This is
the period during which the DNR initiated the zone and quota system, restricting the
number of bear hunting permits issued. Visser estimated there were 8,000 bears that

Females in the Lower Peninsula breed for the first time when as young as 1 1/2 years old and they produce more cubs than females in the U.P., too, resulting in bears increasing at a faster rate.

were yearlings or older in the U.P. on September 1, 1995. By 1999, he estimated there were 11,000 adult black bears in the U.P.

He said an additional 2,500 cubs were present, for a total U.P. population of about 13,500 bears. He added that there were approximately 2,000 additional bruins, including cubs, in the Lower Peninsula in '99, putting the total bear population in the state in September of 1999 at 15,500.

Remember that the DNR estimates represent minimum figures for the bear population in the state. Visser said that the U.P. bear population has been experiencing a three to four percent increase annually, while bruins in parts of the Lower Peninsula have been increasing at a rate of 10 percent per year.

The reason that bears are increasing faster in parts of the Lower than the Upper is that females breed at younger ages and produce larger litter sizes. Visser has documented female bears breeding as young as yearlings in the L.P. and the average litter size there is three cubs. Females have bred as young as two years old in the U.P. and have average litter sizes of 2.57 cubs. The bottom line is that Michigan currently has a healthy bear population that is experiencing a slow annual increase. Current hunting seasons and regulations are presently controlling that increase, which is important to manage bear numbers.

If bear hunting were dramatically curtailed, which is what would have happened if a 1996 referendum to ban hunting with bait and dogs were approved, the population would increase dramatically over a span of a few years.

The DNR may not know exactly how many bears we have, but they do know approximately how many there are, based on sound scientific studies. They also know that bear numbers are steadily increasing at the same time hunters remove a carefully controlled portion of the population each year. And that's not likely to change as long as current management practices continue.

Bear Researcher Terry DeBruyn records information about a bear's behavior on a portable computer while walking with the animal.

Chapter **8**

Walking With Bears

Most people try to avoid contact with female black bears that have cubs because of the animals' reputation for being defensive of their young. Terry DeBruyn of Chassell is an exception. The bear biologist used to spend as much time as possible seeking contact with sows and cubs to learn more about them. He spent so much time tracking one five-year-old female with triplets during 1991 that the family got used to his presence and would let him tag along with them for hours at a time.

DeBruyn had the unique opportunity to observe firsthand, bits and pieces of what the life of a mother bear and her young is like in the wild. He saw how they interacted with one another, reacted to other wildlife, what they ate, how far they traveled, what type of habitat they preferred and much more. That year was the first time such detailed information about black bears had been gathered in Michigan, but it was far from the last.

Terry continued his unique relationship with the same adult female through 1996, walking with her and her offspring during spring and summer months and checking on them each winter when they were in dens to monitor their progress. Over that time, the bear gave birth to cubs three more times. A pair of males were born during January of 1993, she had triplets again in 1995 at the age of nine and a single female was born during 1997. Two of the cubs born during 1995 were females while only one of the three offspring she had in 1991 was a female.

The daughter born during 1991 claimed a portion of her mother's territory and became an important part of DeBruyn's bear research. He alternated between walking with her and her mother to gather even more insights into the life and times of Michigan bears. The daughter had her first cub when she was three years old, giving birth to a lone female. She gave birth to a pair of males during 1996 and triplets in 1998, two of which were females.

DeBruyn has always had an intense interest in black bears, which eventually led him to enroll at Northern Michigan University (NMU) as a graduate student with the intent of studying bears, having Professor Dr. William Robinson as his advisor. The study got underway during the summer of 1990 with the cooperation of the Department of Natural Resources (DNR) and U.S. Forest Service. A 63-square-mile study area in Alger County, composed primarily of land within the Hiawatha National Forest, was selected. The DNR provided live traps, tags, radio collars and other equipment necessary to catch, handle, mark and keep track of bears.

The DNR and Forest Service also provided personnel and vehicles for them to use, to assist DeBruyn. DNR Bear Researcher Dr. Larry Visser from Houghton Lake spent a lot of time with Terry training him in the trapping, drugging and handling of bears and Elaine Carlson also provided valuable assistance. Visser played an active role throughout the project. The DNR hired Yu Man Lee to assist DeBruyn in trapping and monitoring bears during 1990 and '91. Forest Service Wildlife Biologist Kevin Doran also played an active role during the course of the study. The Forest Service hired Dan Cote during the summer of 1991 to help DeBruyn along with Yu Man.

The objective was to catch as many bears as possible. Ear tags were attached to males and females were fitted with radio collars in addition to tags. The reason females got collars was to learn about their productivity; at what age they first produce cubs, how many cubs were born and how many of those cubs survived to become yearlings. One of the adult females DeBruyn and Yu Man caught and collared that first summer was the animal he would come to know so well the following year.

Even though determining cub production and survival for all of the females on DeBruyn's study area was the project's major objective, one of the goals was to "habituate" a female to his presence to get detailed information about habitat use and food selection. He tried working with a yearling female on the chance a young animal would be more likely to get used to a person's presence than an adult, but those efforts didn't work out. The 1 1/2-year-old was intolerant of people, as most wild bears are, running off as soon as she detected them.

It wasn't until the spring of 1991 that DeBruyn recognized the female with triplets as a perfect candidate to habituate. On a number of occasions soon after they left their den he was able to sneak up close enough to observe the family. When DeBruyn got too close, the female would send the cubs up a tree and follow them. Other females would tree their cubs and leave the area.

Each time Terry visited the foursome, he left the female a treat. He left food near the tree she was in on one occasion and under the tree the family climbed, the next. On each visit, he also talked to the bears in a reassuring tone to help calm them.

Eventually, the female no longer climbed a tree with her cubs, but remained on the ground at or near the base of the tree. Terry then threw her treats and gradually extended the time he spent nearby. Over a period of weeks, the wild bear learned that Terry didn't represent a threat and, in fact, could be trusted. The relationship between man and bear progressed slowly until the female finally allowed the cubs to descend to the ground in his presence and would let him follow when they moved off.

It took a lot of patience, care and dedication (more than 100 hours of time) to get

(Right) An adult female that followed her cubs up a tree when disturbed became a prime candidate to get used to DeBruyn's presence (habituate) through repeated contact. Other females frequently left the area after treeing their cubs.

the bears to accept DeBruyn, but he wanted the project to be successful and he did what was necessary to make it happen. Gaining the trust of a wild bear so it will let a human follow where ever it goes, is definitely a difficult task. It's only been accomplished in a few other special cases. Former Michigan resident Dr. Lynn Rogers, who now lives in Ely, Minnesota, was the first researcher known to accomplish the feat while studying bears in Minnesota. DeBruyn's contact with the adult female was modeled after Rogers' pioneering work.

In each case, study bears were fitted with radio collars, which enabled researchers to maintain constant contact with the bears' locations and to find them whenever they wanted to. In most cases, it would be impossible to habituate free roaming, wild bears that are uncollared, because it would be difficult to find the animals on a regular basis. It's the constant exposure to people that eventually causes some bears to accept the researchers' presence.

However, the bears' acceptance of Terry wasn't unconditional. Some days they would only tolerate his presence for an hour or two. On other occasions, he could stay with them longer. Windy days were often the worst because the animals could not use their hearing as well as on windless days and their sense of smell was also negatively affected, making it more difficult for them to detect danger. As a result, they were nervous and seldom relaxed. Under those circumstances, they were less likely to accept an onlooker.

DeBruyn could usually tell when he had worn out his welcome by the bears' behavior. The adult female, which was eventually named Carmen, also made it clear when Terry got too close. This usually happened when the bears entered thickets. The vegetation was so dense that if Terry didn't stay right behind the animals, it was difficult to impossible to keep track of them.

One time I was with DeBruyn and the family of bears when they entered a thicket littered with fallen trees. It was not only hard to see, walking was difficult and noisy. I was following Terry and had gotten a little behind when I heard Carmen snort or blow and DeBruyn suddenly came backpedaling out of the brush and fell down while calling, "Sorry Carmen! Sorry Carmen!"

The bear had stopped in the thicket and Terry didn't realize it, walking out on a log right above her. She simply told him to back off, which he did without hesitation. Terry admits to experiencing some tense moments while following the bears, but he was never in danger. The mother bear made it clear through vocalizations and actions when she was uncomfortable or had a problem with Terry. He felt threatened on a number of occasions, due to the bear's actions, but she never made physical contact with him.

The times Carmen did show aggression toward Terry it was in an effort to communicate something to him like the occasion he unknowingly got too close to her in the thicket. The first time she showed aggression toward him, her behavior had something to do with a deer blind that they encountered one day. Terry said Carmen got agitated when she saw the blind, walking stiff-legged up to it, stood up on her hind legs and pushed against it with her front feet.

Her cubs followed her lead, according to DeBruyn, and did the same thing. She was probably trying to communicate something to her cubs about the blind. Perhaps she was shot at or scared by a hunter in the blind at one time.

At any rate, when Carmen dropped down from the blind, she seemed to make a connection between Terry and the blind's former occupant. She did a paw swat toward Terry, which consisted of quickly advancing a step or two then swatting a sapling or the ground with a front paw while blowing. The display was probably part of the

Adult female that DeBruyn was eventually able to habituate that he named Carmen.

demonstration for the cubs, but was obviously meant as some type of warning for Terry, too.

I was fortunate enough to accompany DeBruyn and Carmen during many of their walks and I got some valuable insights into bear behavior during those times. I also got my share of warnings from Carmen during those walks when I made too much noise, got too close to her cubs or did something else she didn't like. You never get over the temporary feeling of apprehension as a 200 pound bear quickly approaches to within a matter of feet and slaps the ground or a handy tree with a powerful paw, while blowing a blast of air through its mouth.

I was with Terry and the bears one day when another deer blind was encountered. Carmen stood up against it and one of the cubs went inside to investigate, but the tension was absent that DeBruyn had observed previously.

One of the most exciting moments Terry experienced while following Carmen happened another day that I was along. The female was walking through a semi-open swampy area and we were about 40 yards behind her when she stepped up on a fallen tree. Her attention was immediately riveted on something on the opposite side of the big log and she suddenly leaped forward.

The cries of a fawn came to our ears as soon as the bear disappeared. The young deer's screams scattered the cubs and sent them up trees. The fawn had been laying next to the fallen tree and Carmen pounced on it in its bed before it had a chance to move. We had witnessed something that isn't unusual in the wild, but is seldom seen.

Since then Terry has been present when both Carmen and her daughter (she was eventually name Nette after Terry's wife Annette) have caught and killed additional fawns and he's documented this predatory behavior on video tape. In each case, the bear seemed to stumble upon the young deer and take advantage of the opportunity. A short chase was sometimes required to catch fawns. If they weren't caught quickly, however, they usually outran the bears. Terry watched one fawn escape Carmen's grasp with a fast getaway.

One of the most unique examples of bear predation of fawns that DeBruyn filmed was the taking of a pair of fawns that had just been born on June 5, 1996. He was filming Nette and her two cubs as they walked along the edge of a wetland, when a doe bolted about 30 yards away. The adult bear rushed toward where the doe had been and quickly pounced on a fawn that had been near its mother. The small fawn may have been less than an hour old.

Terry stepped up on a log to get a better vantage point to film the bear with the fawn. Minutes later, he spotted a second fawn hiding on the forest floor in front of him. The bear carried the first fawn off and fed on it for a while, then returned to the area where the doe had been.

The researcher's camera captured the bear sniffing around the area and eventually spotting the second fawn. Amazingly, the fawn made no attempt to run, even as the bear sniffed it. The tiny deer remained motionless on the ground. The fact that the fawn was small and perhaps too weak to run, may have been a factor.

The close proximity of both fawns near their mother indicates they may have just been born before the bears came along. The doe apparently had not yet had a chance to separate them. Most does do separate their fawns as soon as possible after they are born to reduce the chances that a predator will find more than one of them, if a bear, coyote or wolf does happen along.

The pair of cubs had climbed a tree when Nette killed the first fawn. They started calling for their mother from their perch after she grabbed the second fawn. Upon hearing them, the mother bear dropped the second fawn and went to the base of the tree they were in to make sure they weren't in any danger. Cub bears are just as vulnerable to predators as fawns are.

It was at least 15 minutes later before the three bears returned to the vicinity of the second fawn, which was still alive. As if by design, for the purposes of training the cubs for the time when they would have a chance to pull down fawns on their own, the adult allowed the cubs to paw and bite at the struggling fawn. After a few minutes of that, the mother bear led the cubs a quarter mile away to rest.

Their lessons with the still living fawn resumed 2 1/2 hours later. DeBruyn said the bears chewed the fawns ears and nose off before eventually killing it, hours after it was first caught. Terry said the incident was difficult for him to watch, but he knew it was not his responsibility to intervene. His job was to observe and document bear behavior, not to modify or judge it, and he did an excellent job of it.

Others will learn to better understand black bears and their interaction with wildlife such as deer through his work. Life in the wild is seldom as rosy as most people would like to believe, as this episode clearly illustrates.

Fawns are most vulnerable to bears or any other predator, soon after they are born. Few of them are killed by bears after they are a month or more old. Bears are opportunistic predators, taking advantage of circumstances they encounter while roaming their territory in search of more normal food.

DeBruyn emphasized that fawns didn't make up an important part of Carmen's diet. She and her cubs fed mostly on vegetation, fruits and nuts. Insects such as ants, their pupae and wasps were the most important part of their diet consisting of animal matter.

They also occasionally obtained fish found along the shore of rivers and lakes. One fish that Terry saw Carmen eat was obtained courtesy of an osprey. Carmen's daughter walked up to the base of a tree a pair of osprey were nesting in as if she intended to climb it, which started the osprey that was on the nest calling. Its mate soon appeared carrying a fish and also got excited. As the flying osprey approached the nest, it dropped its catch, which practically landed on top of Carmen. DeBruyn said the bear wasted no time eating the unexpected bounty.

After Carmen killed that first fawn when Terry and I were with her, two of her cubs joined her to feed on the carcass. The third cub had gone out of sight and apparently got lost. We heard the missing cub calling to its mother and Carmen grunted back to it, but it never came to her. Carmen started to go to the cub, but didn't. It appeared as though she didn't want to leave the fresh carcass. Under normal circumstances, Carmen would have gone to the cub. Terry observed her do so a number of times when a cub got separated from the others.

We watched Carmen and the two cubs feed on the fawn at least three times over a period of hours, then left. The third cub still hadn't showed up, but they were all together when Terry made his next visit with the family. He said one cub was off on its own for intervals varying in length from hours to a day, on a number of occasions, but the foursome always got back together.

In view of what Terry saw, it's probably not unusual for cubs to become separated from their mothers in the wild. In most cases, they probably get back together. However, when cubs are on their own, they are vulnerable to predators, including other bears, and some are undoubtedly killed during those separations. Carmen lost one of her cubs born in 1995, probably to a predator, and that's the only one under her care that died during the study.

On two occasions during that first summer, other bears came near Carmen and her cubs while DeBruyn was with them. The first time was August 8. Terry said the small bear was making some sort of vocalization as it approached, perhaps a submissive sound. When the bruin got close, Carmen popped her teeth at it to warn it away. When it didn't leave, Carmen chased it off.

The second episode happened exactly one month later. Carmen was sleeping soundly at the time. One of her cubs was resting in a tree and the other two were on the ground. Terry said that when he first saw the strange bear, he thought it was one of the cubs, but a quick count revealed that was not the case.

The small bruin walked straight toward DeBruyn, unaware of his presence. When it was 10 yards away he said, "Who are you?" Caught by surprise, the strange bear put its front feet on a log to assess the situation and saw Terry. The animal slowly turned its head away then bolted back the way it had come from.

Carmen slept through the incident. By then the adult female was perfectly comfortable in DeBruyn's presence. In fact, she was probably able to relax more when Terry was with them during nap time because she knew he didn't pose a threat to the cubs and had been accepted as a part time member of the family. Carmen

Carmen and her three cubs born in 1991 walk a log in Alger County.

certainly viewed the researcher as some type of benefactor and I wouldn't be surprised if she may have considered him a protector as well.

When Terry started working with Carmen, he had to jot notes down in the field to keep track of what he observed and then expand on them when he got home, to do his best to record everything that happened. By late June he acquired a portable computer similar to those used by bear watchers in Minnesota that made it much easier to keep track of the action. A set of computer codes enabled him to punch in everything the family did as it happened. When he got home, it was a simple matter to transfer data from the portable unit to a larger computer for storage.

Although there was a lot of support within the DNR for the bear research DeBruyn did, there was also concern that Carmen and Nette, having gotten used to Terry's presence and the corresponding handouts, would approach other people looking for food or would become nuisances at camps or rural homes. That didn't happen.

The truth of the matter is Carmen and Nette were intelligent enough to tell the difference between Terry and other people. They did not trust other humans like they did Terry. If someone did stumble upon either bear, they were more likely to run away than approach. In fact, Terry was with Carmen on at least one occasion when she avoided a pair of people that were talking as they approached. The unsuspecting couple had no idea a family of bears and an observer were nearby, hidden quietly in the brush, as they walked by.

When other people were with Terry as he walked with Carmen and Nette, the bears were seldom as comfortable or relaxed as they were with him alone.

One week when Terry was out of town I offered to monitor Carmen and her cubs while he was gone. Afterall, she had seen me when I was with Terry a few times. If she trusted anyone else, she should trust me, but she didn't. I homed in on the signal from her radio collar several times one day, but I never did see her. She wouldn't let me. Whenever I got too close, she took off before I could get a look at her.

Even when Terry approached Carmen, she did not always stay put for him. He located her by the signal from her collar. When he started getting close, DeBruyn called her name and talked to her, so she knew who was coming. It wasn't unusual for her to move off a time or two before settling down and letting Terry get close enough to see her.

After hunting seasons opened in the fall it became harder and harder for DeBruyn to get close to Carmen. The presence of increased numbers of people in the woods probably made her more skiddish and there was evidence that she had been chased by hounds a time or two. Terry seldom saw Carmen during the fall due to the fact he didn't want to risk pushing her into a hunter and she simply wasn't as trusting as she was during summer months.

Every spring, Terry had to reacquaint himself with Carmen and her young due to the months they spent apart. After not being followed for seven to eight months, allowing for the four or five months she was denned, it took Carmen a while to get used to DeBruyn's presence again. It sometimes took up to a month for them to allow Terry to walk with them once more.

After Terry received his Masters Degree from NMU he transferred to Michigan Tech in Houghton and enrolled in their Doctoral program to continue his research. He not only got the degree, he eventually was hired as an adjunct professor. DeBruyn said he is extremely grateful for the support he has obtained from a variety of sources during the course of his bear project. Besides the DNR, U. S. Forest Service, NMU and Michigan Tech, he has gotten funding from MUCC, the U.P. Bear Houndsmen Association, the Michigan Bowhunters Association, Commemorative Bucks of Michigan, the Michigan Bear Hunters Association, the Frey Foundation, Wildlife Unlimited of Delta County, Michigan Polar Equator Club, a Negaunee grade school class and a number of individuals.

During the course of the study, hunters were asked to voluntarily pass up collared females that they saw and DeBruyn said he would like to express his appreciation to hunters who did so. Terry said he's talked to a number of hunters who were hunting over bait and with hounds who chose to let collared females go, including Carmen and Nette, because they support his research.

That made him feel good. So did Carmen's and Nette's trust and tolerance of his presence. Both the bears and the person have played a major role in furthering a better understanding of Michigan's black bear.

Chapter 9

The Rest of the Story
Part 1

Although walking with bears was an important part of the bear research that Terry DeBruyn conducted in a 63-square-mile study area in Alger County, there's far more to it. Many more bruins were captured, marked and monitored than those he was able to walk with. A lot was learned from those animals, too. The next two chapters will cover other highlights from his research, some of which is as interesting and exciting as the walks with bears.

The study started during 1990 and much of the work that first year was geared toward capturing and marking as many bruins as possible. Baited barrel and culvert traps were employed to catch the animals. Once caught, bears were drugged through holes in the traps with a syringe on the end of a jab stick so they could be weighed, measured and marked. Small premolar teeth were also removed from each animal so they could be aged.

Males were ear-tagged. Females were fitted with radio collars and ear tags. Collars were put on females because they were the main focus of the study. DeBruyn's primary goals were to determine at what age females first produce cubs, how many cubs each had and how many bears, both cubs and adults, survived. He also gathered data about habitat and food use and home ranges of females.

The researcher and his assistants marked 18 different bears that first year, six of which were females. One of the females and five of the males were known to have been taken by hunters during the fall of 1990. The five remaining females wearing radio collars were checked in their dens the following winter.

One of the females had three cubs at the time it was collared. All three of those cubs survived and denned with their mother. The youngsters were more than a year old when the den was checked. The four animals were drugged and removed from the den for examination.

(Left) Terry DeBruyn video tapes a bear that's already marked as he releases it from a live trap.

As many as 18 radio collared/ear-tagged bears were in DeBruyn's 63-square-mile study area at one point.

Two of the three yearlings were males weighing 46 and 49 pounds and the young female weighed 38 pounds. The female was fitted with a radio collar and the males were ear-tagged. The yearlings' mother weighed 150 pounds.

Three more adult females gave birth to cubs that winter. Two of them had triplets and one had twins. The larger of the pair with triplets weighed 175 pounds and that's the bear Terry eventually named Carmen. The other two adults weighed 135 and 140 pounds. The cubs ranged in weight from two pounds to 4 pounds, 12 ounces.

The final collared bear that DeBruyn checked in its den that winter was two years old. It was too young to have cubs yet.

Eleven more bears were trapped and tagged as part of the study during the summer of 1991, including an adult male that was brown in color. The vast majority of Michigan black bears are black, but brown coated animals occasionally turn up. The brown color phase is more common further west in the United States and Canada. Up to six percent of the black bears in Minnesota are brown, for instance. Interestingly, that brown male had a black coat when it was killed by a hunter during the fall of 1993 at the age of 10 3/4 years, so bears don't always have the same coat color throughout their lives.

Four of the new animals were females and they were collared, giving the researcher a total of 10 collared bears to monitor. As many as 14 males wearing ear tags were in or near the study area by the fall of 1991. One of the males tagged during 1990

Barrel traps like the one Terry DeBruyn and Larry Visser are shown carrying in this photograph are lighter and easier to place away from roads than culvert traps.

was recaptured during '91 and the numbers on its tags were no longer visible, so new tags were put in that male's ears.

One collared adult female was lost in the fall of 1991 during hunting season and contact was lost with a second female after hunting season ended. The missing female had been collared during 1990 and was three years old. There's a strong possibility that the young female was shot illegally, according to DeBruyn.

Cub production and survival was excellent among the eight remaining females wearing collars in the study area the following winter. Three of the females had not yet reached maturity, so they didn't have young with them. During den checks in March of 1992 Terry discovered that seven of eight cubs born the previous winter survived and five more cubs were born.

The five cubs were born to a pair of females, both of which were seven years old, according to DeBruyn, with one weighing 170 pounds and the other 180 pounds. The larger bruin had triplets and the slightly smaller female had twins. Most cubs are born during January, so they were about two months old when checked in March and weighed between 4 pounds, 7 ounces and 5 pounds, 10 ounces.

Two of the three adult females that had cubs the previous winter were five years old and the third was six. One of the 5-year-olds only weighed 110 pounds and she also had the smallest yearlings. The year-old male weighed 40 pounds and the female 34 pounds.

The second five-year-old weighed 170 pounds, according to DeBruyn and her two male yearlings weighed 52 and 53 pounds. He said that female gave birth to three cubs the previous winter, but the young female from the litter did not survive. She died of unknown causes some time during 1991 after the mother and cubs left their den.

The 6-year-old female (Carmen) had the largest yearlings and she weighed 175 pounds. The largest male tipped the scales at 86 pounds, his brother weighed 70 pounds and the yearling female (Nette) weighed 75 pounds.

By 1992 DeBruyn's bear research was expanded slightly to include study of male dispersal. Yearling males were collared that year to find out what happened to them. Yearlings normally separate from their mothers by June. Females usually establish a territory within a portion of their mother's home range, but males commonly leave country they are familiar with to establish a home range. Researchers wanted to find out when males disperse, how far they go and where they end up.

Males were fitted with black radio collars rather than white ones like those that were put on females, to reduce their visibility. Hunters were asked to voluntarily pass up collared females, so that the age at which they first produce cubs as well as cub production and survival, could be determined. Hunters were not discouraged from shooting males and the different color collars made it easier for them to know when they saw a female.

The trio of juvenile females that DeBruyn had collared during March of 1992 included a three year old and a pair of two years olds. The older animal weighed 145 pounds and the 2-year-olds weighed 75 and 95 pounds.

Four bears handled during the study were taken by hunters during the fall of 1992, three of which were males. One of the males and the female were wearing radio collars. The hunter who shot the female didn't see the collar. As the hairs in a bear's coat lengthen during the fall, they sometimes obscure most of a collar. During poor light conditions and at a distance, collars can be tough to see under those circumstances. For clarification, it is not against the law to shoot a collared female. Hunters who pass up collared females, do so voluntarily.

The two adult males that were marked with ear tags had dressed weights of 285 and 428 pounds. The larger male was 11 3/4 years old and was the biggest and oldest bruin DeBruyn live trapped. The oldest bears are often the toughest to capture, so there might have been older bruins in the study area that escaped capture.

Eleven dens were visited during 1993, three of which had females with newborn cubs and two had females with yearlings. The other five dens contained three immature females and two immature males. Putting black radio collars on yearling males continued that year. A total of 15 bears were wearing collars by the time den work was completed, 10 of which were females.

Each of the adult females that had cubs that winter produced twins. Four of the cubs were males and two were females. Cub weights ranged between 3 pounds, 13 ounces and seven pounds. One of the five cubs born the previous winter was lost some time during the year, according to DeBruyn.

The adult female bears DeBruyn had collared that winter ranged in age between six and eight. Their weights were spread between 147 and 210 pounds. A pair of 3-year-old females weighed 95 and 125 pounds.

Four 2-year-olds were wearing collars at the time, two of each sex. The females weighed 60 and 120 pounds while the males weighed in at 70 and 124 pounds.

Trapping and tagging more bears in the study area was done during the summer of 1993 and 14 more animals were marked during an intensive trapping effort. Three new females were fitted with radio collars and 11 males were tagged. DeBruyn and his assistants attempted to capture all of the bears in his study area and spent a lot of time at it, but his results illustrate that it's impossible to accomplish that under most circumstances. There are always some animals that escape capture.

By the fall of 1993, 18 Alger County bears were wearing radio collars, five of which were young males. The trapping done that year was part of an effort to estimate the bear population in the study area. Some of the bears marked during 1990 and '91 were recaptured and information about the number of marked versus unmarked animals in the area was used to help Michigan Technological University Graduate Student Jodi Helland make that estimate.

Helland and assistant Pam St. Louis from Massachusetts did most of the work associated with trapping bears that year. They also set cameras to monitor hanging baits visited by bears that they may not have been able to catch in traps. Animals that grabbed the suspended baits took their picture by tripping the camera shutters when pulling on the string attached to the cameras.

Two other student assistants from U.P. colleges worked with DeBruyn on the Alger County bear study during 1993. Lake Superior State University Senior Natalie Fahler did telemetry work to monitor movements of collared bears. NMU Graduate Student Laurie Johnson gathered as much information as possible about ants in the study area, especially those utilized by bears, for a masters thesis.

DeBruyn said he's found that ants are an important part of the black bears' summer diet in the study area, especially during years when other foods such as berries are scarce. He added that by gathering data about where ants are found, it may be possible to improve the availability of ants to bears in the future through some type of management strategy. A number of species of ants are eaten by Alger County bears.

Another new aspect of DeBruyn's bear research starting in 1993 was the use of a Global Positioning System (GPS) Unit during his walks with Carmen. He carried the equipment in a backpack with him along with his other gear. The unit plotted the course he and the bear followed while traveling through the forest. The sophisticated piece of equipment is designed to calculate the speed of travel as well as plotting the course that's followed.

Hunters tagged eight marked bears in or near DeBruyn's study area during the fall of 1993, two of which were females. One of the males was collared and the remaining five had ear tags. Only 15 percent of the collared females were taken by hunters that year compared to 21 percent of the marked males. At the end of three years of research, 11 collared females and 23 marked males remained in the population.

The study took another new twist during March of 1994 when DeBruyn followed up on one of the young males that dispersed from the study area and ended up on the Seney National Wildlife Refuge in Schoolcraft County. Terry had to use a dart gun to secure the animal so it could be examined and the radio collar removed. The 3-year-old male was the last of a group of collared animals he tranquilized in their dens that winter. The fact that the young male had traveled to the refuge from Alger County was a valuable piece of the puzzle in helping DeBruyn understand bear behavior.

Most male black bears disperse from their mother's home territory when they are between one and two years old. The bruin that traveled to Seney started his cross country travels during the spring of 1994 when he was two years old, according to DeBruyn. He said the straight line distance from the male's starting point in Alger County to where he denned on the refuge was about 39 miles.

However, the wandering bear covered more than twice that distance before settling on the refuge. DeBruyn pinpointed the bear's location as far south as Delta County's Garden Peninsula before it changed course and headed northeast to the refuge.

One other 3-year-old bruin (Carmen's son from 1991) that also dispersed from

Alger County the same year denned south of Thompson in Schoolcraft County, according to DeBruyn. He said the straight line distance from the animal's starting point to its den was about 34 miles. The second male that Carmen had during 1991 dispersed from his mother's home range during August of 1992 as a yearling and he was shot by a hunter that fall.

The bear that ended up on the Seney Refuge proved to be more of a problem for DeBruyn to tranquilize than all of the others he handled up until that time. The others remained in their dens while they were injected with a drug from a syringe on a jab stick. The animal on the refuge left its den as the researcher was preparing to drug it.

He had a syringe ready to go on a jab stick when the bear started to vacate the premises and he had the presence of mind to inject the drug as the bruin went by him. The dosage probably would have been enough to put the bear down if the animal had been inactive, but the bruin kept moving after leaving the den and that activity apparently counteracted the effects of the drug. DeBruyn, U.S. Forest Service Wildlife Biologist Kevin Doran from Munising and Refuge Wildlife Biologist Richard Urbanek followed the animal for two hours and it stayed on its feet.

When DeBruyn returned to the refuge on March 25th for another try at the bear, he was prepared for the bruin to make a run for it again. That's why he had a dart gun provided by the DNR. The dosage of drug in the dart was also adjusted accordingly.

Urbanek and Bruce Smith from Marquette accompanied DeBruyn to help handle the bear, if the animal was successfully tranquilized. When the group encountered fresh bear tracks in the snow close to where the signal from the bruin's collar indicated it should be, they thought it had heard them coming and moved out ahead of them. Sign at that location indicated the bear had scavenged a snowshoe hare killed by a coyote.

Theorizing that the bear may have heard the coyote kill the hare from its new den, then returned to the den after feeding, DeBruyn followed the bear's tracks. His hunch proved to be correct. The animal was denned about 40 yards from where the hare had been killed. As expected, the bruin started to leave its den as soon as the researcher spotted it.

DeBruyn was fast enough to put a dart in its neck before it could leave.

"Tally ho! He's coming out," he hollered to alert the others as he backed away from the den entrance to make room for the animal's exit.

The bear's shiny black coat and blue ear tags stood out in sharp contrast to the white background as it trotted through the snow. It was a beautiful sight. This time the animal's escape was cut short by the drug.

The main objective of the effort was to remove the bear's collar since it had left the study area and provided information about its dispersal. The bear was also weighed and measured. It weighed 135 pounds, more than double the 60 pounds it weighed a year earlier.

DeBruyn also obtained valuable information during March of 1994 about the age at which black bears in the U.P. first produce cubs. One female was 3 years old and another was 4 when they gave birth to their first cubs. Each animal had a single cub.

Information about cub production from three other females in the same age classes (two were 3 and one was 4) was lost when their radio collars fell off prematurely during the fall of 1993. Leather links in those collars broke after only a few months of

(Right) Jodi Helland and Terry DeBruyn measure the length of a drugged bear caught in the barrel trap in the background while Pam St. Louis records the data.

An ear-tagged male that took its own picture when grabbing a bait attached to a preset camera. (Photo courtesy Terry DeBruyn)

wear. The links are supposed to remain intact for up to a year. Collars also fell off of a pair of yearling males.

DeBruyn said a 9-year-old female produced three cubs that winter, all of which were males. Terry added that all six cubs born the previous winter to three other females survived their first year and were denned with their mothers. Carmen was 8-years-old, she weighed in at 180 pounds and had a pair of yearling males weighing 90 and 95 pounds. Another female the same age that weighed five pounds more had a male weighing 69 pounds and a 50 pound female denned with her.

A 7-year-old female that was much smaller than the other two adults also produced smaller offspring. The adult weighed 135 pounds. Her yearling male tipped the scale at 45 pounds and his sister only weighed 25 pounds, which is the smallest yearling DeBruyn encountered during his Alger County study.

DeBruyn had radio collars on 13 bears by the time den work was completed during 1994. Seven of those were adult females and six were yearlings. Two of the yearlings were females.

Terry and his assistants spent some time during the summer of 1994 trying to recapture the two females that had lost their collars prematurely the previous fall. They managed to get the 3-year-old, but not the 4-year-old. However, they did catch something almost as good; a pair of cubs belonging to the 4-year-old female, and radio collars were put on the cubs. Interestingly, one of the collars Terry put on a cub was

DeBruyn started recording his walks with Carmen with a GPS unit in 1993.

purchased by my wife and I during 1986 for use on a pair of cubs we helped raise and returned to the wild (see "A Tale of Two Cubs"). We donated the collars to the DNR after the cubs slipped out of them.

It was pleasing to realize at least one of those collars was eventually put to good use. The collared cubs enabled Terry to locate the den they occupied as yearlings with their mother during March of 1995. The adult female was then recollared. At that point, the researcher also verified that the female had produced her first cubs at age 4, having twins.

Five new males were captured during the limited trapping efforts in 1994 and four

Terry DeBruyn with a collared male that dispersed to the Seney National Wildlife Refuge and the dart gun he used to drug it as it left its den.

of them were fitted with ear tags before being released. Ed Rumbergs signed on as one of DeBruyn's assistants during '94 along with Jodi Helland and he helped out during 1995 as well. He monitored the locations of collared bears and helped Jodi with trapping. Dave Bach did some telemetry work during April of 1994, too.

Two radio collared females and four ear-tagged males were reported taken by hunters in Alger County during the fall of 1994. One female was shot by a hunter using

In 1994 DeBruyn played a role in documenting the first bear known to have been killed by a porcupine. The single cub born to Nette died when quills got in its chest after pouncing on a porky, working their way into its heart and lungs.

bait and the other was killed when bayed on the ground by hounds. The dog hunter was a member of a group of houndmen who had passed up collared bears previously and would have again, if the collar had been seen. The collar was not visible to the hunter before the bear was shot.

During the fall of 1994 DeBruyn played a key role in documenting what may be the first reported case of a porcupine killing a black bear. The bruin that was killed was Nette's first cub, which was 10-month-old at the time. When DeBruyn found the cub's carcass during October, he thought it had been killed illegally by a hunter. Cubs are protected by law and external injuries appeared as though they might have been made by an arrow.

The carcass was transferred to DNR Veterinarian Steve Schmitt at the Rose Lake Lab for examination and he determined the external damage was done by scavengers after the bear's death. The cause of the animal's death was located internally. Schmitt said a pair of porcupine quills interfered with operation of the bear's heart and four more quills were lodged in the lungs.

He determined that the quills had entered through the chest and estimated that it probably took about a month for the tiny spears to work their way into the bear's internal organs before finally killing it. Schmitt theorized that in order for the quills to be imbedded in the chest, the young bear must have pounced on a porcupine it encountered.

Terry spent many hours with Nette and her cub during 1994, observing their behavior and habitat use and was disappointed about the loss of the cub.

One of the radio collared females in DeBruyn's study area is carried from its den for examination.

Chapter 10

The Rest of the Story Part 2

If the condition of female black bears that were part of DeBruyn's study during 1995 are any indication, U.P. bears were in the best shape they had been in for years. Radio collared females with cubs had their heaviest average weights and produced more and larger cubs than previously, according to den checks conducted during early March. A bumper crop of natural foods the previous fall, resulting in superb nutrition, was responsible for the heavier weights and excellent cub production.

One 9-year-old female that Terry had fitted with a radio collar since the summer of 1990, for example, weighed 210 pounds during March and had four cubs. The most that bruin weighed any other winter was 185 pounds during 1994 when she had two yearlings with her. The same female had three cubs during January of 1991 and she weighed 140 pounds when checked in the den.

Those three cubs ranged between 2 pounds, 5 ounces and 2 pounds, 11 ounces, with a total cub weight of 7 pounds, 8 ounces. The four cubs she had during 1995, three of which were males, ranged between 4 pounds and 4 pounds, 12 ounces for a total cub weight of 16 pounds, 12 ounces. Larger cubs have a better chance of survival when they leave the den.

Carmen was also nine years old and she weighed 205 pounds when checked during March of 1995. She had three cubs ranging between 5 pounds, 10 ounces and 6 pounds, with a total cub weight of 17 pounds, 8 ounces. She weighed 175 pounds during March of 1991 and the cubs that year were between 3 pounds, 11 ounces and 4 pounds, 12 ounces for a total cub weight of 12 pounds, 7 ounces.

The most dramatic increase in weight for the winter was evident in an 8-year-old female that had also been part of the project since the beginning. She weighed 185 pounds and had two cubs weighing 5 pounds, 14 ounces and 6 pounds, 2 ounces. The heaviest that bear had been any other winter was 150 pounds in 1993 when she had another pair of cubs weighing 3 pounds, 13 ounces and 4 pounds, 1 ounce.

Her lightest winter weight of 110 pounds was recorded in 1992. She was 135 pounds during 1991 and 1994. The bruin had another set of twins weighing 2 pounds and 2 pounds, 12 ounces in 1991.

DeBruyn credits the abundance of natural foods such as beech and hazel nuts for the increased size and health of females and cubs in 1995. He said the diets of at least two of the females was supplemented the previous fall by food put out by hunters, but he added that food source had been utilized by the same animals during other years as well.

The female that DeBruyn recollared during the summer was 4 years old when her den was checked. She also had a pair of cubs, which were probably her first young. The adult weighed 130 pounds and the two male cubs weighed 6 pounds each. The 5-year-old female that Terry recollared during the winter after collaring her cubs the previous summer, weighed 150 pounds and the two yearling males that were in the den with her tipped the scales at 72 and 73 pounds.

The oldest female Terry had collared was 10 years old during January of 1995 and she had three yearling males denned with her. She weighed 160 pounds and the yearlings were 35, 42 and 44 pounds.

Cub production was the highest in the study area during 1995 since the project started, according to DeBruyn. Four females produced 11 cubs for an average of 2.75 cubs per adult. The next best year for cub production was 1991 when three females produced eight cubs for an average of 2.6 cubs per adult.

By 1996, both Carmen and Nette were fitted with Global Positioning System (GPS) collars. Carmen was the first bear in the United States to wear such a collar in '95. The collar was programmed to link up with satellites every three or four hours to pinpoint the bear's location. With the use of satellites, it is possible to determine where an animal is or was within 100 meters, at the time readings are taken. Conventional radio collars are only accurate within 300 meters.

Data collected by the collar was stored in it until the device was removed by De-Bruyn during the first week of March 1996, when Carmen was checked in her den. The used GPS collar was replaced by a new one that gathered more information. The collar that was removed was returned to the manufacturer where the data was retrieved and the device was refurbished for use in the future.

Carmen was 10 years old in '96 and she weighed 175 pounds. The two yearling females that were denned with her weighed 74 and 83 pounds.

The second GPS collar was put on her 5-year-old daughter. Those two females were chosen to wear the special collars because DeBruyn was able to walk with them and could periodically monitor how the devices were functioning. He could test their accuracy by taking readings with a hand held GPS unit to compare with those in their collars, when he was with them.

Nette was in better shape than her mother during the first week of March, weighing in at 205 pounds. Of course, she had to be to care for the pair of male cubs she gave birth to while in the den. The cubs weighed about six pounds each.

A total of nine cubs were born during January of '96 to four adult females that De-Bruyn had fitted with collars in Alger County. Two other females had twins besides Nette and one had triplets. His study animals produced 11 cubs during 1995, one of the best years he recorded. However, the survival of the cubs was worse than normal. During all other years, an average of one cub was lost per year.

A total of five cubs born during 1995 did not survive. DeBruyn isn't sure what might have happened to increase cub mortality, but it may be due to increased predation. Other bears, wolves, coyotes and bobcats prey on bear cubs. Both bear and wolf

100

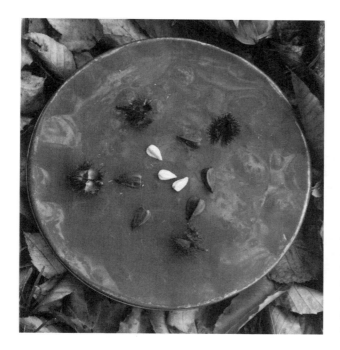

An abundance of natural foods like these beech nuts resulted in heavier weights among bears and greater cub production in DeBruyn's study area during 1995.

populations were increasing at the time and they continue to do so. With excellent cub production during 1995, there were also more cubs for predators to prey on.

Terry was in for a lot of surprises when he checked radio collared females in their Alger County dens during March of 1997. One adult female that should have had cubs didn't, another bruin had cubs two years in a row and two more older females that had always produced multiple cubs in the past only had one cub each.

"When you think you start to know what should be happening, things like this happen," DeBruyn said. "I'm always left with more questions than answers. That's the problem with short term studies like this one. I've learned a lot about bears here, but there's a lot more I would like to know."

Due to an abundance of natural foods during 1996, DeBruyn expected cub production to be high in his study area during 1997, but the opposite proved to be true. Fewer cubs than normal were produced by the bears he had collared. However, there are plausible explanations for what happened.

The female that should have had cubs, but didn't, for example, was 11 years old and in excellent physical condition. She weighed 245 pounds, the heaviest she had been during March since she was collared in 1991. In March of '91, she only weighed 140 pounds and had three cubs.

He said she had two cubs during 1993 and weighed 170 pounds. That same bear gave birth to four cubs in 1995 and weighed in at 210 pounds.

The bruin's selection of den sites was different during the winter of 1996-'97 than the others during which she had cubs. She elected to spend the winter in a nest on top of the ground as opposed to an enclosed den like she had during previous winters when she had cubs. DeBruyn suspects the open nature of her winter quarters might have

101

Carmen was the first black bear in the United States to be fitted with a
GPS collar to maximize the opportunity to learn as much as possible about
how this special bear used the habitat in her home range.

made her cubs more vulnerable to predators. It's possible she had cubs, but they were taken by coyotes, wolves or bobcats.

The female that gave birth to cubs two years in a row was 12 years old. She gave birth to twin female cubs during January of 1997 and she had a pair of male cubs in 1996 when she was 11 years old.

Mature females normally produce cubs every other year, but if they lose their cubs or become separated from them for a period of days as late as July, they will stop producing milk and become fertile, allowing them to breed two years in a row. In this female's case, she must have been separated from her male cubs long enough to come into breeding condition because DeBruyn saw her with the cubs from 1996 during late August or early September. He was surprised to find another set of newborns with the female when he checked her in the den.

Since the previous year's cubs were males, she may have instinctively separated from them before denning due to her pregnancy. Ten-month-old cubs normally den with their mothers and are forced to go on their own when about 1 1/2 years old. The male cubs from 1996 were ear-tagged, so they can be identified if they show up in the harvest.

The two adult females that had one cub each were 10 and 11 years old and each had a history of producing multiple cubs. Carmen was the 11-year-old and she produced twins or triplets every other year since 1991. The 10-year-old always had twins previously.

Both females were in excellent physical condition, weighing 198 and 235 pounds. Something else the two bruins had in common is that they were drugged during December, while they were pregnant, so malfunctioning radio collars could be replaced with ones that were working properly. There's a possibility that the drug may have impacted cub production on those bears, according to DeBruyn.

After den work was completed during '97, DeBruyn left the U.P. for Florida where he accepted a job with the Game and Freshwater Fish Commission. He was in charge of that state's bear management program for a year. While working in Florida, he took time off from that job during the winter to return to the U.P. for den work on the remaining study bears. After working in Florida for a year, DeBruyn took a job at Michigan Tech, which allowed him to finish his Alger County bear study. The project ended during February of 1999 when remaining radio collars were removed from bears that were still wearing them.

The loss of Carmen during the fall of 1997 when Terry was in Florida and Nette during 1998 after he had spent another field season with her, was one of the factors that led to ending the project. Carmen was 11 3/4 years old when she was killed during the 1997 bear season. Although she's gone, she won't be forgotten. She will live on in an educational video and a book planned for the future. DeBruyn has written a book about his Michigan bear research, with emphasis on his many hours walking with Carmen. Much of the video he took during his research is being used to produce an educational video about bears by Frida Waara of Marquette.

Although Terry developed a close relationship with Carmen during the course of his study, he never lost sight of the fact that she was a wild bear and the reason for his contact with her was to learn as much as possible about her daily life that could be applied to managing the state's many other bruins. As a hunter himself, he understood the role that hunting plays in managing game animals, including bears. He knew Carmen could be killed during any of the bear hunting seasons that came and went during his study, but he worked hard to reduce the chances of that happening.

The fact that Carmen wasn't killed while DeBruyn was in Michigan made him feel good. Her death in his absence was disappointing, but not unexpected.

"I knew there was a good chance she would be killed during hunting season," Terry said upon learning about Carmen's death. "If she wasn't shot during 1997, I figured she would be during 1998. There is a lot of hunting pressure in the study area and she was bound to be taken sooner or later. I'm glad she lived as long as she did. I learned a lot from her that I hope is put to use in managing bears and their habitat."

The fact that Carmen played such a valuable role in DeBruyn's research contributed to her longevity. She is known to have been passed up a number of times by hunters using both bait and hounds during the course of the study, as were other collared females. The hunter who failed to do so during 1997 said he did not see the bear's collar or ear tags before shooting.

Through 1996, DeBruyn had spent more than 1,500 hours walking with Carmen. At least two of Carmen's daughters born during the study were still alive at the time of her death and so was one son. Nette and the surviving male were born during 1991. The second daughter (Bows) was born during 1995.

During the winter of 1997–'98 Nette selected the same maternity den that she had used two years earlier. Black bears in the U.P. don't often reuse dens because potential den sites are plentiful across the region. However, a huge, old, triple-trunked white cedar tree in Alger County proved to be an exception to the rule. There's a protected cavity at the base of those trees that serves as a perfect bear nursery.

That's obviously why Nette returned. She had a pair of male cubs there during the first months of 1996. The pregnant female gave birth to triplets in the ideal den during the beginning of 1998. Two of the cubs were females.

A feature that adds to the appeal of this particular den is the trunk of the largest tree of the threesome is hollow and the cavity where the female and her young spend the winter, is at its base. The hollow tree trunk probably serves as a playground for the cubs once they are mobile enough to climb. The cavity also provides added security, giving cubs an avenue of escape should a predator try to enter the den.

Carmen's 3-year-old daughter had her first cubs during January of 1998. She gave birth to triplets, two of which were males. The adult weighed in at 145 pounds. Her 7-year-old step sister (Nette) weighed 200 pounds.

Two more of the collared bears DeBruyn checked in their dens that winter also had cubs and each had triplets, too. In both cases they produced a pair of females and a male. Those adult females weighed 190 and 230 pounds.

Three of the collared females had yearlings with them in their dens. One of those adults gave birth to a pair of cubs during 1997, but it only had a single yearling with it, so one of the cubs was probably lost sometime during the year. The female that apparently lost a cub born during 1997 was five years old and had the lightest weight among the adults, tipping the scales at 135 pounds.

Carmen was killed by a hunter when she was 11 3/4 years old. Although she's gone, she won't be forgotten. She will play a prominent role in an educational video about bears and a book written by DeBruyn about his research. What was learned from this valuable animal will help our understanding of bears and their management in Michigan.

Nette gave birth to two sets of cubs in the den Terry DeBruyn is checking out here. A cavity at the base of a triple-trunked cedar tree proved to be a perfect maternal den. The rate of den reuse is not high among black bears.

She also had the lightest yearling with her, a female that weighed 33 pounds. However, that yearling weighed more than her mother did at the same age. DeBruyn said that female had the lightest weight of any yearling he handled at 25 pounds.

Three other yearling females that DeBruyn weighed during March of 1998 were 46, 52 and 60 pounds.

Terry resumed his walks with Nette during the spring and summer of 1998. After a year's absence, it took him a while to reacquaint himself with the wild bear. She ran from him with her cubs during his first attempts to make contact with her. Terry was persistent, however, and Nette eventually accepted his presence again. Unfortunately, Nette was killed during the fall of 1998 when she was 7 3/4 years old, but, like her mother, her genes live on through the cubs she bore that remain alive.

Three of the adult female bears that radio collars were removed from during February of 1999 had been a part of the study during most of its duration. A 12-year-old that was originally collared during 1990 when she was three years old, was one of them. She gave birth to cubs in her winter den during each odd numbered year, including 1999.

She produced twins each of those years, except 1997, when a single female was born. Her cubs were most often a male and female, however, she had two males during 1995. This female gave birth to a total of 9 cubs during the course of the study and she could have many more in the future.

Another female that was 14 years old was seven when she was collared in 1992. She started having cubs on even-numbered years, but then she had cubs two years in a row during '96 and '97. Due to the birth of cubs two years in a row, this female had 12 young since 1992. She had triplets during '94 and '99.

A third female that was eight years old in 1999 had been collared since she was a year old in 1991. She gave birth to her first cub, a female, when four years old during 1994. She then had triplets during 1996 and '98. Two of the triplets were males in '96 and two were females during '98.

The fourth female that a radio collar was removed from was four years old. She had her first cubs during 1998, having triplets, two of which were males. One of the male cubs died sometime during the year because only two yearlings were denned with the adult when her collar was removed.

The final Alger County bear that was uncollared in '99 was three years old and she had her first cub, a female.

Due to the excellent bear research that has been conducted in Michigan and the work that's currently underway, we now know far more about the animals than ever before. However, there's still more to learn. Hopefully, this research will continue into the future and will provide more information to better help us understand Michigan black bear.

Tables at the end of this chapter summarize the information gathered by Terry DeBruyn during his Alger County research. The entries for females that were part of the study during most of its length provide those animals' reproductive history and weight variations from one year to the next. The letters "HK" denote hunter kill followed by the year the animal was shot.

Many of the names selected for study bears were those of people helping out on the project. Some of the names were chosen by participants in the project. In some cases, bruins got named based on something they did or that happened while they were part of the study.

Carmen's female cub from 1991 with Terry's wife Annette.
The bear was later named Nette after her.

107

Bears	1991						1992					
	Age	Weight	Cubs		Yearlings		Age	Weight	Cubs		Yearlings	
			Sex	Weight	Sex	Weight			Sex	Weight	Sex	Weight
CARMEN	5	175	M	3, 11			6	175			M	70
			M	4							M	86
			F	4, 12							F	75
JOHNSON CREEK (JC)	5	140	F	2, 5			6	175			M	52
			M	2, 8							M	53
			M	2, 11							F	NID
TAMMI							7	170	F	5, 6		
									M	5, 10		
SANDY	4	135	F	2			5	110			F	34
			M	2, 12							M	40
PRISCILLA (Tammi's Daughter)							2	75				
LIL (Sherri's Daughter)	1	70					2	95				
NETTE (Carmen's Daughter)												
Sandy's Male												
Sandy's Female												
SHERRI	5	150			F	38	6	180	F	4, 7		
					M	46			M	5, 1		
					M	49			M	5, 8		
RUNT (Carmen's Son)												
PHYLLIS							3	145				
VICKI												

This two-page table shows some of the information obtained from the research conducted in the Alger County Study, which began in 1990. Bears are listed by name for ease of distinguishing them rather than numbers, with their age and weight for each year the winter den check was done. The sex of their young, cubs or yearlings, with their weight, are also listed. Cub weights are listed as pounds and ounces. The letters

1993						1994						1995					
Age	Weight	Cubs		Yearlings		Age	Weight	Cubs		Yearlings		Age	Weight	Cubs		Yearlings	
		Sex	Weight	Sex	Weight			Sex	Weight	Sex	Weight			Sex	Weight	Sex	Weight
7	210	M	6			8	180			M	90	9	205	M	5, 14		
		M	7							M	95			F	5, 10		
														F	6		
7	170	F	5, 14			8	185			F	50	9	210	F	4		
		M	6							M	69			M	4		
														M	4, 2		
														M	4, 12		
8	150			M	50	9	170	M	2, 13			10	160			M	35
				F				M	2, 14							M	42
								M	3, 6							M	44
6	150	F	3, 13			7	135			F	25	8	185	M	5, 14		
		M	4, 1							M	45			M	6, 2		
3	95						Dropped Collar					5	150			M	72
																M	73
3	125					4	155	F	3, 5			5	135			F	?
2	120					3	155	F	4, 10			4	180			F	Dead
																P Quills	
2	70											2	110				
2	60											2	80				
7	147	F	47				HK '93										
		M	52														
		M	57														
2	124					3	Too Heavy										
							Collar Removed										
						3	115					4	130	M	6		
														M	6		

NID (Not In Den) denote yearlings that were not found in dens with their mothers. In most cases, the young bears did not survive, but in some instances, yearlings may have denned separately from their mothers. A ? means the weight is unknown. P Quills refers to the porcupine quills that killed Nette's first cub.

Bears	1996						1997					
	Age	Weight	Cubs		Yearlings		Age	Weight	Cubs		Yearlings	
			Sex	Weight	Sex	Weight			Sex	Weight	Sex	Weight
CARMEN	10	175			F	82	11	270(Dec)				
					M	74		235(Mar)	F	6.91		
					M	NID						
JOHNSON CREEK (JC)	10	185			M	71	11	245				
					F	52						
					M	NID						
					M	NID						
TAMMI	11	200	M	5.5			12	207	F	5.9		
			M	5.28					F	5.19		
SANDY	9	145			M	NID	10	237(Dec)				
					M	NID		198(Mar)	F	6.12		
PRISCILLA	6	157	M	6.75				HK '96				
TAMMI'S DAUGHTER '90			M	6.49								
LIL	5	182	M	4.18			6	155			M	62
SHERRI'S DAUGHTER '90			M	4.09							F	50
			F	3.8							M	NID
NETTE	5	205	M	6.86			6	210			M	101
CARMEN'S DAUGHTER '91			M	6.18							M	85
VICKI	5	135			M	62		Missing				
					M	41						
BOWS							2	137.5				
CARMEN'S DAUGHTER '95												
NO NAME												
SHERRI'S DAUGHTER '97												
SUSIE	3	115					4	147	F	3.5		
SANDY'S CUB '93									M	3.19		
BIGLY		HK '96										

A scale to weigh cubs was not available during den checks in 1999, so the weights of cubs for that year are unknown. Cub weights are in fractions of a pound, except for Lil's litter during 1998. NID (Not In Den) is for yearlings that were not found in their

1998						1999					
Age	Weight	Cubs		Yearlings		Age	Weight	Cubs		Yearlings	
		Sex	Weight	Sex	Weight			Sex	Weight	Sex	Weight
	HK '97										
12	230	F	4.91				HK '98				
		F	4.16								
		M	4.09								
13	195			F	52	14	225	F	?		
				F	46		New Tags	M	?		
								M	?		
11	180			F	60	12	235	M	?		
								F	?		
7	185	F	4, 15			8	175			M	60
		F	4, 9							F	60
		M	4, 10							F	55
7	200	F	5.6				HK '98				
		F	4.75								
		M	5.39								
3	145	F	4.88			4	140			M	65
		M	4.66							F	55
		M	4.33								
2	77					3	130	F	?		
5	135			F	133		Missing				

mother's den. HK stands for "Hunter Kill." Carmen and Sandy were each weighed twice during the winter of 1996–'97, during December of '96 and March of '97. Those two weights are listed under 1997.

Section 2

Problem Bears

(Left) The mere presence of a black bear can be threatening to some people. A few bruins are more aggressive than others and they usually cause the bulk of the problems, but bear problems increase during years when natural food supplies are scarce.

Chapter **11**

Dealing With Nuisance Bears

Escanaba Public Safety and DNR personnel involved in the capture and relocation of a black bear in the city on May 14 one year deserve a pat on their collective backs for the way they handled the situation. Their actions prevented possible confrontations between local residents and the confused animal, but, more importantly, they did what was best for the welfare of the bruin. A dart gun owned by the Public Safety Department was used to drug the bruin so it could be captured.

Few years go by that bears don't end up in one or more Michigan communities. The animals are usually either attracted by food or venture into city limits while exploring new territory. Many of the bruins that end up in cities and towns are young males that are striking out on their own for the first time after leaving their mother's home range, which happens at one or two years of age.

These dispersing males often set out in a specific direction and keep going until they find a location to their liking, sometimes covering 50 miles or more. Cross country jaunts through unfamiliar terrain occasionally bring bears in contact with cities. They normally detour around them, but in some cases attempt to go through towns, especially if it's late at night or early in the morning when there's little human activity.

Occasionally, the animals are spotted or surprised by people or dogs before they make it back into the woods and that's probably what happened in Escanaba. One of two things usually happens when bears are surprised in towns. In most cases, they climb the nearest tree, but they sometimes try to escape as the Escanaba visitor did and become confused by the urban setting and interference from humans.

All too often, these frightened, disoriented animals are killed under the guise of protecting the public. They are either shot or drugged while in a tree and allowed to fall to the ground, resulting in injuries that sometimes kill the animal. The safety of bears

(Left) Bears don't often attempt to break into homes or cottages, but those that do can also pose a threat to people.

that end up in cities is actually more at risk from what humans might do to them than any threat bruins pose to people under those circumstances.

One of the best ways to handle bears that end up treed in cities, especially if they are on the edge of town and woods are nearby, is to keep people away and let them climb down and leave on their own. That's what authorities in Iron Mountain did a number of years ago when a sow and her cubs became stranded in a tree. The family waited until midnight, when things had quieted down and they felt the coast was clear, before leaving their perch and the city.

The same scenario has worked countless times in other cities throughout the state. That's what eventually led to one young bear in Wexford County leaving its perch in a tree after three days on June 2, 1999. What was unusual about that situation is there wasn't any cover close to the tree the bear was in. The bruin was probably traveling cross country in unfamiliar territory under the cover of darkness and got surprised in the open near a rural home.

Bears aren't commonly seen in the area, so the animal's presence created a stir among local residents and passersby alike. In view of the commotion created by people as a result of the bruin's presence, it felt safest in the tree. After the bear was in the tree for three days, a fire truck was brought in and a hose from the truck was turned on it from the ground, on the chance the pressurized stream of water would force it from its perch. When the fire truck's water tank was empty, the bear was still there.

DNR Wildlife Biologist John Hendrickson from Marquette commented he was involved in the successful dislodging of a bear treed in a Baraga County community with a fire hose one time, but he said a cherry picker was used to get the hose above the bear before it was turned on. With the stream of water coming at the bear from above, it left the tree. When the fire hose trick didn't work on the Wexford County bear, DNR Bear Researcher Larry Visser cleared the area of people to see what would happen. Larry hid across the road from the bear to watch.

With the elimination of all distractions, the bear finally came down from the tree on its own. When it left the tree, the bear headed for a nearby house. The home owner had been watching it through a window. The guy came outside as the bear got close to his house, spooking it back toward the tree the animal had been in. Larry knew he had to get to the tree before the bear did to prevent it from going back up and he managed to do that, causing the bear to go elsewhere.

Black bear expert Gary Alt from Pennsylvania, who is an employee of the state Game Commission, demonstrated another technique for handling treed bears that he frequently uses, when I visited him one summer. After darting the young bear, he enlisted the help of bystanders to hold a net at the base of the tree to break the bear's fall if it fell before he could reach it. As the bruin got drowsy from the drug, Alt climbed the tree.

When it was ready to lose its grip, the bear biologist slipped a set of rope "cuffs" around the bruin's feet and then it was gently lowered to the ground with a rope. In most cases, a net would be sufficent to protect a bear from injury when falling out of a tree after being drugged.

That same week, I photographed Alt as he darted a free roaming adult female that lived in a subdivision. Alt had put a radio collar on the sow a few years earlier that was no longer functioning. He wanted to put a new collar on the animal, but she avoided live traps.

He got the opportunity to dart her when the bear paid a visit to the yard of one of the subdivision's residents. As the bear stood up on her hind legs to check a feeder, Alt

*When young males disperse from their mother's home range, they sometimes
end up in cities and towns where they climb trees when disturbed by people.
This bruin was photographed in the city limits of Marquette.*

117

A dart gun can be an effective means of dealing with nuisance bears, as shown here, if done properly. A dart is visible striking the bear's neck in this photograph.

put a dart in her neck as the home owner watched. People in Pennsylvania have a higher tolerance of bears than in the U.P. A new collar was soon in place after the drug took effect and the bear went on her way none the worse for wear, just like the bruin that paid Escanaba a visit.

But not all bears that find their way into Michigan cities are handled as well. A young bear that ended up in a tree in Calumet during late August of 1998 wasn't as lucky. It was killed by local law enforcement personnel as soon as it descended the tree it had been in. The animal wasn't given a chance to leave on its own. Claims that the bear was sick and that it was a threat to local residents were used to coverup the needless killing.

Nuisance bear activity is on the increase in Michigan and that trend can be expected to continue into the future as bear numbers escalate and they expand their range in the state. More human encroachment into bear habitat also contributes to the problem as has the closure of open dumps and poor availability of natural foods that bears depend on some years.

As an example of what can happen when natural foods that bears eat are scarce during spring and summer months, consider what happened one year during the early 1990s. The Department of Natural Resources (DNR) received more complaints about black bears during 1992 than they had for many years. Exactly how many complaints were received isn't known because they weren't all recorded, but there were hundreds of them. Some conservation officers in the U.P. received multiple calls about problem bruins during the course of one day, for example.

The food shortage in the woods brought the animals in contact with people as they searched for alternative meals. Their noses led them to table scraps in garbage cans, dog food, bird food, deer food and bee hives. They sought anything that was edible at campgrounds, rural residences and city dwellings alike.

Open pit dumps used to serve as buffers against nuisance bear activity during years when natural foods were scarce. Bruins were usually able to scrounge up enough food at these locations to satisfy them until alternative food sources developed. That's no longer possible due to the closure of most open pit dumps. Despite their advantages as buffers against nuisance bears, open dumps had far more disadvantages environmentally and it's good that they are no longer in use.

The good news is that despite the fact the potential for nuisance bear activity is increasing, there are plenty of ways for individuals to prevent problems from developing and for dealing with those that do occur. Learning how to prevent problems from nuisance bears and how to react to those that develop will benefit Michigan residents and the DNR as well as the state's growing bear population. Unfortunately, bears like the one in Calumet are sometimes killed when their search for food brings them in contact with people or their property. In most, if not all, of these cases, nonlethal measures would have been effective.

Many complaints about bears that the DNR receives have more to do with individual tolerance of the animals and perceptions about what a bruin might do rather than anything it's done. Bob Baty of Trufant cited an extreme example.

"Some guy bought property in Crawford County and one day while walking around the land he found a bear track. The first thing he did was file a complaint with the DNR because he felt unsafe knowing a bear was around."

Even when bears are hungry, they don't generally pose a threat to people or their pets. Despite all of the nuisance activity from bruins in the state during 1992, there were no reports of anyone being injured by one and there's no reason for that to change in the future, as long as current hunting seasons and harvest levels are maintained. Black bear can be dangerous, but they generally aren't because they have learned to fear man after years of being hunted and killed. Most black bear attacks on people that have occurred involved bruins in parks or remote settings where they aren't hunted or lightly hunted. However, females with cubs and wounded animals have been responsible for attacks in areas where they are hunted.

As someone who has had close contact with hundreds of black bears of all sizes, including females with cubs, over the years while photographing them, I can verify that the danger these animals pose to humans is often grossly exaggerated. I've never come close to being attacked or injured. On the occasions bears have made threatening gestures toward me, it was because I got too close to them or surprised them, not the other way around.

Leaving food of any type where it will be accessible to black bears is responsible for most nuisance complaints. The problem can be eliminated by removing the food or securing it in a location not accessible to bears. If that procedure is followed to begin with, most problems from bears can be avoided entirely.

Some specific examples of complaints from 1992 will help illustrate what I mean. A Grayling resident that continued feeding birds into June, for instance, attracted more than he bargained for. The bruin not only ate the bird seed, it damaged the feeders and did some minor damage to his house.

119

Open pit dumps used to serve as buffers against hungry bears during years when natural foods were scarce and many people went to landfills to watch bears. Most open dumps are now closed.

The bear left when the food supply stopped. The home owner was given a shell cracker, a device that makes a loud bang when fired, to scare the bear away if it returned.

Damage done to the house in that case may have been related to breeding behavior. Black bears normally breed from late May into July. Adult males travel over large areas looking for receptive females and leave their scent as well as bite marks on trees, signs and even buildings that they encounter during their travels.

Some homes and out buildings are also damaged by bears in an attempt to get food that is inside. In some cases, that food is in the form of ant colonies, bee hives or hornet nests that become established in the walls.

A Marquette County resident was feeding deer with corn during July that four bears also took a liking to. The home owner wanted deer in the area, but not bear. He was advised to quit feeding and informed no attempt would be made to live trap the bears if he continued feeding. With a steady supply of food, other bears were sure to show up even if the original four were moved. Black bear travel long distances in search of food and will settle in locations where food is abundant.

Individuals who want to feed wildlife where there is a chance of attracting bears should do so at sites where the presence of bears will be acceptable. Under current laws it is legal to feed wildlife, including bear, during the summer. However, it is

Some people feel threatened just knowing a bear is in the vicinity based on sign such a track like the one Dave Raikko is pointing out to his son.

illegal to hunt bear at a spot where they have been fed for more than 30 days before bear season begins. To be safe, there should be at least one-half mile between summer feeding sites and locations where bears are hunted. A distance of 50 to 100 yards is not acceptable.

One of the most common types of nuisance bear complaints involves raiding of household garbage cans containing table scraps and/or containers that still retain food odors. Rural home owners can eliminate the attractiveness of their garbage by keeping it inside the home, garage or shed. Household garbage that's stored outside can be kept "clean" and free of food odors by recycling bottles and cans. Food containers and wrappers that are discarded should be rinsed first. Table scraps such as fat, bones and grease should be stored in a freezer until garbage day.

When garbage is stored outside, bear proof cans and dumpsters will prevent bears

121

from helping themselves to the contents. Dumping household garbage in the woods on your property is definitely not a good way to avoid visits by black bears.

One of the bear complaints the DNR handled in Luce County during July involved a large bruin attracted to a dump in the woods behind a home where household garbage was disposed of. The bear hadn't bothered anyone or anything, but the home owner was concerned about its presence due to children that live in the area. The animal ended up leaving on its own, but others are sure to be drawn to the vicinity in the future, until the garbage is cleaned up.

Honey produced by bees and larval bees are irresistible for bears at any time, so bruins raiding bee hives account for a lot of problems. As an example, a pair of bruins showed up at commercial bee hives in Benzie County during May of 1992. A barrel trap and two leg snares were set in an effort to catch the animals and move them. One bear was captured and moved to the Pigeon River Country State Forest. The fate of the second bear is unknown.

Owners of bee hives who are interested in protecting them from bears can do so in one of two ways—electric fencing or an elevated platform. Pennsylvania Bear Biologist Gary Alt has had a lot of experience with bears and bees and he said if electric fencing is chosen, three strands of barbed wire spaced 10 inches apart works best. The first strand of wire should be 10 inches from the ground. Alt added that barbless wire is less likely to administer a shock to bears because of the length and density of their hair. To attract attention of bruins interested in honey, he recommends wrapping beef suet around wires so they are sure to get a shock when trying to grab the fat.

One bee keeper told me that he has a couple of his bee yards fenced with six strands of wire spaced eight inches apart at a cost of $200 per yard and the fencing works. However, due to the expense involved, he said he can't afford to fence all of his bee hives. As a result of slow response time from DNR personnel when he has bear damage, he's constructed a live trap of his own to capture offending bears.

Platforms about 10 feet high that are supported by metal legs will also prevent bears from getting at bee hives, according to Alt. He said that in Pennsylvania, state Game Commission personnel do not provide assistance to bee keepers who have problems with bears unless they have their hives fenced or elevated. Bee keepers in bear country who need assistance to protect their investment through fencing or in dealing with nuisance bears should contact the Michigan Bear Hunters Association or the U.P. Bear Houndsmen. Refer to the chapter "Bears and Hounds" for addresses and phone numbers of contacts for both organizations.

Corn and oat fields are also attractive to black bear and fencing the fields is the best way to protect the crops from both bear and deer. The problem is that the type of fencing that will keep bear out (electric) won't deter deer because they can jump over it and fencing that will block access for deer won't necessarily keep bear out. Mike Pollard from Stephenson said an 11-foot-high page wire fence his family erected around a 120-acre cornfield in Menominee County keeps deer out, but not bear. He said bruins used to go through the fence, but they now crawl under it through holes they've dug.

Protecting crops from bears is obviously more difficult than bee hives, especially in large fields. Elimination of as many problem bears as possible through live trapping and hunting would appear to be the best alternatives where fencing isn't possible or effective. Farmers who would like problem bears removed from their property by hunters should contact the bear groups mentioned above, local DNR personnel or county extension agents for assistance in notifying harvest permit holders.

Most nuisance bear are live trapped by conservation officers and other DNR person-
nel and relocated to areas where they are less likely to cause problems.

Since some crop damage from bears may occur before hunting season normally begins, the DNR might consider implementing regulations similar to Wisconsin and Minnesota for dealing with these nuisance animals. Those states issue bear harvest tags through a drawing like Michigan does. When preseason nuisance complaints develop, permit holders who want to are given the opportunity to fill their tag with a problem bear, under the guidance of a game warden. That program goes a long way toward meeting the needs of all parties who are involved. When a bear has to be destroyed, it's far better that the resource be utilized by a licensed hunter.

Bear guide Lawrence Edwards and his hounds from Republic helped get rid of a nuisance bear one fall after hunting season opened that was breaking into cabins and outbuildings in Dickinson County. The hounds were put on the nuisance animal's trail where it left a shed it broke into and the dogs eventually treed the 225 pound bruin.

When camping in bear country, food should not be cooked or stored in sleeping quarters. Food and sweet smelling toiletries such as toothpaste, perfume and deodorant should be hung in a canvas bag or pack from a rope over a tree limb so the items are too far from the ground, the limb and tree trunk for a bear to reach. Some campgrounds have "bear poles" to hang food from. State parks in bear country such as Porcupine Mountains Wilderness State Park also have bear proof food lockers for rent or sale to store food in. These lockers offer the most dependable means of keeping food from hungry bears when backpacking. If at a campground accessible by vehicle, food should be stored in the vehicle where it is out of sight.

During August of 1992 a big bear in Luce County tore the canvas on a camper in an attempt to get at food inside. What's the best way to deal with nuisance bears that

When camping, food should be hung from a tree with a rope over a tree limb so items are too far from the tree trunk, the limb and the ground for a bear to reach. Bear proof food lockers that can be rented or purchased at Porcupine Mountains Wilderness State Park are the most reliable means of keeping food from bears while camping.

*Spray cans of bear repellant can be very effective for individuals to use
in dealing with nuisance bears*

show up at campgrounds or rural residences when you are present? Bear expert Lynn Rogers' advice is to be aggressive toward them.

"What I do is run screaming at the bear," he said. "I wave my arms and throw things in the brush. Their biggest fear is other bears. They're not going to want to deal with you if they think another bear is coming.

"You can even throw rocks at the bear. A bruise is better than a bullet."

The bear biologist also said spray cans of dog repellent called Dog Shield like those used by mail carriers or Counter Assault, a repellent designed specifically for use on bear, are effective at getting rid of problem bears. To work, bears have to be sprayed in the eyes and face.

"Some people are afraid to use a repellent because they're afraid it will make the bear mad," Rogers said. "The times I've used it, I've never seen a bear go away mad. They just go away."

Cans of Dog Shield can be obtained from Viking Industrial North, 3825 Grand Ave., Duluth, Minnesota 55807 (218-624-4851). Counter Assault is available from P.O. Box 4721, Missoula, MT 59806 (800-695-3394).

Use of spray repellents is an excellent way to get rid of nuisance bears without killing them. The unpleasant experience should not only prevent them from returning, it should discourage them from causing problems elsewhere.

Chapter 12

Nuisance Bear Increasing

Although there were generally a lot of nuisance bear complaints in Michigan during 1992, 1993 was one of the worst for veteran western U.P. Conservation Officer Gary Lindquist. He said he filled out 146 nuisance bear complaint forms himself that year. There was poor natural food production in his area during '93.

Interestingly, 1994 was the worst year since 1992 for bear complaints in Porcupine Mountains Wilderness State Park, according to park employee and author Dave Young. "We gave refunds to campers right and left that year," he said. "We had people come in planning to camp for three or four days and they would be leaving after a day. They didn't have any food left. I estimated that half of the food carried into the interior of the park that year was taken by bears."

There were a whopping 114 bear complaints registered in the Porkies during 1994, according to Young. That compares with 35 during 1992, 64 in 1993 and 45 nuisance bear encounters for 1995. Young wrote a book titled *True Bear Tales* about bear/people interactions in the wilderness park. The third edition of the book was published during 1995.

If it weren't for Young's interest in documenting problem bears in the park, there probably wouldn't be as many reports on file as there are. He said some negative interactions between campers and bears are not written down. An example is a report he filled out about a bruin that followed a couple and their 5-year-old daughter for two miles on the South Mirror Lake Trail. He wrote the incident up a month after it happened when he learned about it.

The couple thought the bear was after their daughter, but it was actually after a ham sandwich in a fanny pack. In desperation, they eventually threw the small pack off

(Left) Pennsylvania Bear Biologist Gary Alt carries a young bear that got in trouble when it found its way into a city. Alt shot the treed bear with a dart gun to temporarily put it to sleep while it was being transported back to suitable habitat for its release. The bear was ear-tagged for future identification.

to the side of the trail, which also contained the man's wallet and $300. The bear forgot about the people and ripped the pack open to get the sandwich. The camper's wallet and money were retrieved later.

The DNR Wildlife Division has been trying to get a handle on the number of nuisance bear complaints filed in Michigan during recent years, but they've obviously got a long way to go. The figures that are available represent a fraction of the complaints that are made because they do not include all sources. The information is also incomplete from some sources that are reporting such as the Porkies.

It's easy to figure that out by simply looking at the total number of bear complaints the division had recorded for 1993—217. Lindquist handled close to that number himself and he was not the only officer who kept busy dealing with nuisance bears that year. Nonetheless, the division's nuisance bear records during recent years show a trend that is generally increasing in keeping with the upward trend in the bear population.

There were 133 complaints listed for 1991 and 168 for 1992. The number of nuisance bear recorded for 1994 was up to 330 compared to 217 the year before, but the actual number was probably much higher because complaints practically doubled in the Porkies alone between those years. By 1995, the tally of problem bear reports went down slightly to 279. There was a noticeable decline in nuisance bear activity during 1996 (196 reports), probably due to an increase in natural foods that year, and remained at moderate levels for 1997 (236).

DNR Bear Specialist Tim Reis said nuisance bear complaints dropped to 99 for 1998. He said he suspects that poor reporting was responsible for that decline as much, if not more, than anything else. Reis said he suspects there was a better effort on the part of DNR employees to document nuisance bear activity before, during and immediately after the bear referendum in 1996 and that reporting has fallen off since then. It appears as though the DNR still has a long ways to go to accumulate accurate information about the nuisance bear activity in the state.

Due to the inaccurate reporting system currently in use for recording bear/human conflicts, it's difficult to communicate to Michigan residents how serious a problem it is. I suspect that as few as 10 percent, and possibly even less, of the complaints are currently being recorded and there's no estimate of the dollar value of damage that bears cause each year. The figure for bear damage is easily in the tens of thousands of dollars, but it could be as much as $100,000 or more. If bear damage to bee hives and agricultural crops such as corn and oats are considered, the economic loss to bears could approach $1 million.

Another known that a price tag can't be put on is that problem bears often scare people besides causing property damage. They scare some individuals so badly that they fear for their lives or those of family members. Following are some real examples of nuisance bear activity.

Black bears don't have to attack Michigan residents to strike fear into their hearts or terrify them. It happens hundreds of times each year without tooth or claw touching anyone. Some of the most frightening experiences occur when bruins show up on the door step of rural homes or cottages looking for food, but humans are most vulnerable when the paths of hikers, anglers or campers cross those of aggressive bears on their own turf.

Unfortunately for some campers, bruins sometimes claim campgrounds as part of their territory. One young male bear in Pictured Rocks National Lake Shore, for example, frightened a party of teen-aged boys and group leaders from a Petoskey school

A boy peers out the window of a trailer as a black bear tries to look in.
Such an encounter might scare many rural residents, but bruins normally
stay away if there is no food to attract them.

during late May of 1993. They set up camp at a group campsite near the mouth of the Mosquito River on May 19, where the bruin eventually showed up, following and "pestering" group members.

The persistent bruin hung around most of the night and into the next morning, during which time it thoroughly scared the campers. Efforts to get it to leave proved unsuccessful and the animal seemed to be getting more aggressive. It ripped one backpack apart in its search for food and damaged a pair of tents.

Imagine the fear those people must have felt. They were concerned the bear might attack someone, and it certainly could have. Fortunately, it didn't before park rangers reached the scene the morning of May 20th. Attempts to chase the bear away with spray cans of repellent failed, so the bruin was killed to eliminate the opportunity for that bear to terrorize more campers. There's a good chance its behavior would have continued. The same bear is thought to have been involved in two other incidents in the park before its death.

Two more bears, both of which were also males, were killed in the U.P. during the summer of 1993 under similar circumstances. During July, a "medium size" bear was killed by staff members in Porcupine Mountains Wilderness State Park near the mouth of the Big Carp River. Park Manager Ron Welton said that bruin was responsible for a lot of problems and that's why it was eliminated. On one occasion, 38 people crammed inside a park cabin and 17 took refuge on the roof to escape the ornery animal.

Those campers and hikers were obviously scared and they had every reason to be. Welton said that if the bear hadn't been killed it probably would have eventually hurt a park visitor. Bears in the Porkies have been responsible for a number of attacks on people in the past, one of which resulted in the death of a camper.

Conservation Officer Tom Courshaine from Sault Ste. Marie killed the third aggressive male after it chased a jogger into a lake at a church camp north of Strongs. That bear seemed to have no fear of humans and had gotten into trouble on numerous occasions. The bruin started causing problems along the Mackinac Trail near St. Ignace.

It was then live trapped and released in a remote area between Brimley and Paradise. A day later, trouble started again. The problem bear was easy to identify due to blue ear tags that had been attached as a cub on Drummond Island. DNR Bear Researcher Larry Visser from Houghton Lake said he's sure the bear swam to the mainland from the island like others have done.

The U.P. is not the only part of the state where close calls with bears can be expected. Soil Conservation Service employee Joe Dumont was working in the Missaukee County portion of the Dead Stream Swamp one spring on April 29th when he encountered an aggressive bruin.

"I was about 1/3-of-a-mile into the swamp on a faint trail when I heard some unusual noises," Dumont wrote. "The unusual noise was coming from a mature black bear circling me at about 200 feet. I had never seen a bear in the wild, but instinctively I knew that I was in for trouble. Not knowing what else to do, I pulled a whistle from my emergency kit. One blast on the whistle resulted in the bear charging me and I went up the nearest leaning tree.

"The bear stopped about 30 feet away and spent the next two hours threatening me with deep-chested noises, snapping teeth, short charges and swipes at the nearest tree. I was convinced that there would be a fight to the death if I was on the ground.

"The emergency started about 2:30 p.m. and by 4:30 I had thoughts of a search party being formed to look for me. By 7:00 I was sure that it would be unlikely that anyone would be able to find me that far in the swamp with the wind blowing so hard that yelling couldn't be heard. Hypothermia was starting to take its effect and I was sure that I didn't want to spend the night in this situation.

"I beat my muck probe on the tree next to me, whistled, yelled, talked to the bear and prayed to help forget the danger of the situation. Nothing seemed to have any effect on the bear. I experienced moments of fear in that first two hours when my every move would bring a short charge and then retreat from the bear. I had another fright when I dropped my canister of Halt (spray can of repellent) which I had intended to try if the bear got close enough."

At 7:15, Joe finally decided to try hitting a map board with his muck probe. That sound caused the bear to move off about 100 feet and he took advantage of that opportunity to drop to the ground and leave. The bruin didn't make any further advances toward him once he was on the ground.

Although Dumont obviously felt safe in the tree he climbed when the bear initially came toward him, his elevated position is not what saved him from the bruin. If the bear was serious about attacking him, it could have easily done so where he was. I suspect the bear in question might have had cubs nearby and was uncomfortable with the human so close. Joe probably could have escaped the situation much sooner and saved himself a lot of worry, by staying on the ground in the beginning and moving away from the bear slowly, but steadily.

Never turn and run from a bear. Either back away or move sideways, always keeping an eye on the animal. If the bear had actually attacked when Dumont was on the ground, he had two weapons to defend himself with—his muck probe and canister of Halt.

It's not necessary to go into the deep woods to find aggressive bears. Some people have encounters of the scary bear kind by staying at home or camp. More bold bruins are traveling to homes and cottages each year to frighten unsuspecting people. Imagine arriving home at 3:00 p.m. as one Grayling woman did during May, to find a hungry bear destroying your bird feeder.

She wisely honked her car horn in an effort to chase the animal away, but it ignored the sound. Too scared to leave the safety of her vehicle with such a bold and obviously hungry bear in her yard, the woman left. The bear was gone when she returned. However, once she was inside the house, she was afraid to leave for fear of encountering the bruin. She's not the only person who has been afraid to venture outside in her own yard, especially after dark, where a bold bear has been sighted.

A Wexford County bear reportedly attacked the house of a Cadillac resident during June, ripping a screen off. During September, a bruin that could have been the same one, ate plums from a tree in the yard of another Cadillac resident. After done with the plums, the bear walked up to the house and stuck its head inside an open bedroom window. Shots fired over the animal failed to drive it off.

Pets, poultry and livestock are normally in more danger from bears that visit peoples' yards than the home owners themselves. One September, a couple from Alpena watched a bear break into their rabbit cage then kill and eat a rabbit. A second rabbit was injured. They chased the bear away and retrieved the injured rabbit, only to have the bear come back once they were inside. The bruin returned the next day, too.

Once bears obtain food in a location, they often return to try for more. Another Presque Isle County bruin killed as many as eight caged rabbits at a Posen residence during August of 1995. Chickens, turkeys, goats, sheep and pigs were also killed and eaten by bears in Michigan during 1994, according to the DNR's huge stack of nuisance bear complaints. Dogs have also been injured and killed by bears.

Bruins that make a habit of searching for and obtaining food at homes can become dangerous and destructive. Fences have been torn down by the animals, out buildings broken into and anything that smells like or contains food such as bird feeders or barbecue grills, are ransacked or carried off. DNR employees make an effort to live trap and move as many of these bears as possible and that usually helps, but some of the animals end up being destroyed.

A home owner from Marenisco in the U.P.'s Gogebic County killed a 300-pound male on his porch one summer after it broke a window. He was afraid the bear would try to go inside and that might have been the bruin's intention. A Luce County bear did enter an occupied cabin that same summer and it was also killed.

Ronald Caron from Gladstone had a 250 pound bear break into his screened porch and then it left. However, it returned two hours later. Caron yelled at the bruin in an effort to scare it away. Instead of leaving, the animal came toward him and he shot it.

Fortunately, no one was at home when a bear on Drummond Island entered a house and opened the freezer to get some food. Conservation Officer Matt Dallman set a trap for that animal and caught it within four hours. Another bruin that broke into the Bakers Oven Bakery on Drummond, damaging a microwave oven and a window and helping itself to baked goods, was also trapped and moved.

State Park Ranger Joe Jacobson had a run-in with an aggressive bear that was eventually trapped and moved one July at the Presque Isle Campground in Porcupine

131

Mountains Wilderness State Park. He was in the small park office building at the campground when the bruin pushed against all of the windows in an attempt to get in. When that didn't work, it checked out the bed of Joe's pickup truck. From there, it went to a dumpster.

After going through seven bags of garbage, the animal ravaged two campers' coolers. When the bear was in the dumpster, Jacobson drove up to it and laid on the horn, but the noise had no impact on the bear. The following day, the animal was live trapped and relocated. If problem animals are released in an area where natural foods are available, which is what Ontonagon Conservation Officer Jackie Strauch said she always tries to do, that helps them stay out of trouble.

Strauch told me about a young male, which she trapped and moved, that became a serious problem in Silver City. She said the bear began hanging around a store that sold ice cream cones adjacent to a miniature golf course. The bruin learned that by charging people coming out of the store, they would usually drop their ice cream and run. The bear then ate the food.

That bruin obviously provided some people with serious scares before Strauch moved it. She said the bear bluff charged her several times while preparing to set a trap for it. The animal was fitted with ear tags before it was released and she hasn't heard word of it getting in trouble again. Jackie commented that nuisance animals are often shot by hunters during the fall, eliminating their opportunity to cause further problems.

Conservation officers and wildlife biologists often refer bear hunters to areas where bears have been problems, so they can target the specific animals. That's what happened one August on a bruin that had been hanging around a rural Baraga County residence, having damaged the garage. As soon as hunters put baits in the area, the bear spent time feeding on them and was no longer seen at the home.

From 1991 through 1995, live traps were set in 349 instances, with the intent of capturing nuisance bears. There were 152 bruins caught. However, two of those animals managed to get out of traps. In one case, a bear managed to get out of a trap after the home owners moved the trap.

Another two bears that had been trapped were destroyed due to serious injuries that they suffered from gunshot wounds. In both cases, property owners had shot problem bears, but had not killed the animals. One of the bruins had a shoulder wound that was badly infected and the second had suffered injuries to its head and jaw.

Relocated bears sometimes return to locations where they were captured. One adult male that Jackie Strauch moved 85 miles on May 1 was back where it had been caught on the 7th. Adult males have such large home ranges, distances of up to 100 miles are easy for them to navigate. However, they often get distracted with other food sources or obstacles on their way home, either slowing their return or preventing them from returning.

Black bears also do their share of damage to vehicles. Doug Bundy from Epoufette told me about a black bear estimated to weigh 150 pounds that beat logger Lee Karridge of Rexton to his lunch one day during early July while working at a site near Gould City. Karridge left a window open on his pickup truck and the bear climbed

(Left) Bird feeders are frequently the target of hungry bears during spring and summer. Once the food is removed, the animals usually move on.

A total of 150 nuisance black bears were live trapped and relocated in Michigan between 1991 and '95. Some relocated bears return to where they were trapped in a matter of days, but that is less likely to happen if they are released in an area with abundant natural food.

inside to help itself to the meal. The bear scratched the door and ripped the side mirror off when gaining access to the truck.

The animal had to open a cooler the food was in, damaging it in the process, before dining. When Karridge opened the door on his truck, the bruin went a short distance and laid down. Fortunately, the bear didn't feel cornered or threatened. Otherwise, it might have attacked the logger.

Bears damage vehicles as well as other property, usually in an effort to get at food that's stored inside. Bruins have been known to bite tires and flatten them as well as knock off mirrors and antennas among other things.

In another case, bear researcher Terry DeBruyn of Marquette had an unexpected surprise waiting for him one evening during August upon returning to his pickup truck after spending more than 8 hours following a female with a single cub in his Alger County study area. Another bear had tried to gain access to food in his vehicle during his absence, leaving prints all over the vehicle and a bed nearby. Frustrated about not being able to get at the food, the bear damaged all four of his tires by biting them before leaving.

One of the tires was flat upon his arrival and he replaced it with a spare. A second tire went flat as he started driving. He ended up having the truck towed and all four tires had to either be replaced or repaired. The DNR's Larry Visser told Terry about a bear in the northern Lower Peninsula that flattened the tires on a number of vehicles by biting them, before his experience.

Convertibles are poor choices for storing food in bear country. The soft tops of these vehicles have been ripped open by hungry bruins on a number of occasions. Other types of damage has been done to vehicles by bears, too, in their efforts to secure food that's inside.

Game bagged by hunters can also be targeted by hungry bears. On October 1, 1995, a bruin took a bow-bagged 4-point buck that was hanging from a buck pole in Delta County. During June of '94, a bear ripped a bow and arrow target apart that resembled a deer on an archery range in Chippewa County.

There will always be nuisance bears in Michigan as long as we have a healthy population of the animals and their food supply fluctuates from year-to-year. It will be impossible to totally eliminate them, however, one of the purposes of hunting is to eliminate as many problem bears as possible on an annual basis. That will continue to happen as long as current bear hunting practices are legal.

Black bears often kill young wildlife such as fawns. Children also qualify as prey, which is what happened in Michigan's most tragic and widely known bear attack, resulting in the death of a 3-year-old girl. Bears don't have to be big to kill a fawn or child.

Chapter 13

Michigan Bear Attacks

Black bears are not normally considered predators because they don't depend on killing prey for survival, but they are opportunistic predators. When they get the chance to kill an animal such as a fawn, moose or elk calf, cub or beaver for food, they usually take advantage of it. Since bruins are not fulltime predators, they are most effective at catching prey that are vulnerable and can't easily escape such as young animals.

I've witnessed bears killing fawns on two occasions while following a pair of female bears in Alger County with Bear Researcher Terry DeBruyn and he's seen them prey on others. In each case, the bruins simply stumbled upon the young deer and immediately transformed into killers to secure a meal at a time when most of their normal foods are not yet available. Deer are so abundant over the black bear's range in Michigan that most bruins in the state probably kill fawns every year. Those DeBruyn has followed have.

The reason I bring this up is that such a predatory attack is probably what was responsible for the most tragic and widely known bear attack on a human being in Michigan, which occurred on July 7, 1948 at 2:30 p.m. It involved a 3-year-old girl named Carol Ann Pomranky who was playing in the back yard of the remote U.P. firetower cabin where her family lived. She played near a set of three steps leading to the back door. An inside door was open, but a screen door at the top of the steps was closed. The closest town was Brimley. Carol Ann's father worked for the U.S. Forest Service and he was elsewhere at the time the attack occurred.

The girl's mother was inside the cabin and endured the horrible experience of watching a black bear grab her daughter and carry the toddler into the woods. A cry of alarm from Carol Ann attracted her mother's attention and when the woman reached the screen door the girl was on her hands and knees on the porch, with a hand on the screen. The bear was coming up the steps at that point and soon had the girl, pulling her off the porch. It wasn't a big bear, but it doesn't take a large bruin to kill a fawn or a child. Bears can and have become predators when they are yearlings weighing less than 100 pounds. The animal that killed the girl was weighed after it was destroyed and it was 125 pounds.

It's obvious the bear in this case viewed the little girl as prey because it ate part of the child. Former state trapper and woodsman Alex Van Luven from Brimley located the victim's body with a leashed hound that followed the bear's scent. A commercial fisherman named Wayne Weston was left to guard the body while Van Luven continued on with his dog in an effort to find the bear. Minutes after Van Luven left the scene, the bruin returned to its victim and Weston killed it.

Based on the black bear's predatory preference for young mammals, it's amazing there aren't any other cases of children being attacked and/or killed by them in the state. Michigan has obviously been lucky in that regard, probably because most residents learned a valuable lesson from the Pomranky child's death, and I hope such a case never happens in the state again. However, it could be repeated at any time. There are plenty of examples from other states and provinces where children have been attacked by bears to confirm that youngsters are preferred prey over adults for hungry and/or aggressive bruins.

There are two other documented cases from Michigan in which people have died as a result of bear attacks, the most recent of which occurred during 1978 in Porcupine Mountains Wilderness State Park. I was able to locate a number of other records of nonfatal attacks and lots of other cases that could be described as dangerous encounters between bears and people, all of which involved adults. I'm sure there are additional accounts I was unable to locate.

My research shows that the chances of anyone in the state being attacked by a black bear are not high, considering the thousands of potential contacts between humans and the animals annually. In many of these cases, a bear detects a person and leaves the area without the person ever knowing a bruin was nearby. This is typical behavior because the animals normally try to avoid people. Part of the reason for the avoidance of humans is that bruins have learned to fear man because they frequently have bad experiences when their paths cross. They are either killed or trapped and moved. The fact that bears are actively hunted in the state contributes to that fear and avoidance.

Although bear hunting is more controlled now than it has ever been, there is still enough hunting pressure on the animals to promote continued wariness and avoidance among most bruins. Current bear hunting regulations actually reflect better management more than anything, but that could have all changed if the DNR's ability to regulate bear hunting was usurped through a ballot referendum during 1996. Fortunately, the referendum failed. If the two most popular bear hunting methods—the use of bait and hounds—had been eliminated through passage of that referendum, hunting success would have declined and the bear population would have experienced a dramatic increase.

The more bears there are, the greater the chances for interaction between them and people, especially during years when natural food supplies normally utilized by bears are scarce. Hungry bears are often bold and a decline in hunting of the animals might increase their boldness even more. When coupled with the fact that there are more people than ever before in the outdoors and the number of humans is expected to continue to increase, the odds of someone being injured or killed by a bear go up even more. Let's hope that doesn't happen—either an increase in attacks or a major change in bear hunting.

Michigan's first known fatality from a black bear happened in the Lower

*The odds of being attacked by a black bear in Michigan are extremely low,
even when being surprised by a bruin at close range as shown here.
Most bears fear people due to the fact they are hunted.*

Peninsula during the late 1800s. The victim was Frank Devereaux, who lived on a lake south of Cheboygan. The Civil War Veteran was killed by a bear on September 4, 1883, according to Reginald Sharkey from Petoskey. Devereaux died from a blow to the head from a bruin he wounded with his muzzleloader. He also had a severe injury to one leg where the bear bit him.

It's unknown whether the attack occurred before or after Devereaux shot the bear, but the bruin also died from its injury. The carcass was located not far from the man's body. The small lake that Devereaux lived on was named after him and Sharkey said there's a monument there marking his grave. The bear he killed was also buried there. An inscription on the headstone reportedly reads, "Here lie the bodies of a man and bear . . . it was a draw!"

Pomranky was the next victim of a bear attack, followed by 71-year-old Arthur DeGault from Engadine on June 5, 1960 at 3:30 p.m. The attack occurred near his home in Mackinac County. DeGault managed to fight off his attacker, but at least 100 stitches were required to close his wounds and he spent five days in a hospital recuperating. The evidence in that case indicates a female with cubs may have felt her cubs were threatened by DeGault's presence and took action. The man unknowingly came within 100 feet of where she had left the cubs in a yellow birch tree.

The outdoorsman went out that afternoon to look for a hand hook and axe that had been left in the woods during March when they were covered by a heavy snow-fall. DeGault was walking along a logging road on a ridge when he saw the bear below him a "stone's throw away." It appeared as though the bruin was stalking him. When he tried to walk away, the bear ran up behind the man, biting his left thigh.

DeGault responded by hitting the bruin in the face and she released her grip to stand on her hind legs to face him like a boxer. He used his hands and arms as much as possible to protect his face and punch the animal as he slowly backed away from the bruin. Eventually, he remembered a jackknife in a pants pocket and managed to get that out.

When he started jabbing at the bear with the knife, it dropped to all four feet. He tried to stab the bruin in an eye and he thinks he succeeded because he felt the blade sink in. Whatever damage he caused, it was enough to bring the attack to an end. The bear left and DeGault staggered to his truck, stopping to rest a number of times along the way.

When he reached his vehicle, he discovered the pocket his keys were in had been ripped open and they were gone, so he had to continue on another half mile to reach his house. He had gone about three-fourths-of-a-mile from the scene of the attack to his truck. If the U.P. resident's injuries had been more serious, preventing him from covering that distance, he might have died before help reached him. Fortunately, that wasn't the case.

Later that day, District Conservation Supervisor Ernest Ruecker and a pair of bear hunters from Newberry with hounds—Tom Singleton and Arnold Norman—returned to the scene in an effort to find the bear that attacked DeGault. They found

Females with cubs have been involved in many of the bear attacks in Michigan.

140

plenty of blood and evidence that the bruin had left cubs in a birch tree near where the attack occurred. The blood trail led to that tree, which bore claw marks thought to be from cubs, indicating the female retrieved her cubs before leaving the scene.

The hounds were eventually pulled off of the injured bear's trail late in the day when it failed to climb a tree in front of the dogs. DeGault's experience illustrates the importance of fighting back, if attacked by a black bear. Authorities on black bears such as Dr. Lynn Rogers from Ely, Minnesota recommend that course of action, if at all possible.

Five years before the attack mentioned above, DeGault said he was charged by another female with cubs. The cubs were with the mother in that case. Another major difference is the woodsman had a rifle with him that time and he used it to kill the aggressive animal at point blank range. That incident happened about 300 yards from where the later bear encounter took place.

Joe Newman, Sr. of Palmer had a similar experience while grouse hunting near town during the fall of 1976. He had his seven-month-old bluetick hound, Jake, with him on the chance it might get some experience chasing snowshoe hares and it's a good thing the dog was along. When going through some thick balsam trees, Newman almost stepped on a pair of napping bear cubs. The startled cubs bawled and climbed the nearest tree.

The cubs' mother suddenly charged from the brush and the hunter was forced to shoot in self defense at point blank range with his 20 gauge shotgun. The injured bruin retreated momentarily, but quickly returned. Newman then discovered his gun had jammed in the excitement.

At the last moment, Jake dashed between the enraged bear and his master and held the sow at bay until Newman got his shotgun reloaded. Two more shots finished the episode.

During November of 1974 an unnamed deer hunter from Marquette was injured by a small bear that was sleeping soundly under a log when the man grabbed it, thinking it was dead. The 80 pound bear appeared lifeless to the hunter, so he grabbed it by the ears to pull it in the open. That was enough to wake the bruin and it responded by clawing the hunter's hand and biting his leg. When the man retaliated by slugging the bear in the jaw, it ran away.

That bear obviously acted defensively, so this incident doesn't qualify as an attack. The person's actions were responsible for his injuries, but that is sometimes what brings bear attacks on. Campers, for instance, should never cook or store food in tents while in bear country and should try to avoid pitching a tent in locations frequented by bears. Those mistakes were responsible for a bear attack in Porcupine Mountains Wilderness State Park during July of 1975.

Sixteen-year-old Paul Cameron from Dearborn originally pitched his tent near Mirror Lake, cooking and eating dinner in his tent that evening. He had apparently spilled cooking oil on the tent during a previous meal, creating an even more appealing attraction for any bears in the area. Paul put his backpack containing most of his food outside his tent that night, leaving it on the ground where a bear would have easy access to it. A bruin was attracted to Cameron's tent that night and ate most of the food in his pack.

That experience forced the camper to move the next day, but the spot he moved to was a bad choice. He pitched his tent near a trash barrel along M-107 near the beginning of the Government Peak Trail. On top of that, he stored his backpack and remaining food in the tent with him that night.

About 8:00 a.m. the next morning Cameron heard something walking outside the

Campers have been among bear attack victims in the state, especially in Porcupine Mountains Wilderness State Park.

tent. When it started scratching at the shelter, he realized his visitor was another bear. It left the tent temporarily to rummage in the nearby garbage can, but soon returned.

The bear then knocked the tent down and began biting through the fabric in search of the food it could smell. Paul remained motionless, playing dead, hoping the bruin would lose interest and wander off.

"I thought the bear was nibbling at me to see if I would jump," Cameron said. "If I did I thought it would pounce on me and tear me up."

When the bear started dragging the tent, Paul was able to roll out through an opening and continued playing opossum. The bruin soon walked up to him, grabbed him by the throat and lifted his head. At that point, Cameron screamed and the animal released its grip. He then took advantage of the opportunity to make his escape.

The offending bear was later killed as it was rummaging through Cameron's tent. It proved to be a female weighing 125 pounds with two cubs and the cubs were also killed.

Nineteen-year-old Michael Patterson from Alma wasn't as lucky as Cameron had been. His body was found on June 20, 1978 along the Lake Superior Trail in the state park at the base of a balsam tree he fell out of or was pulled out of during the course of a black bear attack. Claw marks in the tree indicated the bear also climbed it. The man's legs and lower back bore puncture marks and scratches from a bear, but a ruptured lung and kidney resulting from the fall were responsible for his death. If the bruin pulled him out of the tree, which it may have, the animal was responsible for his death.

Since Patterson was alone, no one is sure exactly what happened. He could have lost his balance or grip in the tree, causing the fall or a limb he was on might have broken. A number of the tree's limbs had been broken sometime during the horrifying life and death struggle that must have taken place.

Park officials did determine that an aggressive female with four cubs was responsible for the attack on Patterson. If the cubs had been in the same tree the camper climbed or he surprised the family or acted in a threatening manner toward the cubs, his actions would have been enough to bring on the female's wrath. It can be difficult to always do the right things under a stressful situation, but the camper would have been better off facing his attacker rather than climbing a tree. A black bear is far better at climbing trees than any person, so doing that is not a means of escaping them and expends precious energy that might be useful in fighting off an attack.

The aggressive female that attacked Patterson is thought to be the same animal that developed a bad habit of stealing backpacks from campers in the Porkies the year before. She developed a routine of charging at visitors to get them to drop their packs. She damaged some tents, too, one of which had a woman inside.

Her behavior cost the bruin her life nine days after the camper's death. The day after Patterson's body was found, the female resumed her aggressive habits and reports poured in about her actions. Initial efforts to kill the female failed when she moved, but she was relocated on June 29th when she charged three women on the North Mirror Lake Trail. Her reign of terror soon came to an end.

The Porkies weren't the only area of the state where bears were causing problems that year. On June 14th, 1978 Alger County resident Wayne Pangborn had a close call with a bruin while stream fishing in his home county. When he first encountered the animal at close range he reacted by hollering at it, which temporarily scared it off. The trick worked for Pangborn once before in turning the charge of a sow with cubs.

This time when the angler crossed the creek he had been fishing, the bear followed him. He threw his creel at the bear next, which had several trout in it, and that distracted the bruin for a short time, but it soon turned its attention back to the fisherman. Pangborn thought about climbing a tree, but it's fortunate he didn't.

Instead, the desperate angler grabbed pieces of wood for clubs and used them to fend off the bear during a three-quarters-of-a-mile struggle to his car. He made it through the harrowing experience without suffering a scratch from the bear. The following day, I returned to the scene with Pangborn and former DNR Conservation Officer Leo Erickson, so Wayne could retrieve his fishing equipment and there was no sign of the bear.

A sow with cubs was involved in another attack that happened in Gogebic County on September 19, 1982. John Skosnik from Warren was bear hunting that evening when the female and two cubs approached his blind. The hunter reportedly wounded the adult, which attacked immediately, biting him over most of his body. Surgery was required to tend to his wounds.

Former K. I. Sawyer resident Gary Wudtke was bowhunting for deer over bait on October 1, 1991 in southern Marquette County when he was attacked by another sow with cubs. This female had three cubs. After the family of bears appeared, the cubs concentrated on feeding while their mother checked out the area, according to Wudtke. She was grunting as she circled the tree he was in. The presence of another bear earlier may have made the bruin nervous.

After circling the tree, the female stood up between the tree and cubs and looked directly at Gary. She then went to the base of the pine and the hunter thought she was ready to climb the tree, so he hollered at her in an effort to discourage her from doing so. The hunter's voice scared the cubs and the pine Gary was in was the biggest and closest tree, so that's the one they climbed. Wudtke kicked at a cub to try to keep it below him and then started climbing higher to stay above the cubs.

The pine was broken off 16 feet above his stand. He hadn't climbed far when the

143

mother bear grabbed his right shoe. She pulled him down several feet as Gary kicked at her with his other foot.

The bear then grabbed his left shoe. Wudtke was able to pull free and climb away from his attacker, but he soon lost his grip on the tree and fell on top of the bruin. She pushed him away from the tree and he fell 36 feet to the ground. The bowhunter could have suffered the same fate as Michael Patterson. Fortunately, he didn't.

Once on the ground, Gary walked to his car as fast as he could, which was parked three blocks away. The fall from the tree ended Gary's bowhunting for the year. He dislocated his left shoulder, having landed on it when he hit the ground. The only other injury he received was a cut to his left ear, which may have been sliced by one of the bear's claws.

Wudtke's mistake was hollering. He should have made his presence known to the adult bear in a more subtle manner such as waving his hands at it or standing up to make sure she saw him. Once a potential threat was recognized, the mother probably would have led her cubs away from the site and the chances of an attack would have been eliminated.

Mark Johansen from Harbor Springs endured a similar encounter with a female that had three cubs while bowhunting for deer on opening day of Michigan's 1998 bow deer season. However, in that case, the bruin never actually touched him. Nonetheless, a front paw she swatted at him with, came within a foot of making contact.

Like Wudtke, Johansen was hunting over bait, sitting 25 feet from the ground in a double-trunked hemlock tree with a 55-pound-pull Bear compound bow. The sugar beets and apples he was using for bait are just as appealing to bears as they are to whitetails. However, the appearance of bears was a surprise to the bowhunter because he had never seen any on the property during three years of hunting there.

He didn't have a clue any bruins were in the area until the three cubs appeared and started eating the bait. When Mama Bear arrived, she picked up Johansen's scent and began checking the area out. She eventually looked up the tree the hunter was in and stood up against the trunk as though she intended to climb.

Mark then hollered at the bear, hoping to scare it away. The sudden sound did scare the cubs off, but it had the opposite effect on the adult female. She started up the tree toward Mark.

Johansen then tried to maneuver his bow for a shot at the bruin directly under him and his arrow came off the string, falling to the ground. To give himself time to undo his safety harness, Mark then threw his bow at the bear. It hit the bruin, slowing her down long enough for him to undo the harness.

That's when Johansen's job with a tree service company came in handy. He climbs trees on a daily basis and was confident he could jump the three feet to the hemlock's second trunk, which he did as the bear came closer. That worked temporarily.

The bruin descended the trunk Mark's stand was in, but only so she could get to the smaller trunk. Once she reached it, she started climbing again. Johansen responded by returning to his stand, but the bear switched trunks again, too.

This time, Mark climbed out on a limb beyond his stand as far as he dared go, continuing to yell at the angry bruin and throw twigs at her that he was able to break off. The bear didn't attempt to climb out on the limb after him, but swatted at him from a position near the stand. The female eventually lost interest, descended to the ground and started to leave.

144

A walking stick can help fend off an attacking bear when used as a club.

Figuring the encounter was over, Mark returned to his stand. That proved to be a mistake because the bruin came roaring back up the tree as soon as he did. He climbed out on the limb until she lost interest again, but he made the same mistake twice more before realizing it was important to stay out on the limb until she was gone for good.

When the female was finally gone, Johansen left the tree and ran the 200 yards to his vehicle, fearing the female would follow, but she didn't. He asked a friend of his who lived nearby to retrieve his bow and arrow, which he did. The arrow rest on the bow was bent, but it was in good shape otherwise.

Once the bow was repaired, Mark returned to the same tree stand on the evening of October 4, hoping he would see deer instead of bears and he did. In fact, he

145

A can of bear repellent called Counter Assault is the best means of stopping a bear attack.

managed to arrow a 3-pointer. He hunted the same spot a number times after that and never saw the bears again.

Bowhunters will be happy to know that bear's behavior was unusual. Most females with cubs would have left with their cubs. Perhaps Johansen's yelling and being hit with the bow made the bruin more aggressive than it otherwise would have been. Even though that bear was more aggressive than most blacks, it's important to realize it could have actually attacked Mark if it wanted to, but it stopped short of doing so.

Bow deer hunters who use bait and want to avoid attracting bears should consider using cabbage as bait, where legal. That's one type of food that deer will eat, but bears don't seem to like.

The most recent bear attack that I'm aware of involved a bear hunter who was injured by a wounded animal during the fall of 1998. The Bay City resident, who asked not to be identified, bagged a trophy black bear weighing about 400 pounds while hunting in the U.P. However, he and his partner neglected to make sure the bruin was dead before trying to load it in or on their vehicle. One of the men suffered a broken wrist and bite marks before the bear was "killed" a second time.

There have been many other cases in Michigan that could be described as close calls between people and bears, but in most of those incidents there was no actual physical contact between man and animal. The encounters were obviously still scary for the individuals involved, however, they don't qualify as attacks. As long as a healthy bear population remains in the state, which most of us want to see, those scary episodes will continue. The odds of future bear attacks can be minimized by properly

146

managing bear numbers, as they are today, through REGULATED HUNTING, WHICH INCLUDES THE USE OF BAIT AND HOUNDS.

Hunters often have the means to protect themselves on those rare occasions that a bear attack does occur during the fall, but what about outdoor enthusiasts that are in bear country during the rest of the year? There is a means for all people to protect themselves should a bear attack happen to them that will effectively repel a bruin without hurting it. Spray cans of bear repellent have been developed specifically for that purpose. Some hunters, especially those carrying bows and arrows, should consider carrying these products with them while afield and they are highly recommended for hikers and campers. Refer to the chapter on "Dealing With Nuisance Bears" for specifics about repellents.

An alternative to spray repellents are walking sticks that can double as clubs. Hikers, campers and other outdoor enthusiasts should get in the habit of carrying a sturdy walking stick with them while afield. If the need arises, it can serve as a club to fend off a bear. Hitting a bear on the end of its sensitive nose can be enough to discourage an attack. That's what I did one time on an adult male that got too close and it worked.

Parents with young children should always be cautious when taking them in bear country. Families who live in the U.P. are always in bear country and should be especially careful if residing in a rural setting like the one where Carol Ann Pomranky lost her life. Black bears are opportunistic predators and I hope and pray that one never has the chance to use those instincts on a child in Michigan again.

Chapter **14**

Hunter Mauled By Bear

John May from Blanchard, Michigan can no longer hear out of his left ear. A 500 pound black bear is responsible for the hearing loss. May is thankful he didn't lose his life in the encounter with the big bruin.

The attack happened during the course of a bear hunt with hounds like so many others John had been involved in over more than 30 years of participation in the activity. He said he had encountered some aggressive bears during his years of hunting them, but none of them made physical contact with him. When they charged, he managed to kill them before they did. The closest any bruin managed to get to him was four feet.

That all changed on September 22, 1997. John was hunting with a group of friends in the northern Lower Peninsula that day. Fortunately, emergency medical technicians were members of the party.

The track of a big bear was located in the soft sand of a woods road that morning and the group decided to put dogs with the best noses on the trail. "I knew it was a big bear based on the size of the prints," John said, "but I didn't know it was as big as it turned out to be."

The bruin had walked through the area where his tracks were found hours earlier, so there wasn't a lot of scent associated with them, but there was enough for the experienced hounds to follow. A pair of the group's best dogs were put on the bear's trail.

"The dogs did an exceptionally good job following the bear," John commented. "They cold trailed him for five or six miles. Once the bear was jumped, he didn't run. He wasn't afraid of the dogs. He walked them into a thick slashing and tried to fight them off."

The bruin wasn't successful in his attempt to get rid of the hounds in the slashing, so he eventually moved on, crossing a road in the process. A member of the hunting

(Left) A large male black bear like this one that weighed more than 500 pounds mauled John May during a hunt with hounds.

They knew the bear their dogs were following was big based on the size of its tracks that they located before the hunt started that day.

party got a hasty shot at the bear when it crossed the road, but the bullet missed. Although the bear kept going, the hunters managed to put three more dogs on the bruin's trail when it crossed the road. Michigan law limits hunters to a maximum of six dogs during a bear hunt.

Eventually realizing after traveling another two miles that he couldn't successfully fight the dogs off, the big bear decided to get away from them by climbing a tree. All of the members of the group joined the hounds at the base of the tree as soon as they could. Standard procedure among most dog hunters is to wait for all participants to reach the tree a bear climbs before any action is taken. Most small bears and females are left to run another day.

When a big male like that one is treed, a decision is made who will shoot it. The option usually goes to the first hunter with a tag who gets to the tree, but novice hunters or those who may have never shot a bear before, are often given preference, too. In this case, it was decided that Sharon Agren from Lewiston would be the shooter.

Sharon and her husband Doug have been actively involved in bear hunting with hounds for 17 years. They have dogs of their own, two of which were trailing the bear on that hunt.

"For us, bear hunting is an excellent opportunity to exercise our dogs," Sharon said. "It doesn't matter if we get anything."

In fact, that was Sharon's first opportunity to shoot a bear. She said the bear climbed high into the tree it was in, with leaves and branches blocking most of the animal from view. The hunter had a difficult time getting a clear shot with her .30-06. Most treed bears are killed instantly with a head or neck shot and Sharon aimed for the bruin's neck.

As a precaution, most hound hunters designate a backup shooter to be ready to finish off any bear that may not be dead when it hits the ground. The hounds are all tied to trees before any shots are taken because they can be vulnerable to a wounded bear, as can the hunters. John May generally fills the position of backup shooter, as he did that day.

When Sharon shot, the bear fell out of the tree, but it wasn't seriously hurt.

"I was more surprised than you'll ever know when the bear took off after hitting the ground," Agren commented. "I was awed that it got up and took off."

"I knew the bear wasn't hit too good when he came out of the tree," John said. "As soon as he hit the ground, he took off at a fast run going away from all of us downhill and I ran after it. I wanted to be ready for a followup shot in case I was wrong and the bear went down."

John was carrying a .44 magnum handgun. He figured if the bear wasn't seriously hurt, it would soon outdistance him and the hounds could be released to resume the hunt. The interference of one of the dogs too soon complicated matters.

"All of a sudden, a dog ran by me after the bear," May remembered. "It must have broke loose from the tree it was tied to. The dog caught the bear and grabbed its butt. Then the bear turned and came charging straight toward me after the dog."

Still traveling downhill, John had built up a head of steam. His frame of mind quickly changed from monitoring the bear's retreat to stopping a full blown charge. John's concentration on the charging bear was probably responsible for less focus on his surroundings, causing another mistake that contributed to the attack.

"I wasn't worried or concerned at all when I saw the bear coming," May said. "It was 25 yards away at that point. I had confidence I could deal with the situation after having done so before. It was at that time that I hit a tree and fell.

"I knew I had to get up if I was going to stop the bear, because he was coming fast. When I got on my hands and knees and looked up, the bear was only six feet away. He was three feet away when I fired a shot and turned my head to try to protect it.

"I knew I was had when I fired the shot and turned my head. I was thinking of shooting again, but there was nothing I could do with that kind of weight on me. You're at the bear's mercy when you're in the jaws of a 500 pound animal."

The bruin grabbed John by the back of the neck and shook him. After releasing its grip on the neck, the angry bear bit down on May's face. That's when damage was done to John's left ear. He said he could feel his skull being crushed.

For some unknown reason, the bear released John after biting him twice. As a religious man, May feels divine intervention is what saved him.

"If it hadn't been for the Lord, I wouldn't still be here," he said. "The bear released me. He didn't have to. I believe an unseen angel stepped in after the bear bit me twice and said, 'That's enough.' If anymore had happened, I wouldn't be here."

John said the shot he fired when the bear was only three feet away hit the animal, but it obviously was not enough to stop or turn the charge. It was probably a glancing blow. When the bear left him, he thought about shooting again, but he didn't know if anyone else was nearby, so he held his fire. As the bear ran off, he heard shooting from other members of the party.

"I knew I was hurt and needed help," John said, "but I didn't know how bad I

151

***Sharon Agren did not have a clear shot at the treed bear due to the presence
of interfering limbs and leaves where it was perched.***

was hurt. I wanted some one to tell my wife and family that I love them, in case I
didn't make it."

Once the medical technicians reached John, they determined his injuries were not
life threatening. They took good care of him until an ambulance arrived about an hour
later. John was stabilized in the ambulance then transported by helicopter to a Traverse
City hospital for surgery.

"The surgeon, Dr. Harry Borovik, did a tremendous Job," May said. "He told me
that if the cut on my neck had been a half inch either way, the bear would have gotten
the major artery and nobody could have saved me then. He told me there could have
been a lot of nerve damage, too, if the injury had been a little different."

John received a total of 188 stitches to repair the wounds caused by the bear, but
he made a quick recovery. He said he was back bear hunting two weeks after the
attack.

"Accidents do happen," John commented, "and this was just an accident. I don't blame anyone for what happened. Three things happened that should not have happened to contribute to the accident. If any one of those three things hadn't happened, the accident might not have occurred, but it's not always possible to avoid mistakes."

One of the three things that John said contributed to the attack was the initial shot at the treed bear; the fact that it was not a fatal hit. The dog getting loose and turning the bear back toward the hunter was a second factor. The final variable was John hitting a tree and falling during a critical time as the bear charged.

None of the shots fired at the big bear after the attack proved fatal. After John was airlifted to safety, the hunt for the bruin continued. A leashed hound was used to follow the blood trail while the remainder of the group waited along a woods road that the bear was expected to cross when it was jumped. Everything went according to plan, and the bruin was finally killed when fleeing the trackers.

It was the biggest bear that had ever been taken on hunts John May participated in. The dressed weight was 488 pounds. It's live weight was estimated at 540 pounds.

Besides the fatal wound, the bear suffered three nonfatal hits. One of them was a glancing blow to the skull, which was probably the round fired from John's gun. If that bullet had hit the skull a little differently, the attack probably would not have happened.

John's hearing isn't as good as it used to be, but other than that, he's fully recovered. He's also thankful to be alive so he can continue hunting black bears with hounds.

Sharon Agren with the bear that mauled John May. The bruin was killed after the injured hunter was transported to a hospital. (Photo courtesy Doug Agren)

153

How to manage Michigan's black bears has become controversial during recent years.

Section 3

Management

Chapter 15

Michigan's
Bear Hunting History

A new movement is afoot to protect Michigan black bears from hunters, especially those who use bait and hounds, as though they need it. The truth of the matter is that these very hunters realized the value of this large omnivore as an important part of the state's renewable natural resources a long time ago and deserve credit for any level of protection black bears now have in Michigan. If it weren't for hunters and the state agency largely funded by their dollars—the Department of Natural Resources (DNR)—there probably wouldn't be as many bears in the state today for everyone to enjoy.

As a matter of fact, the present bear situation in Michigan is a good news story. The population of bruins in the state is as healthy as it has ever been, with numbers on the increase, and there's no reason for that to change with the continuation of current hunting practices. But the outlook for Michigan bears has not always been so rosy. Even though hunters and DNR wildlife biologists were among the first state residents to recognize the value of black bears and the importance of protecting their future, it took a while for that to happen.

Bears were first given statewide protection in 1925, for example, when they were designated as game animals. However, the level of protection they actually received over the years that followed see-sawed back and forth. The animals were sometimes treated more like pests than game. What follows is a look at the history of bears in terms of how, when and where they could be hunted, which will be helpful in putting the current bear hunting situation in Michigan in perspective.

Prior to 1925, black bears in Michigan could be taken at any time by any means. The animals were trapped as well as shot. Catching bears in traps became illegal during 1925 and a statewide bear season was established to coincide with gun deer season (November 15-30).

(Left) Historically, hunters and the DNR have taken responsibility for managing bears in the state. They hope to continue in that role during the future. How bear hunting has evolved reflects concern for the resource among hunters and DNR personnel.

Year round protection for bears in certain parts of the state was begun in 1935. This was not done for the benefit of bruins, however, but rather because deer hunting was closed in those areas. The closure on bear hunting in 1935 included all of the southern Lower Peninsula and a handful of counties further north—Mecosta, Isabella, Osceola, Oceana, Benzie, Grand Traverse and Leelanau.

By 1936 the area closed to bear hunting had been reduced in size and was limited to everything south of Highway M-46 (including the Thumb), with Leelanau County being the only exception. Two years later, bear hunting was also closed on the Keweenaw Peninsula at the request of local people.

The first major turnabout for the state's bears came in 1939 when the legislature removed all protection for the animals, including the use of traps to catch them, but the Natural Resources Commission (NRC) retained authority to close counties to bear hunting. The only location where Blackie was totally protected from 1939 through 1942 was the Keweenaw Peninsula.

No protection whatsoever was afforded the animals during 1939 in all of southern Michigan in addition to four counties in the northern Lower Peninsula (L.P.) and three in the Upper Peninsula (U.P.). Those counties were Missaukee, Ogemaw, Benzie, Leelanau, Menominee, Baraga and Ontonagon Counties. All other counties were open to bear hunting from November 15-30, with no dogs and traps allowed during that 16-day period. Those regulations remained in effect through 1947, with a few minor changes. Bears on the Keweenaw Peninsula became legal game during gun deer season starting in 1943, for instance, and there were a few additions or subtractions to counties where the animals were unprotected.

Two U.P. counties—Houghton and Gogebic—were opened to the first early fall bear hunt during 1948, with hunting also permitted during gun deer season. Dates for the special season were October 15 through November 5 and dogs could be used for bear hunting then. However, cubs were protected, a restriction that has remained in effect since then. Both dogs and traps could still be used to collect bears at any time in counties where they were unprotected.

It was 1952 before another early fall hunt during the same dates was held in three counties—Gogebic, Montmorency and Otsego. The trapping of bears became illegal for good that same year. As experiments to test bear hunting at various times of year, four separate bear hunts were held in the entire U.P. from spring through fall during 1953. Fall seasons proved to be the most acceptable.

Dates for the spring hunt were April 1 through May 31, with no dogs allowed and cubs protected. A summer season was held from August 15 through September 15. The early fall hunt was from October 1 through November 5 and the long standing fourth season coincided with gun deer season. Bear hunting with dogs was permitted during summer and early fall.

Early and late fall bear hunts were in effect in all L.P. counties the same year that spring and summer seasons were tried in the U.P. The next two years, uniform seasons were in effect statewide, with the exception of Chippewa County. A September 7-15 bear hunt took place in Chippewa County during 1954 and September 1-15 in 1955 in addition to the October and November hunts in effect everywhere else. A September 1-15 bear hunt was tried U.P.-wide during 1956 and '57, with October and November hunts held in the L.P. those year.

Dates for the early fall bear hunt in the U.P. eventually evolved to September 10 through October 31 and was in effect for many years. Bears also remained bonus animals on gun deer licenses during the last half of November. Early and late fall bear hunts were continued statewide through 1964.

The entire L.P. was closed to bear hunting starting in 1965 due to concern about a declining population of the animals. The timing of the closure was obviously good because it didn't take long for the animals to rebound. Bear hunting on a limited scale was resumed in designated counties of the northern L.P. in 1969 after four years of protection. Hunter numbers were controlled under a permit system, allowing the population to increase further. The permit system was eventually dropped when more permits were available than the number of applicants.

However, a more sophisticated bear hunting permit system has since been revived on a statewide basis and now plays a very important role in protecting bear populations for the future. This current permit system is covered in the next chapter.

Since 1969, the regular bear season has ranged between 7 and 10 days in the L.P. and it usually falls during late September. Hunters have the option of hunting with firearms or bow and arrow during the regular season and hounds can also be used during that period. A special archery bear season of the same length in October, during which hunting with hounds is not permitted, also evolved in the Red Oak Bear Management Unit. Dates for the 1999 general bear season in Red Oak are September 17-23 and October 8-14 for bow and arrow only.

Refer to a map in the next chapter for the boundaries of bear management units in the L.P.

Resumption of bear hunting during gun deer season in the L.P. did not take place because that's when the highest harvest occurred. That hunt was probably largely responsible for the decline of black bears there. An estimated 280 bears were shot by deer hunters in the L.P. during November of 1964, the last year of hunting before the closure. Such a high kill was especially significant in view of the fact only nine bears were taken during the early season that year and a record low harvest of 76 bruins was recorded for the entire 1963 season.

There are other problems associated with a November bear season in Michigan besides the number of animals shot, one being that most of the state's bears are already in dens then. As a result, many bruins shot during gun deer season were being shot in dens when their ability to elude hunters was greatly reduced. While in dens, the black bear's normal ability to sense danger and to attempt escape are greatly diminished, if not eliminated.

I have personally observed and photographed Michigan black bears in dens during November on two occasions. The first case involved a female and cub before November 15. The cub climbed a tree near the den at my approach, with the adult remaining inactive other than slowly lifting her head a couple of times.

The second occasion was during gun deer season and the animal never moved while being examined and photographed from only a few feet away. In both cases, adult bears could have been easily killed under circumstances that could hardly be considered sporting. Since cubs usually den with their mothers, all members of a family group have been killed when stumbled upon by deer hunters, despite the fact cubs are protected. The chances of cubs that haven't yet entered dens being mistaken for a legal animal are also highest during November because this is when they are at their largest size. Their hair is also at it longest, making the young bears look larger than they really are.

Former DNR Wildlife Biologist Al Erickson gathered some valuable information about bear denning in relationship to November hunting while conducting bear research in Michigan. He reported in his findings that 67 percent of the bears shot during the 1954 gun deer season were in dens at the time. For 1955, 47 percent of the bears deer hunters shot were in dens. The percentage of denned bears in the kill for 1956 was 31 percent and 52 percent for 1957. An average of 50 percent of the bears shot during November of those years were killed while sleeping.

There was obviously good reason to prohibit bear hunting in the L.P. during gun deer season and the problems associated with November hunting were even more severe in the U.P. However, it took persistent lobbying on the part of concerned bear hunters before U.P. bruins were finally protected during November. U.P. bears were initially protected during November of 1981 and then again in 1985, but in both cases the late hunt was reopened as a result of political pressure despite overwhelming public support for protection of the animals then.

One of the stipulations that went along with reopening bear hunting during November in the U.P. during 1986 is that no bear licenses would be sold after November 14. That rule was supposed to prevent deer hunters who didn't have a bear license from shooting a bear, expecting to buy a license afterward. However, the regulation had little impact on the November bear kill. Unlicensed hunters who shot a bear (these people are actually poachers rather than hunters) often found a friend who had a license to tag the animal. If caught with an untagged bruin, poachers usually claimed they were attacked or charged by the animal and there was seldom any attempt to prosecute.

The efforts of bear hunters who were concerned about the welfare of the animals started to produce results once again in 1989 when, for the first time, bear hunting regulations clearly stated, "It shall be unlawful to disturb, harm or molest a bear in its den at any time." Although a major step in the right direction, this regulation alone wasn't enough because bears could still be hunted during November and some of them could still be shot in dens. By 1990, U.P. bears finally got the protection they deserve during November with a prohibition on hunting them then. That same year, a statewide permit system was established to control the number of bear hunters by management unit, thereby better controlling the annual harvest of bruins in Michigan. As mentioned earlier, the permit system is discussed in the next chapter.

Hunters who use bait and hounds, in cooperation with the DNR, were responsible for bears getting the protection they deserve starting in 1990. They should receive credit for their efforts, not be unjustly criticized for allegedly taking advantage of the resource. Hunters have voluntarily restricted themselves to help protect the future of black bears for the benefit of all residents of this state.

Something else that may come as a surprise to those unfamiliar with the history of bear hunting in Michigan is that everyone who hunted bear in the state didn't have to buy a license until 1980. During most of the years prior to that, they could be taken by anyone who had a small game license or as a bonus on a gun deer license. This illustrates how bruins fit into the scheme of things prior to 1980. The laws were designed to encourage hunters to shoot bears with little or no value placed on the resource.

Bears could be shot on a small game license until 1959. An effort was started to put some value on the bear resource that year when a law was passed requiring hunters who were interested in shooting a bear to purchase a stamp at a nominal fee to affix to

(Right) The entire Lower Peninsula was closed to bear hunting in 1965 to protect the animals. A limited hunting season was resumed in 1969 after the animals had increased enough to allow it.

Bear hunters and the DNR were responsible for ending the practice of shooting bears in dens during gun deer season, which was a problem in the U.P. until 1990.

their small game license. Bear stamps were issued through 1963, but bears remained as bonus animals on gun deer licenses during this time.

The state's first bear license was issued during 1964, the year before hunting was shut down in the L.P. Some realization of the importance of bears was obviously recognized as the animals declined there. Until 1980 bear licenses were still only required of hunters trying for a bruin during early fall seasons. Gun deer hunters in the U.P. could shoot them at will. By 1980, deer hunters who were serious about shooting a bear were also required to buy a bear license, but the tradition of shooting bruins as bonus animals was tough to break. Some deer hunters who were unconcerned about the new license continued to shoot bear in November even if they didn't have a tag.

Fortunately, the elimination of November hunting in 1990 finally put a stop to most of the unregulated harvest of black bear in Michigan.

Successful bear hunters have been required to register their kills at DNR offices and designated check stations since 1974, with the exceptions of 1982 and '83 in the U.P. Statewide registration requirements were resumed during 1984 and are expected to continue into the future to gather as much biological information as possible about the state's bears. Small premolar teeth are taken from as many bagged bears as possible to determine their ages. Reproductive tracts from female bears are also collected to determine whether or not the animals have had cubs and, if so, how many.

With few, if any, exceptions, bear hunters have harvested a higher percentage of males than females annually, which is important in protecting the future of the population. Bears are polygamous, meaning males mate with more than one female, therefore, not as many males as females are necessary for reproduction. That makes males the most expendable segment of the population.

Bear hunters have been required to register bears they bag with the DNR since 1974, so the state agency can monitor the number of animals taken along with their ages and sex.

The use of bait and hounds is responsible for the higher harvests of males because both methods normally allow hunters to get a good look at animals they are about to shoot and most hunters are inclined to shoot the biggest bear they see. Since males average larger than females, bear hunters are able to selectively shoot males and they most often do.

The highest bear kill recorded for Michigan since 1974, according to DNR registration records, was during 1998. This is clear evidence that current bear management practices are working! A total of 1,512 bruins were registered by hunters during 1998, 1,322 from the U.P. and 190 from the L.P., and more record harvests can be expected in the future as the state's bear population continues to increase. The DNR's desired bear harvest for '98 was 1,594. That was the third year in a row that bear hunters did not tag as many bruins as wildlife biologists expected. I predict that it won't be long before annual bear harvests approaching 2,000 or more will be the norm rather than the exception.

The alltime highest estimated bear kill for the state as this was written during 1999 was 1,720 in 1958 when most bears were shot during gun deer season. Such a high harvest was obviously not a concern then, but that example helps illustrate how easy it can be to overharvest bears during a November hunt when a maximum number of hunters are in the field. There were only about 450,000 deer hunters in Michigan during 1958. That number has been closer to 750,000 during recent years. A November season is definitely not advisable for harvesting bears in Michigan for many reasons.

163

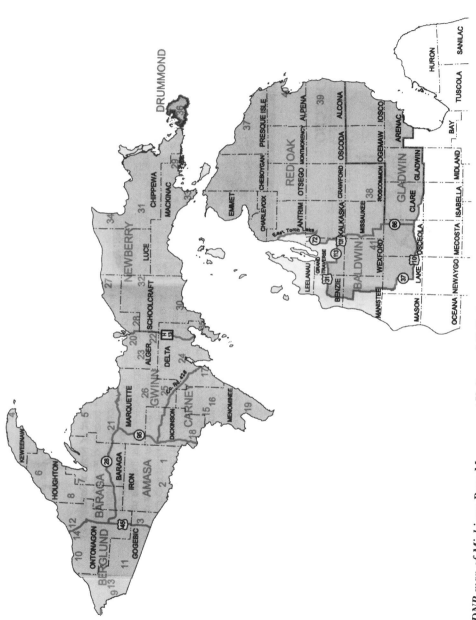

DNR map of Michigan Bear Management Units as of 1999. Most units are named after a town within the unit. Numbers denote locations of check stations.

Chapter **16**

Understanding
The Permit System

As long as bear hunting in Michigan is regulated under a permit system, as it is now, there's no need to worry about legal hunting of any type threatening the state's bear population. In fact, bruins have been thriving since the statewide permit system was started in 1990. The number of bears has increased steadily as a result of controls placed on hunting pressure, which also restricts how many animals are taken by hunters each year.

In other words, more bruins are born each year than the number killed by hunters, allowing the population to increase. The annual harvest of a portion of the bear population is important to prevent them from increasing too fast. The presence of too many bruins can increase conflicts among bears for available space and food supplies as well as conflicts between bears and people.

The establishment of bear management units in all areas of the state where healthy populations of bruins live, is an important part of the permit system. DNR wildlife biologists determined boundaries for management units based on bear numbers and differences in habitat. A total of seven units have been designated in the U.P. and three in the northern L.P.

Drummond Island is one of the U.P. bear management units and the other six are named after towns located within their boundaries. A map in this chapter shows the state's bear management units as of 1999. Refer to a current copy of a pamphlet published by the DNR about "Bear Hunting Seasons" for any changes that may occur in units during the future. These annual booklets, which also include permit quotas for each unit and other important information, are available at DNR offices and from hunting license agents.

A permit quota is established for each management unit, which is based on the number of bears that biologists would like to see harvested and the previous hunting success achieved by hunters. The number of permittees who actually hunt is also taken into account. An example will help illustrate how this works.

Consider the Gwinn Management Unit, where 952 kill tags were issued during

1994, but only 855 permittees actually hunted, and those hunters shot 174 bears. Hunting success was 20 percent during the fall of 1994 in that unit, only considering the number of people who actually hunted. However, if the total number of permits that were issued is used, success for the unit was 18 percent.

Let's assume wildlife biologists set a harvest goal of 200 bears for the Gwinn Unit in 1995. How many permits would they have to issue to achieve that goal? Based on the number of permittees who didn't hunt during 1994 and success among those who hunted, a permit quota of 1,100 would be appropriate. Eighteen percent of 1,100 would be 198.

If biologists want to adjust the harvest up or down, they can easily do so by modifying the number of permits they issue. This type of system can be adapted to any change in bear numbers or hunting success from one year to the next. If, for some reason, more bears than necessary are taken by hunters from a particular management unit one year, harvest and permit quotas can be reduced the following year. By the same token, permit quotas can be increased for units where a greater harvest is desirable.

Because there are more people who want to hunt bear in Michigan each year than the number of harvest permits available, hunters participate in a type of lottery. They apply for a permit in the management unit they want to hunt by June each year. The deadline was June 15 in 1999. A nonrefundable fee of $4 is required to apply for a kill tag. Hunters who are drawn, must purchase a harvest tag before they can hunt. The chances of being drawn varies by unit, depending upon how many applicants and permits there are.

During 1998, for instance, there were 7,305 permits available and 35,915 applicants, so only about 20 percent of them got permits. However, the chances of being drawn in some units were higher than that and lower in others. Since most bear permits are reserved for residents of the state, they have much better odds of obtaining a tag than nonresident hunters. A maximum of two percent of Michigan bear tags are allocated to nonresidents each year.

Until 1990, an unlimited number of resident bear licenses were available and they could be purchased over the counter at DNR offices and from license agents. The first quota on nonresident bear licenses was established in 1985 when a cap of 875 was put on the number that could be sold. That quota was reduced to 600 during 1989. Under the current system, fewer bear licenses go to nonresidents.

The number of bear hunters who could try to kill a bear annually has been reduced by 60 to 65 percent under the permit system, but many hunters supported the change, even though it meant more restrictions for them, because they knew it would help protect the state's bear population and bear hunting for the future. Despite what many people who don't understand hunting might think, hunters care a great deal about the animals they hunt. Hunters understand that hunting plays an important role in managing wildlife populations by eliminating part of the surplus, at the same time they acquire healthy food for their table.

Hunters don't want bear populations threatened any more than anyone else. In fact, as is pointed out elsewhere in this book, hunters have done more to protect bears in this state than anyone else, doing so in cooperation with DNR personnel. And much

(Right) The statewide bear permit system started in 1990 limits the number of people who can hunt bears annually and effectively controls the harvest. The bear population has been increasing since the permit system began.

of the money for those whose job it is to protect bears—wildlife biologists and conservation officers—comes from hunters through license fees they pay.

Revenue from the sale of bear licenses has been reduced due to the fact fewer licenses are now sold, but hunters found a way to offset that difference by winning approval for a nonrefundable application fee for bear licenses. That fee generates more revenue for the DNR because everyone who applies contributes, not just those who receive kill tags. That nonrefundable fee generated $143,660 during 1998 alone.

A total of 12,293 bear licenses were sold in Michigan during 1989, the year before the permit system started. That figure was about 250 less than the record 12,542 bear licenses sold in 1988. Hunters registered 1,237 bear in the state during 1989 compared to estimated harvests of 1,448 during 1988 and 1,374 for 1987.

It became obvious that the potential of overharvesting bears was too great with the number of bear licenses unlimited. That's why the permit system was started. Limiting hunter numbers not only gives better protection to Michigan bears, it increases the quality of the hunt for those who obtain harvest tags. With fewer hunters in the woods at one time, there is less competition and a better chance to enjoy the experience and perhaps be selective rather than shooting the first legal bruin that's seen.

By reducing the number of bear hunters in the woods at one time, there's also less chance of conflict between hunters and nonhunters. There's more room to roam for hikers, backpackers, bird watchers and other outdoor enthusiasts where the chances of encountering a bear hunter are reduced. Not that there's a problem when hunters and nonhunters cross paths in the outdoors. The quality of any outdoor experience is often enhanced, however, when communing with nature isn't interrupted by strangers.

The value of a permit system for bear hunting was tested in two locations in the U.P. before it was adopted on a statewide basis. Drummond Island had permit hunts during 1988 and '89. The Carney Unit had its first permit hunt during 1989. Another chapter in this book is devoted to Drummond Island, so specifics about the unique situation in that unit, including the state's first intensive black bear research, can be found there.

The year before the permit hunt was tried in the Carney Unit, bear season was shortened by 31 days as an alternate means of reducing the bear harvest. Instead of going from September 10 through October 31 like the rest of the U.P. mainland, bear hunting ended on September 30 in that unit during 1988. With no control on hunter numbers, hunting pressure was intensified during the shorter season and there were actually two more bears shot than had been the year before. Shortening the season alone obviously didn't reduce the bear harvest.

Hunter numbers were controlled under a permit system in the Carney Unit during 1989 and the season length was the same as the rest of the U.P. mainland. This time the desired results were achieved. Only 76 bears were accounted for by hunters in the unit during 1989 compared to 86 in 1988. The size of the unit was increased between 1988 and '89. When considering the portion of the unit open to bear hunting in 1988, only 69 bruins were actually registered during the permit hunt.

Another excellent example of the value of a permit hunt for black bear is the state's first use of such a system in the northern L.P. during 1965 when there was concern about the population in that part of the state. Bear hunting was closed for four years to allow the animals to increase and when hunting resumed, hunter numbers were controlled by permit until the population rebounded.

A bear permit system is like putting money in the bank, except you're saving bruins instead of dollars. By saving some bears now and letting them collect interest (reproduce), more will be available in the future for every resident of the state to enjoy,

168

The permit system was started to eliminate the possibility of overharvesting bears in Michigan, so all state residents, not just hunters, might have the chance to see a bruin like this one in the wild.

not just hunters. That's exactly what has happened in the neighboring states of Wisconsin and Minnesota where bear permit systems were started much earlier than in Michigan.

Minnesota started its bear permit system in 1982. Only 1,960 permits were issued then, resulting in the harvest of 429 bears. But the bear population increased steadily, along with the number of hunting permits issued. By 1989, the state's bear permit quota was 5,520 and 1,907 bruins were registered. There were 9,400 permits drawn for 1994 and 2,329 bears were taken by hunters. The permit quota for 1995 was 11,950, more licenses than were issued before the state went to a permit hunt. By 1999, the permit quota was up to a whopping 20,840.

There are now enough adult bears in Minnesota, estimated to number between 25,000 and 30,000, that it is possible to remove between 3,000 and 5,000 annually without having a negative impact on the population. In fact, it is necessary for hunters to take as many as possible to keep nuisance complaints in check. Permit quotas have steadily increased in an effort to control problems experienced from bears.

*The permit system is like putting money in the bank, except you're saving bears
instead of dollars. More females reach adulthood and produce cubs
when a permit system is in effect.*

The last year an unlimited number of bear licenses were available in Minnesota
was 1981 and 11,429 tags were sold then. Hunters registered 1,660 bruins in the state
that year. Now the bear population is healthier than it was then rather than declining
and more bruins are available for everyone and the same thing is happening in Michigan and Wisconsin.

Wisconsin went to a statewide permit system for bear hunting in 1986, four years
before Michigan. After three years under a permit system, Wisconsin's adult bear population increased from an estimated 4,500 to 6,000 adults and has increased to 14,000
since then. Like Minnesota, the permit quota and harvest have steadily increased in
Wisconsin under the permit system. Only 840 permits were issued during '86, resulting
in the harvest of 503 bears. A total of 5,860 permits were issued during '98 and 3,184
bears were bagged.

In Michigan, bear numbers were estimated to be 8,000 to 10,000 during 1994 and
were higher still by 1995. The state's population of adult bears was estimated at 12,500
by 1999. Annual figures for Michigan's permit system are listed in table form below.

A larger portion of a bear population is comprised of adults when managed under
a permit system. This means there are more females producing cubs each year, resulting in excellent annual recruitment of new animals. It also increases the chances that
large males will be seen. Such a system produces both quantity and quality because
there are a lot more young animals present than adults.

BEAR HUNTING UNDER STATEWIDE PERMIT SYSTEM

	1990	1991	1992	1993	1994
Applicants	8,820	9,195	11,695	16,367	19,628
Tags Available	4,191	5,519	5,115	5,063	5,096
# Hunted	3,733	4,936	4,442	4,591	4,613
Harvest Goal	996	1,000	963	1,066	1,279
Harvest	723	1,057	1,125	1,262	1,258
% Males	65	65	56	59	58
% Females	35	35	44	41	42
Hunter Success	20%	22%	28%	28%	27%

	1995	1996	1997	1998	
Applicants	23,645	26,728	29,118	35,915	
Tags Available	5,652	6,641	6,602	7,305	
#Hunted	5,095	5,610	5,693	5,935	
Harvest Goal	1,379	1,475	1,475	1,594	
Harvest	1,459	1,302	1,294	1,512	
% Males	55	64	55	61	
% Females	45	36	45	39	
Hunter Success	30%	23%	23%	25%	

Chapter 17

A Case For Baiting Bears

Black bear in Michigan have been hunted with the benefit of bait for at least a century and perhaps longer. According to Ben East in his book *Bears,* Ike Cooper and Cap Littlefield from Cheboygan routinely used this method to shoot bears in the late 1800s and early 1900s. However, they seldom had to put bait out themselves. The pair frequently hunted over logging camp slop holes where food and grease were discarded by cooks or the carcasses of horses that died during the winter. In those days, horses were used to haul logs instead of machinery.

Most of their bear hunting was done during the spring after the logging camps closed. Bruins were routinely drawn to food sources left near logging camps at that time of year. When Cooper and Littlefield didn't have access to a ready made bait site at a logging camp, they netted suckers from a stream to lure bears into view. Bear hunting was unregulated then, of course, with no seasons or bag limits.

By the time I started bear hunting over bait in the U.P. during 1967, seasons and bag limits had been in effect for a while. Season dates were September 1-15, October 1 through November 5 and November 15-30. The two later hunts coincided with bow and gun deer seasons to give deer hunters who saw bear a chance to shoot them. The bag limit was one adult bear per year and cubs were protected. There were no restrictions on baiting at the time because interest in any type of bear hunting was low and few hunters were using the practice.

There was no bear hunting in the L. P. at the time I got serious about the activity. The season was closed in that region during 1965 and reopened, on a limited basis, in 1969.

It took a while for interest in bear hunting with bait to catch on, but it did and the number of participants increased slowly but surely. Hunting bear with bait became popular during the 1980s. Controls on the practice soon became necessary.

(Left) Bear hunting over bait has been practiced in Michigan for at least 100 years, but has only been popular since the 1980s. The hunting method makes it possible for hunters to avoid shooting cubs, select for males and to make humane kills.

***Bear hunting with bait has been controlled since 1985. Regulations specify
when and how it can be done.***

In 1985 a bear baiting season was established, limiting the amount of time a hunter
could place bait for bear before hunting season opened, which is now 30 days. Other
restrictions were adopted at the same time, making it illegal to have any type of con-
tainer or litter at a bait site. Barrels were popular containers for bait until then. The new
rule made it necessary to place bait on the ground.

Another law limiting each hunter to a maximum of three baits was added in 1989.
Most hunters supported these rules and worked with the DNR in developing them. The
baiting rules basically reflect common sense and were already being followed by most
baiters, but they served as important guidelines for those new to the activity.

Baiters recognized the importance of eliminating possible abuses to project a
positive image. There was also genuine concern for nonhunters. Hunters didn't want

174

anyone's day afield spoiled by encountering a messy bait site. Hunters don't want the woods littered with garbage any more than anyone else. Bait consists of edible food that is completely eaten by bears and other wildlife. The types of food commonly used as bear bait will be discussed later.

Now that a brief history about bear baiting and how it's regulated are out of the way, it's time to touch on the important role baiting now plays in bear hunting and management in Michigan. Although bears are abundant in the U.P. and parts of the northern L.P., the animals are seldom seen because they are secretive, spending much of their time in thick cover where they are screened from view. Their senses are so acute that they normally detect people who might be nearby and leave the area without the individuals ever knowing they were close to a bear. If a bruin is seen by people walking in the woods, it is most likely to be a fleeting glimpse. And that's the same view most walking hunters would get of a bear, too, not giving them enough time to determine the size of the animal much less make a killing shot.

Since cubs and females in the company of cubs are protected during Michigan hunting seasons, it's important for hunters to get a good look at any bear they might see to make sure it isn't a mother or cub. That's where baiting comes in. Food is placed in a location to lure bears out of thick cover where visibility is good enough so that the hunter, who is hiding anywhere from 10 to 100 yards away, can identify his or her target. Cubs are usually in the company of their mother during fall hunting seasons, so when the family is seen in the open it gives hunters the best opportunity to identify them.

It's important to note that even though mother bears did not receive official protection during hunting season until 1995, many bait hunters voluntarily protected adult females with cubs long before that.

Once a determination is made that a bear is legal to shoot, the bait makes it possible for the hunter to make a quick, humane kill. Most hunters always strive for an instant kill and I've always understood that nonhunters support hunting methods that increase the chances for that to happen. If that is indeed the case, hunting over bait fits the bill.

Bears frequently move around while feeding and hunters wait for the animal to be in the best possible position, to insure a killing shot, before pulling the trigger or releasing an arrow. Without something to keep a bear occupied such as food, a bruin can be gone from view before a shot is possible even if a hunter has had time to determine the animal is legal to shoot.

Bait hunters prefer to shoot males over females even when the females don't have cubs because males are larger than females and they are the most expendable segment of the population. Bears are polygamous, meaning one male will breed with more than one female, so fewer males are needed to perpetuate the species. Allowing more females to survive insures plenty of bears for the future through cub production.

All bears shot by hunters must be registered and this is required so the DNR can monitor the number of bears killed, how they were taken and the ages of the animals. Teeth are taken from bagged bears to determine their ages. Data collected by the DNR confirms that bait hunters shoot more males than females every year. The percentage of males in the bear harvest over the past nine years has averaged between 56 and 65 percent and the bulk of the bruins are shot over bait.

Experienced bait hunters such as myself may pass up all but the largest of bears. Being selective in that way increases the difficulty of shooting a bear and allows more time to spend in the woods. In fact, it often results in the failure to shoot a bear at all.

Bait hunters shoot more males than females. The percentage of males in the harvest has been 55 to 65 percent since 1990. Most bear hunters voluntarily passed up females with cubs before they were protected by law.

I've drawn four bear harvest tags in Michigan since 1990 and I haven't filled any of them. During three out of those four years, the reason I didn't fill a tag is not because I didn't have the chance to, but because I chose not to. I will mention more about one of those hunts later on.

The main reason I hunt bear over bait is not to kill a bear, but to enjoy all of the experiences that go with it. I simply enjoy being in the outdoors and watching bears and other wildlife. While hunting over bait, it isn't unusual to see other wildlife such as deer, moose, coyotes, pine marten, fisher, squirrels and all types of birds. I've seen all of those species and more and I've heard wolves howl, which is always a treat. If the right bear comes along and I happen to kill it, that's a bonus.

One of the years I hunted bear over bait in Michigan was during the fall of 1994 and I failed to see any bear that year at all. Part of the reason was that I had limited time to hunt and another was that natural food was abundant in the area I was hunting. Most of the bear were eating wild cherries and beech nuts instead of bait. Those that were eating bait were doing so after dark, making it impossible to see any or shoot them.

Bears that utilize baits frequently become nocturnal in their feeding habits to avoid hunters. They also use their excellent senses of smell and hearing to detect hunters hiding at bait sites by circling them before approaching or sitting down just out of sight to listen and smell. A bear that senses the presence of a person when pulling either maneuver is seldom seen.

176

I learned a long time ago that bears prefer natural foods such as blueberries, strawberries, blackberries, raspberries, wild cherries, apples, hazel nuts, acorns, beech nuts and insects over what's available at baits. This has been verified by research conducted by Dr. Lynn Rogers from Ely, Minnesota. Bears seldom rely on bait as their main source of nourishment either. Food placed in the woods by hunters normally supplements their normal diet.

Bear hunting over bait is often criticized as unethical and unsporting due to a perception that hunters are taking unfair advantage of bruins and that simply is not true. I've already mentioned how bears routinely avoid hunters using bait by relying on their well developed senses and by feeding after dark when it's illegal to hunt. Success rates for Michigan bear hunters verifies further how good the animals are at avoiding hunters.

During the fall of 1998, for example, average hunting success in the U.P. was 25 percent. In the L.P., average success was closer to 16 percent. Keep in mind that bear season lasts for two weeks in the L.P., one week of which is devoted to bowhunting only, and more than 30 days in the U.P. If hunting over bait were unethical or unsporting, success would be closer to 100 percent. Bears are clearly able to take care of themselves when being hunted over bait.

Black bear are smart animals and they've been subjected to significant hunting pressure with this method for more than 20 years. Most bruins who feed at baits have learned how to stay alive. They've adapted by passing the ability to evade hunters on from one generation to the next. Those that don't learn the lessons don't live long and their genes aren't passed on—natural selection at its finest.

During years when natural foods are scarce, bears spend more time than normal eating bait, but there are benefits from this for bears, hunters and nonhunters. There are typically more conflicts between bears and people when food failures occur. Under these circumstances, some cubs may be lost to starvation and adult females that are pregnant may not produce cubs the following year, if they don't get enough nourishment. Research has shown that fertilized eggs don't develop if females don't reach a certain weight by the time they enter dens.

Baits help remedy some of these problems. The supplemental food can prevent some cubs from starving and allow some females to gain enough weight to produce cubs. More importantly, however, the presence of bait from hunters can reduce conflicts with bears. It is far better that hungry bears be feeding on a bait in the woods where contact with people is minimized rather than rummaging for food from garbage cans at rural residences, campgrounds and towns in bear country. Baiting can also reduce damage to farmers' crops such as corn and oats that bears tend to favor.

Bears are adapted for utilizing seasonal food sources and that's what baits are. They are only available during the fall like acorns, beech nuts, hazel nuts, wild cherries and apples just like the natural foods bruins depend on. Bears move from one food supply to another, eating what's available and then searching for another source.

Critics of baiting contend that the practice creates unnatural concentrations of bears, which simply isn't true. Bears will become just as concentrated in a location with an abundance of natural foods such as acorns and beech nuts as they will at baits. Although normally solitary, with the exception of females with cubs, bears do adapt to being around one another when utilizing a common food source by establishing a pecking order. Subordinant animals normally feed at times when they can avoid contact with dominant bears, which are usually large males and sows with cubs.

If you've heard that most baiters only shoot bears for their hides, don't believe it.

177

Bear meat is excellent eating and I take advantage of every opportunity possible to eat the meat from bears I kill. Most hunters I know do the same thing.

Another common criticism of baiting that's false is that baiting trains bears to eat human food, causing them to become nuisance animals. There's no documentation that this is true and clear evidence exists that it's false. Bear Researcher Terry DeBruyn studied two adult female bears in Alger County for seven years that he was able to walk with, which is mentioned elsewhere in this book. DeBruyn provided supplemental food to these bears and neither animal became a nuisance. They also avoided other people. They fed on baits they encountered in the woods, but did not go to homes or camps in the area looking for food.

Dr. Lynn Rogers has done similar research in Minnesota with a number of adult female bears and his findings were the same. Bears that fed on baits would feed at other baits, but not become nuisances or a threat to people.

As far as evidence that bear baiting does not cause human/bear conflicts, one only has to consider the other radio collared animals scattered throughout Michigan. Hundreds of bruins have been collared in the state for research purposes since the mid-1980s. In almost all cases, these bears were captured in baited live traps before being fitted with collars.

If baiting caused human/bear conflicts, all of those animals should have gotten in trouble. The fact is that few of them have become nuisance animals causing human/bear conflicts. Outfitter Marty Quinn from Sudbury, Ontario cooperated in a study that confirmed bears that visit bait sites don't normally become nuisance animals. A total of 16 bears were live trapped and fitted with radio collars at his bait sites so they could be monitored. None of those animals became nuisances.

And there's more solid information along the same lines from other states. In Tennessee's Smoky Mountains National Park, for example, Dr. Mike Pelton with the University of Tennessee had been conducting longterm bear research in the park. Over those years, his students used bait to live trap and radio collar approximately 1,000 black bears in the park's back country.

Over the same period of years, park personnel live trapped 400 to 500 problem bears in areas frequented by people—roads, campgrounds and picnic areas. Dr. Pelton said only 23 (2.3 percent) of the collared bears that were exposed to bait were in the sample of problem bears.

Some people claim that Michigan bears are conditioned to eating human food rather than natural foods as a result of baiting, which is hardly the case. Since baiting bears is limited to the months of August through October, the animals would starve to death if they did not utilize natural food. Even during the months that bear baiting is legal, less than 10,000 bear permits are issued and the bait put out by those permittees is hardly enough to feed all of the state's bears. The bottom line is that Michigan bears prefer natural food to bait, when it's available.

And I've got still another example to prove my point. For a number of years I've fed a group of adult males for photographic purposes in an area that's heavily hunted. I've photographed many of the same animals for as long as eight to 10 years. If their utilization of bait made them susceptible to hunters using bait or turned them into nuisance animals, they certainly would not have survived as long as they have.

(Left) Black bears often visit baits when hunters are absent, as this vacant tree stand illustrates. Average hunting success with bait during 1998 was only 24 percent.

An example confirming bears that learn to obtain food from campers and at campgrounds are most likely to become nuisances rather than those that feed at hunters' baits developed during 1994. A bear that became a major problem in Porcupine Mountains Wilderness State Park that year when it developed a habit of stealing backpacks from visitors, was live trapped and relocated by DNR Wildlife Biologist Doug Wagner from Crystal Falls. Wagner put blue tags in the bruin's ears before it was released, so it could be identified, and let it go in the southern U.P.

The same animal began ravaging bee hives near Cornell in southern Marquette County and was trapped again. The bruin was released in the northern portion of the central U.P. this time. True to form, that bear started causing problems near its new home during 1995 and probably continued doing so until killed. Campers can take credit for that nuisance animal, not hunters. Although bears that learn to associate people with food in campgrounds and parks are most likely to become nuisances, there are probably some animals that are simply predisposed to becoming problems.

Some critics also claim that it doesn't take any skill to bait bears for hunting. If that were true, as mentioned earlier, hunting success would be close to 100 percent rather than the level it actually is. Hunters who look for bear sign and natural feeding areas already being used by bears, then place baits in those areas, have the best chance of seeing bruins. Baits placed randomly may or may not attract bears. Even if bears visit a site, it doesn't mean a hunter will see them.

The act of baiting itself can be a lot of work. Food has to be collected and put at an appropriate site, then replenished as it's eaten and a bear can eat a lot of food. A hunter then has to select a spot to hide where their chances of being detected by an incoming bear are the lowest. While waiting for a bear to arrive, which can take hours, if not days, and it's not unusual for a bruin to never appear, it's important to keep movement and noise to a minimum. Remaining still and quiet becomes critical once a bear arrives, until a shot is offered, to avoid spooking the animal.

As an example of what hunting bears over bait in Michigan is really like, consider the experience of a friend of mine and his son over a two year period. My friend's son drew a bear permit the first year and put bait in a good location. Based on sign at the bait site, a number of bears were visiting the location and they ate all of the food put out for them.

When it came time to hunt, the boy and his father didn't see a single bear. They heard some in the brush around them, but not a single bruin appeared during legal shooting hours.

The following year, my friend also drew a bear permit and he put bait in the same spot. Like the year before, the location was visited regularly by a number of bears, eating all of the food placed there. Once hunting season opened, my friend's efforts to see a bear that he might shoot failed again. And this is not an isolated instance.

All types of foods that are no longer suitable for human consumption make good bear bait. These include table scraps, household leftovers, pastries, bread, fruits and vegetables. Apples and corn are popular choices among fruits and vegetables, but other kinds will also be eaten. Meat scraps and fat from butcher shops and the carcasses of filleted fish work, too. Much of the food I use for bait would have otherwise ended up in a landfill somewhere. In this era of recycling with limited landfill space, I view baiting as a much better use of left over food than having it take up space and rot in a landfill.

Incidentally, you don't have to be a hunter to bait bears. The method is also the best way for nonhunters to view bruins. I use the technique during the summer when

Monitoring of radio collared black bears that were trapped at bait sites confirms that baiting for hunting purposes does not create nuisance animals.

photographing bears. However, it is illegal to hunt at a location where bait has been placed for bears more than 30 days before hunting season begins. So, when I'm hunting, I go to a different area, usually a different management unit, to place bait than where I was baiting for photography.

If bait hunting for bear were banned in Michigan, I seriously doubt enough bruins could be taken by hunters annually using alternate hunting techniques, to properly manage the animals. The methods of bear hunting in Pennsylvania have been suggested by some as the way to go. That issue is dealt with in a following chapter.

A technique popular in the mountain states of Montana and Colorado called spotting and stalking where bears can be located from long distances with binoculars and spotting scopes is simply not well suited for Michigan habitat. There are major differences between the terrain here and in those states that makes the technique effective there, but difficult to impossible here.

Ambushing bears at locations with natural food supplies will work here and has been used on a limited scale all along. Some bruins have been shot every year as they feed on fruits, nuts and corn. However, even if bear licenses are increased dramatically, which they would have to be, I think it would be difficult for hunters to shoot enough bears.

And what about the years when there are food failures? Rural residents will end up shooting bears in their yards. Police officers and conservation officers will kill others as they invade villages and towns before hunting season begins.

If shooting bears as they eat fruits and nuts is acceptable, as I've heard some critics of baiting claim, why is it unacceptable to shoot the animals as they feed on bait? The type of food may make a difference to some people, but there's no difference to the bear and the method is basically the same.

The fact that feeding bears by campers and hikers in most state and national parks is discouraged, but the practice is legal for hunters interested in shooting bruins, creates confusion for some people and that's understandable. It may seem as though hunters are given a privilege other outdoor enthusiasts don't have. However, there is a major difference between the two situations. The key is not to feed bears where you don't want them to return.

Campers and hikers are discouraged from feeding bears because it is undesirable to have the animals frequenting campgrounds, picnic areas and hiking trails where they come to expect food directly from people. Once a bear obtains food in a campground, for example, it will often return looking for more. Bear baits for hunting, on the other hand, are placed in the woods away from locations frequented by people and there is no direct link between the food and people. Bears that return to bait sites in the woods do not create a problem, whereas those that hang around campgrounds do.

I will end this chapter with an account from one of my hunts with bait in Michigan that took place during 1990. There is more to trophy hunting than killing an exceptional bear. The decision not to kill an animal that could have been legally taken can also become a trophy if that special moment can be preserved in some way. My trophy from a bear hunt in the U.P. one fall is a picture of one of those moments.

I drew a harvest tag for Michigan's first statewide permit hunt, enabling me to play an active role in the season. My permit was valid from September 15 through October 21. Although those were the dates hunting with dogs was legal, it was also the period most permits were available and a high percentage of the applicants who applied for those dates were successful in the drawing.

I chose to hunt over bait with bow and arrow and got my trophy October 9. I knew a number of bears were visiting the site, but they were primarily feeding at night. The sign indicated a large male was in the area, but there was also evidence of the presence of at least one female with cubs.

I spent time in a portable tree stand about 10 yards from the bait on six different days without seeing a single bear, although I saw other wildlife such as deer, pine martens and squirrels. It was the evening of my seventh day in that stand that I finally saw a bear. There were actually four animals that arrived at the same time, consisting of an adult female with three cubs.

The cubs appeared first and the adult brought up the rear. The timing of their arrival was bad for me. A pine marten had been running around the base of my tree

(Right) You don't have to be a hunter to bait bears. It's a great way to view and photograph bruins, too, as long as it's done a safe distance from homes and campgrounds.

The reason feeding bears at parks and campgrounds is discouraged is the animals aren't wanted at these locations and bruins invariably return to areas where they've obtained food. They also learn to associate people with food at these sites, which does not happen at baits established for hunting in the bears' natural habitat.

moments before I became aware of the bears and I had just exposed the last frame on the roll of film in my camera as I heard the bears approach.

There I stood with an empty camera as the bear family walked into view. Even though the adult female was legal to kill under my permit, I had no interest in doing so (females with cubs were protected by law in 1995). I chose not to shoot the bruin due to more concern for the resource than filling a tag.

The chances of those cubs surviving would be best as long as they stayed with their mother, although they were old enough and big enough to take care of themselves at that point in their lives. It takes two or three years for a female bear to reach maturity and then she produces cubs every other year. That makes adult females an important segment of the population.

Although I had no interest in killing any of those bears, I did want to try to shoot

This photograph of a female and three cubs was my "trophy" one year that I hunted with bait.

them with my camera, capturing the family with one shot. Concerned that any noise on my part might scare the bears off, I cautiously reloaded my camera with another roll of film and was pleased to accomplish the feat without being detected. The animals were feeding with their heads down when I focused on them and pressed the shutter.

My camera is equipped with a power winder, so film advances automatically. I kept the shutter release down, anticipating that the bears would look up at me after they heard the noise of the shutter opening and closing, and that's exactly what happened. The picture I consider a trophy shows the mother and all three cubs staring at me.

One of the youngsters and its mother were facing me and they simply had to look up. The other two cubs had their backs to me and they had to look back over their shoulders. The expressions of surprise on their faces tells the story.

Those were the only bears I saw on that bait, but I saw three other bruins at another site that I watched the first week of my hunt. At least two of those animals were males, but I decided not to shoot them because they were of average size. The season ended with an unfilled tag in my pocket, but I still got a trophy to hang on my wall!

Bear hunting with hounds plays an important role in managing Michigan bears and has been practiced for more than 50 years.

Chapter 18

Bears and Hounds

Bear hunting with hounds has been practiced in Michigan for more than 50 years. The state's first official hound hunt for black bears was organized in 1946. Veteran Michigan Outdoor Writer Ben East was instrumental in starting the ball rolling. He participated in his first hound hunt in Tennessee during 1945. Although he didn't see or shoot a bear on that hunt, he experienced the thrill and excitement of the chase, one of the main attractions of this form of hunting, and enjoyed the music of baying hounds hot on the trail of a bruin.

Based on his experience in Tennessee, East was convinced the method would work in Michigan and was worth a try. He conveyed his thoughts to leadership of the Michigan United Conservation Clubs (MUCC), who agreed to sponsor such a hunt during October of 1946 and the cooperation of the Department of Conservation (now the Department of Natural Resources) was also obtained. The Dead Stream Swamp in Missaukee County was selected as the site for the hunt and regulations were adopted opening that area to hunting bear with dogs.

At the time, bears were primarily a bonus animal taken during gun deer season, but some were also shot when encountered by small game hunters. Most bear kills were accidental because few people actually hunted them, but a few bruins were taken by individual hunters using bait. A hunt with hounds was a first step toward acceptance of a specific method that could provide groups of hunters an opportunity to see and shoot a bear.

The Department of Conservation limited the number of participants in the state's first bear hunt with hounds to 300, all of whom were issued permits on a first come, first served basis. Interest in the hunt was high. More than 1,000 hunters applied for the limited permits. Hack Smithdeal from Johnson City, Tennessee brought his pack of bear dogs to Michigan for the hunt along with a group of dog handlers and hunting partners.

Ben East describes how that hunt went in his book *BEARS*, which was published by the Outdoor Life Book Club in 1977: "Only two bears were killed in the four-day

Carl Johnson from Cadillac is considered the father of hound hunting in Michigan, having participated in the state's first dog hunt in 1946. He formed the Michigan Bear Hunters Association that same year. (DNR Photo by Dave Kenyon)

hunt, but there were a number of exciting chases. The dog handlers reported running eight bears in one day. Only the dense cover of an almost roadless swamp, coupled with inexperience on the part of the hunters, prevented a higher kill. At the end it was clear that this method of hunting was destined to take deep root among Michigan sportsman."

Carl Johnson from Cadillac was one of the participants on that hunt. He was already involved in hunting other animals such as raccoons and bobcats with hounds and the experience in the Dead Stream Swamp during 1946 hooked him on hounding bears. He bought one of Smithdeal's dogs and began building a pack of his own. The same year as the first official bear hunt with hounds, Johnson formed the Michigan Bear Hunters Association, which is still active today. And Johnson remains one of the staunchest supporters of hunting bears with dogs.

There were more bears in Michigan when bear hunting with hounds got its start than there are today, especially in the L.P., but there were also fewer people and roads and less development. Due to the abundance of bruins, there were still plenty of conflicts between bears and people. Most residents who had bear problems solved them themselves by killing the animals. Afterall, bears had little protection back then. However, there were some nuisance bears that weren't so easy to eliminate because they avoided people.

Johnson built support for hounding bears by offering to go anywhere in the state to solve bear problems with his dogs and he was successful in doing so in both the U.P. and northern L.P. on a number of occasions. And bear dogs played important roles in at least two cases where people were attacked by bears. When 3-year-old Carol Ann

188

Pomranky was killed and partially eaten by a bear near Brimley on July 7, 1948, for example, a hound owned by Alex Van Luven led him to the child's body. The bruin was killed as it returned to the scene.

Without the use of a dog in that case, it would have been more difficult to recover the child's body and to eliminate the offending bear. The process certainly would have taken longer, perhaps long enough for the bear to consume most of the child's remains, making an already tragic event even more of a tragedy. Bear dogs can play just as effective a role in solving nuisance problems and aiding in the event of an attack today as they did back then. Despite the advent of live traps and dart guns now available for use on bear, hounds trained to trail bears remain the quickest and most effective means of targeting a specific bruin. Some of the smartest bears are difficult to impossible to catch in traps.

Fortunately, bear attacks on people are rare in Michigan, but there's no shortage of nuisance complaints from the animals' activities in the northern part of the state and dog owners have been as willing to help out with problem bears now as they were back then. Dog owner Don Overmeyer from Skandia, for instance, helped out in a situation where a home owner was plagued by unwanted visits from bears one summer. A local conservation officer said bears bothered the rural residents during most of June. He said the animals were originally attracted to the home by garbage that was left outside. When the family's household garbage was moved to the enclosed cap of a pickup truck, the cap was damaged by bruins as they tried to get at it.

The officer said problems started with a single bear, but an adult female with four cubs later started visiting the home. He added that the same bear family had caused problems elsewhere, including disruption of a graduation party when the female helped herself to food placed on a table.

The CO put a live trap at the residence where most of the problems occurred, but failed to catch anything. The trap was in place for five days, during which time problems ceased. The trap was then removed and visits from bears resumed.

The officer then issued a permit to Overmeyer to chase problem bears with his hounds. A special permit was necessary since field training of dogs isn't normally allowed until July 15 each year. The houndman had offered his services in helping to deal with problem bears.

Overmeyer said he responded to a complaint on the morning of June 22 and he found the tracks of three different bears. His hounds chased the largest animal to a nearby lake. If and when any bears returned to the home, Overmeyer said he would respond with his dogs, chasing bruins out of the area until they no longer returned.

He added that he and some friends helped solve problems with nuisance bears in the vicinity of Anderson and Charley Lakes in Marquette County a couple of years earlier. After hounding bears on four or five occasions, the animals stayed away.

Another example of the benefits of using hounds to deal with problem bears was proven in Mt. Pleasant on July 1 and 2 of 1996, according to local Conservation Officer Bruce Borkovich. A young male bear estimated to weigh 125 to 130 pounds showed up in two subdivisions within the city on those days. The bruin was eventually treed by dogs on the 2nd and darted, so it could be captured and relocated further north.

"The dog handlers did a wonderful job," Borkovich said. "They were knowledgeable about dealing with bears and took every effort to make sure the animal was not hurt after it was drugged. Some of the guys took time off of work to help out.

"If it weren't for their efforts, that bear might have been killed. Police officers tend to shoot bears that end up in cities and you can't blame them because it's their job to

Hounds can help deal with nuisance bears. One bruin that wandered into Mt. Pleasant was treed with the aid of hounds so it could be captured and relocated to a better area. Otherwise the animal might have been killed.

protect the people. You never know what's going to happen when a bear starts running around where there's a lot of people. The dogs and handlers made it possible for us to catch the animal to prevent it from being killed. Their efforts also eliminated the concern about a bear/human encounter in the city."

Borkovich said the city's central dispatch started getting bombarded with calls about a bear in the Bamber Woods Subdivision, which is in the northwest section of the city, about 9:00 a.m. on July 1. He responded along with other local law enforcement officers. After making contact with the animal, the CO said it appeared comfortable running in and out of yards.

The officer started chasing the bear on foot. His intent was to either chase it out of town or up a tree where it could be darted and moved out. At one point, a woman who was apparently curious about his presence, came out of a house to find out what was going on. Then the bear turned and came running back toward Bruce.

Both people took evasive action. The woman was obviously shocked to see a bear in her yard. Soon afterward, the bruin crossed Pickard Street, the main east/west route through the city, and went into a woodlot. That's when Borkovich contacted hunters who had bear dogs. He figured the hounds would either chase the animal out of town or tree it so it could be captured.

Instead of climbing a tree, the bear went into a nearby creek bottom after the dogs were put on its trail. The canines lost its scent in the water. The fact that it was a hot, humid day didn't help.

Fresh dogs were eventually put on the bear's trail and they followed its scent until

7:00 p.m. that evening without treeing it. When the hounds were pulled off, Borkovich figured the bruin was headed back to where it came from and the problem was solved. However, the bear showed up in the Scully Subdivision the next afternoon about a mile from where the dogs left its trail the day before.

John May of Lakeview and his hounds were then brought in and those dogs managed to finally put the bear in a tree. It was difficult to keep the bruin in the tree though. The animal kept trying to come down despite the fact people and dogs were at the base of the tree. Fortunately, the bear stayed in the tree long enough for Bruce to borrow a tranquilizer gun from local animal control officers.

"The bear came out of the tree like a bullet, after it was darted," Borkovich said. "The dogs took off after the bear again while I went to get another dart in case I needed it."

The bruin covered 200 to 300 yards before the drug took effect and it laid over a log. However, it was not totally out, so the dog handlers used leashes to tie it up and transport it to the CO's vehicle where he had a cage waiting. The bruin was checked by a veterinarian that evening and found to be in excellent condition.

The bear was radio collared and fitted with ear tags and released in the Pigeon River State Forest. Young males like that one typically disperse from their mother's home range during the summer to establish territories of their own and it's not unusual for them to end up in cities as they travel cross country. These bears often encounter larger males that chase them during their travels. Dispersing males are often more afraid of other bears than people.

This incident confirms that bears are doing well in Michigan and extending their range. Borkovich said more and more complaints about bear sightings have been received in his area during recent years. In most cases, bears are only seen by a few people. It was different in this case. This was the first bear that could be classified as a nuisance animal in the Mt. Pleasant area, according to Borkovich, but it may not be the last.

A second smaller bear estimated to weigh about 50 pounds was spotted in Mt. Pleasant by a police officer on his way to work on the morning of July 1. Bears have also been sighted south of Mt. Pleasant near St. Louis, according to DNR Bear Researcher Dr. Larry Visser out of Houghton Lake. He said two bear sightings came in from the north side of Midland, too. Visser said the furthest south a bear has been seen is Pontiac.

He added that a pair of people also encountered a bear on a hiking/biking trail near Cadillac one year. A mountain bike rider saw the bear one day. A woman jogger was reportedly chased by a bear on the same trail another day.

Visser darted a 200 pound male in the city limits of Grayling on June 24th that same year. He said that animal showed up on the south edge of town near a canoe livery on the AuSable River. From there, Visser ended up chasing the bruin through people's yards for a while before finally getting a dart in it.

"The bear was basically surrounded," Visser commented. "Everywhere it went it kept running into people."

He estimated that bear's age at three. It was radio collared and ear tagged like the bruin that was in Mt. Pleasant, before being relocated. It was released in Cheboygan County.

The damage a nuisance bear in Dickinson County was causing to outbuildings near Sawyer Lake was brought to an end one fall with the help of hounds when it broke into a shed where food was being stored during hunting season. After eating all of the food in the shed, the bear ripped open a bag of powdered cement. That bruin left a trail of powder filled prints from the shed into a nearby swamp.

Bear guide L. L. Edwards from Republic was called and he put his hounds on the bear's trail. The chase covered several miles before the 225 pound male finally climbed a tree. Earlier attempts to eliminate that marauding bruin when it had broken into other buildings containing food had failed.

These are only a small sample of the cases in which hounds have helped solve bear problems. The list will continue to grow as long as hounding bears remains legal in Michigan. And hounds sometimes serve another valuable function by helping to recover bears shot by hunters using other methods. It isn't unusual for bruins that are fatally wounded to run as much as 100 yards or more before dying. If the cover is thick and there's little or no blood trail, the animals can be hard to find by sight.

But there's no escaping the nose of a good hound. A leashed dog will follow and find any bear that's down. I've used a pair of dogs over the years, one black and tan and the other a Plott, that have made it possible to recover a number of bears that would have been impossible to find any other way. No dead bears will go unrecovered as long as hounds are legal to use in Michigan for trailing wounded bruins. In fact, as long as bear hunting of any type is legal in this state, it doesn't make sense to outlaw the use of a means that guarantees recovery of bears that are shot. Hunters certainly don't want to risk losing a bear they shoot and I don't think most nonhunters would want to make it more difficult for hunters to find animals they shoot either.

Although bear hunting with hounds remains essentially the same as when the practice started in 1946, there are a few regulations and changes that have taken place over the years to address concerns among the public associated with the activity. In 1976 a law was enacted with the support of the Michigan Bear Hunters Association, limiting the number of dogs that could be used to chase a bear. Pack size was restricted to six hounds at that time and it also became illegal to relay packs, meaning it isn't permitted to pick up the six dogs that were started on a bear's trail after they tire and replace them with fresh hounds.

A requirement that all bear dogs must be registered with the DNR was started at the same time due to concerns about nonresidents bringing large numbers of dogs with them to Michigan for bear hunting. Since then, the number of nonresident bear hunters has been reduced dramatically. Only two percent of the available bear permits now go to nonresidents. Registering hounds is still required for nonresidents, but they are prohibited from chasing bear with their dogs until hunting season opens.

The training season for bear dogs, as mentioned earlier, begins on July 15 each year and continues through September 9. It used to be legal to chase bears with dogs at night, but this is no longer permitted during either training or hunting seasons. Bear hunting with hounds begins in the U.P. on September 15 now instead of the 10th. All members of a dog hunting party are required to have a pursuit permit in their possession, if they don't have a kill tag. Pursuit permits do not allow hunters to carry a gun or bow while participating in a hunt with hounds. Only participants who have harvest tags can legally shoot a bear.

Since bear dogs sometimes chase bruins onto private property, a regulation was adopted giving dog handlers the opportunity to go on private land to retrieve hounds, as long as they do not have a gun or bow in their possession. Most dog hunters start chases in areas where the chances of their dogs ending up on private ground are minimal. When hounds are known to be headed toward private property, hunters often try to catch the dogs before they cross property lines. With the advent of retrieval collars commonly used during recent years, houndmen now have a better opportunity than ever before to find their dogs when they stray from public property. The collars also enable hunters to locate their hounds when they become lost, injured or killed.

Good bear dogs can be worth thousands of dollars. The use of retrieval collars enables hunters to protect their investment in the animals. From a humane point of view, retrieval collars are the best thing that has come along for the care and treatment of hounds. If a dog is injured during a chase, it can be located as quickly as possible and cared for.

Before retrieval collars came along, dog hunters were frequently criticized because days sometimes went by before lost hounds were recovered. The problem was difficult to avoid because dogs often travel long distances and contact with them was sometimes lost. Some hounds dropped out of the chase sooner than others, too, putting them in different locations than the rest of the pack. Lots of time, effort and gasoline was expended trying to find lost dogs.

Now that retrieval collars have eliminated that problem, critics have claimed that the collars give hunters an unfair advantage over bears. Careful study of the issue has shown that the concern is unwarranted. The experience and effectiveness of hounds and hunters as a team most often determines the success of a hunt with dogs, not the collars the animals are wearing. Hunters and hounds work together to occasionally accomplish something that neither could alone.

The trespass issue remains a topic of utmost concern among dog hunters. Most hound owners do the best they can to avoid problems with dogs chasing bears on private property. According to reports received from the DNR, the number of incidents involving trespassing bear dogs have been dramatically reduced during recent years. Dog owners who are members of organized groups would like to work with land owners as much as possible to resolve conflicts. They encourage people with trespass problems to contact their local authorities.

If unable to get satisfaction and the identity of the trespasser is known, please make a report to a representative of the Michigan Bear Hunters Association or the U.P. Bear Houndsmen. Bill Walker is a contact for the Michigan Bear Hunters Association. His address and phone number are 442 Fox River Dr., Bloomfield Hills, MI 48304 (810-334-1101). Joe Hudson or Nancy Reynolds are contacts for the Bear Houndsmen and their address and phone number are N 13421 J1 Rd., Carney, MI 49812 (906-639-2618).

The use of four wheel drive vehicles and CB radios among hound hunters is often unjustly criticized. These tools play an important role in allowing all family members to participate. Radios and 4x4s permit both young and old members of the party who can't go far in the woods on their own, to take part in the hunt. Even among healthy individuals, vehicles are necessary to cover the mileage many chases involve.

Without vehicles, many a chase would end almost as soon as a bear were jumped. A traveling bruin can take baying hounds out of hearing in minutes. Most people on foot are not capable of the speed, stamina and knowledge of the terrain to keep up with, much less intercept, bear and dogs.

Two way radios save on consumption of gas. Most of the time, at least one member of the group has a fix on the current status of the hunt. If a member of the party loses track of the chase or is curious about what's going on, it is possible for him or her to make a call on the radio rather than wandering from one road to another to find somebody who knows what's going on. Neither radios or vehicles give hunters an unfair advantage over bears as success rates listed toward the end of this chapter confirm.

Opponents who claim that hounding bears is stressful on the animals, especially females, obviously are not aware of what takes place during the breeding season. I don't know of any bear dogs that are as persistent in their pursuit of a female bear as a male intent on breeding her. Males probably put more stress on females during the breeding season than the animals endure when pursued by hounds. Male bears begin pursuing females days before they are ready to mate and follow them relentlessly until breeding is complete. Females frequently climb trees to get away from pursuing males and when on the ground have to fight off their advances until the time is right.

Females with cubs are often treed by males as the males try to kill the cubs. Females are sometimes killed or injured by males in an effort to protect their cubs. Shooting bears in front of hounds is certainly more humane than the threats bruins face in the wild during most of the year.

When bears climb trees ahead of hounds, they most often do so to escape danger out of choice, not because they are forced to. One of the first things a bear cub learns to do when it leaves the den is to climb trees for safety. Coyotes, wolves, bobcats and other bears prey on cubs. Cubs can normally avoid predators by climbing trees and this is an instinct that remains with them throughout their lives.

Bear dogs are no different than a pack of wolves to bears. When dogs get close to a bear they are following, some bruins choose to climb a tree to escape them. They aren't forced to. The older bears get, the less inclined they are to climb trees because they become better at dealing with danger on the ground as they age. The reason more bears are not treed by dogs is that, in many cases, the hounds don't get close enough to them.

Hounds follow a bear's scent during a hunt. Bears seldom travel in a straight line for very far and they often enter water, all of which makes the dogs' job harder. Sometimes the dogs lose a bear's trail before getting anywhere near the animal. Plenty of other times, the bears simply manage to stay ahead of the dogs. Far more hunts end when the hounds tire and quit than a bear gets worn out.

What some of the opponents of bear hunting with hounds fail to realize is there is far more to the activity than killing bears. In fact, killing bears plays a minor role. Hounding bears is a way of life for hundreds of families across the state. Caring for and training hounds is a year-round necessity that many men, women and children participate in. Most of the attention is focused on fall months because that's the season dogs and hunters look forward to. That's when their efforts during the rest of the year are rewarded with the chance to spend time in the field. Hounds look forward to the chase as much as their owners.

And the chase with its accompanying hound music is of utmost importance to these hunters. So is reading bear sign. Before a chase can begin, it's normally necessary to find fresh bear tracks to put the dogs on, preferably prints made by a big male. Since males are larger than females and have bigger feet, hound hunters look for the largest tracks they can find.

Since females in the company of cubs are protected, houndmen avoid putting dogs on their tracks. If a female with cubs or a cub happen to be treed by dogs accidentally, the hunters leash their hounds and lead them out of the woods, leaving the protected bears unharmed. How can a female with cubs or a cub be treed by dogs accidentally?

(Right) Male bears frequently tree females and their young and sometimes kill or injure them. Bears that are pursued by dogs climb trees instinctively to seek safety, not because they are stressed or forced to.

In cases where hounds are put on the scent of a big male that's several hours old, for example, the dogs may cross the much fresher scent of a different bear such as a female with cubs, while following the older scent. In most cases, the dogs will switch to the stronger scent.

On rare occasions, a live bear is seen to put the dogs on while in the process of searching for tracks. When this happens, houndmen pass up any opportunity to shoot the bruin when it's seen, preferring to let their hounds chase it. I was on a hunt with hounds a number of years ago near Iron River when such a situation developed.

Our party went all morning and part of the afternoon without locating a track fresh enough to run. Finally, two members of the group spotted a bruin in a two-rut woods road. They watched it walk down the road and eventually cross into heavy cover. There was time to shoot if they wanted to, but they didn't. This illustrates how unimportant the kill can be to dog hunters.

The hounds chased that bear until dark, but no one got another glimpse of it. It was an exciting chase, nonetheless. Several members of the party got close to the bear a couple of times as the animal briefly stood its ground to face the dogs. The sound of the approaching hunters probably caused it to move on in each case. The results of that hunt represents an average day afield with hounds more than those on which a bruin is shot from a tree. On the occasions when that does happen, hunters and hounds most often have earned the success.

More often than not, a bear gets away after the chase begins. It may outrun the dogs or pull a trick to throw the hounds off the trail such as walking or swimming in water or starting to climb a tree then changing its mind. Some bears successfully fight the dogs off. On average, only 10 to 20 percent of chases end up in a bear being bayed on the ground, climbing a tree or being intercepted in front of the hounds.

All bears that are treed are not killed. Cubs and their mothers are protected, of course, and dog hunters often pass up small bears two or three years old that are legal to shoot, too. Hound hunters can often tell the difference between males and females and most frequently shoot males. The chances for humane kills are excellent on bears in trees or bayed on the ground. Virtually all of the bruins shot in front of hounds are recovered.

One of the major benefits of bear hunting with dogs is it is the only form of catch and release hunting available. It is possible to catch a bear by having it climb a tree ahead of hounds, but then let it go if it is a protected animal or one the hunters choose not to shoot.

Only 13 percent of the bear hunters who hunted during 1994 used hounds. They accounted for 20 percent of the bear harvest. By 1998, the percentage of dog hunters was 14 percent and they claimed 24 percent of the harvest.

Success rates for hunters using hounds has gone up considerably under the permit system. Part of the reason for this is that only a small percentage of the members of a dog hunting party are successful in obtaining a harvest tag through the drawing process. Since those tag holders are the only members of the party who can shoot a bear, their chances of success are excellent. Prior to the permit system, all members of a dog hunting party had licenses that enabled them to shoot a bear, if they got the chance, but only a small percentage of those licenses were filled. So even though dog hunters may not be harvesting many more bears than they were before, the odds have gone up of tags being used that now go to hunters who try their luck with hounds.

Another factor that may contribute to the high rate of success among dog hunters is the greatest percentage of bear tags are issued for the second and third hunts in the

U.P. when dog hunting is legal. The longer the season is open, the lower the chances of success among bait hunters because many bruins revert to nocturnal feeding. Since dogs can follow a bear from a feeding to a bedding area, success remains high late in the season and may even increase.

DNR Bear Specialist Tim Reis said dog hunters had a 44.97 percent rate of success during 1998 compared to 42.57 percent success for 1997.

Despite the fact that hounding bears plays an important role in managing the animals in Michigan and provides valuable recreation, it's essential that hound hunters respect the rights of private property owners. In fact, it's important to avoid contact with land owners who are known to dislike bear hunting with hounds such as Jim Rogers from Grand Marais. If they don't, they stand to lose valuable dogs and equipment and possibly much more.

Rogers has made a number of unsuccessful attempts to ban the practice of hounding bears. Houndmen who give him an excuse to try again are asking for trouble. That's what happened during 1997 when three houndmen from the Lower Peninsula were training their hounds before bear season opened.

The men spent time preparing for the season near Grand Marais during late August and early September. All of their hounds were fitted with name tags and retrieval collars. The collars, valued at $150 each, allow hunters to locate their dogs if they become lost.

But when the collars are lost, it's impossible to locate the dogs that were wearing them. The trio got suspicious when the retrieval collars disappeared from three of their hounds.

One of the collars disappeared on August 31 and the other two vanished on September 1. The hunters managed to find the dog without its collar on the 31st. Alger County Sheriff's Department employee Anthony Grahovoc picked up the other two hounds with missing collars from Rogers' residence on September 1st and filed a report about the incident.

Rogers called in a complaint on the morning of September 1, reporting he had caught the two dogs on his property and asked to have someone pick them up. When Grahovoc arrived at the scene, Rogers told him the dogs were not wearing collars when he caught them.

After leaving Rogers' property, Grahovoc encountered the hunters who owned the dogs and turned the hounds over to them. The houndmen claimed that their dogs were wearing retrieval collars until they ended up on Rogers' land and asked to file charges against the land owner.

When Grahovoc contacted Rogers later that day and asked him about the missing collars, he continued to claim the dogs were not wearing any. Rogers added that he might consider shooting any dogs he finds on his property in the future, rather than turning them over to authorities. Grahovoc then asked him to contact the Sheriff's Department if he has any more problems with dogs.

No charges were filed against Rogers.

Chapter 19

They Shoot CUBS, Don't They?

Traditional Michigan bear hunting methods involving the use of bait and hounds were challenged during 1996 in an effort to eliminate them. Opponents of the popular Michigan techniques were and are fond of pointing out that they were not trying to eliminate bear hunting, just the tactics most bear hunters rely on. Pennsylvania bear hunting was often thrown out as an example that Michigan should follow.

That state does not allow the use of bait or hounds for bear hunting and their annual bear harvest averages 1,500 animals. If that's all you know about bear hunting in Pennsylvania, it might appear as an appealing alternative. That's certainly all anti-hunters would like you to know about Pennsylvania bear hunting because the rest of the story is not so appealing.

Pennsylvania's bear season only lasts three days, for example, compared to 46 days of bear hunting in the U.P. and two weeks of hunting in the northern L.P. With the use of bait and hounds, Michigan hunters only harvested 1,294 bruins during the fall of 1997, 1,099 in the U.P. and 195 in the L.P. Without those methods and a fraction of the hunting time, Pennsylvania hunters registered 2,101 bruins during 1997, according to Bear Program Leader Gary Alt. Alt said harvests during hunts of the same length in 1993, '92 and '91 were 1,790, 1,589 and 1,687 respectively.

You might think those Pennsylvania bear hunters really know what they are doing to be so effective. The truth is that they don't. The reason hunters are so effective at killing bears is there are far more of them than in Michigan. There are approximately 15 times as many bear hunters in Pennsylvania as Michigan.

Pennsylvania's Alt said there used to be a quota of 100,000 bear licenses available in the state for bear season. He added that cap was removed because there had been

(Left) The way bear hunting is conducted in Pennsylvania has been suggested as an alternative to Michigan's system. Protection for cubs would have to be removed if Michigan were to follow Pennsylvania's example. An average of 23 percent of Pennsylvania's annual bear harvest is composed of cubs.

fewer hunters interested in bear hunting than the number of licenses available. The number of bear hunters in Pennsylvania stabilized at 90,000 for a number of years, according to Alt. However, bear license sales in the state shot up to 110,180 during 1997 when the tags could be purchased from 1,000 license agents statewide. Previously, bear licenses could only be obtained at the state's seven game commission offices.

With so many bear hunters in the field, some of them are bound to bump into bruins, as harvest figures confirm. However, the chances of seeing a bear during Pennsylvania's 3-day season are low and the odds of actually shooting one are even lower. Bear hunting success ranges between 1.5 and 2 percent.

Many Pennsylvania bear hunters don't really know much about bear hunting, according to Alt. He said most of them stumble around, hoping to see a bear. Some of those who do see and shoot bruins, connect on animals that are trying to escape someone else and cross their path by accident. Alt commented that 13 percent of the hunters who shoot bears in his state have never seen one in the wild before.

One of the most popular hunting methods used by groups of Pennsylvania bear hunters is drives. Drivers walk through swamps and thickets hoping to chase bears that might be hiding in them to partners who are waiting in ambush along the edges. Bears that escape drives, but are displaced by them, run the risk of bumping into one of the many other hunters who are afield.

The number of bear hunters in Michigan is limited under a permit system. There were 7,305 harvest tags issued during 1998, but only 5,935 permittees actually hunted, according to DNR figures. Approximately 36,000 people applied for bear permits in Michigan for '98, so even if everyone who wanted to hunt bear in the state that fall were allowed to do so, hunting pressure would still be three times as high in Pennsylvania.

Without the use of bait and hounds, it's highly unlikely that 36,000 hunters would have been able to harvest 1,000 bears. And even if they did, that wouldn't be a high enough harvest to properly manage the state's bruins anyway. An annual harvest closer to 1,400 or 1,500 would be required to do so. Based on Pennsylvania's best rate of success of two percent, it would take 50,000 hunters to harvest 1,000 bears in the state without the use of bait and hounds and 60,000 to take 1,200 bruins.

However, since Michigan's bear season normally opens during September when foliage is still thick, reducing visibility, there's an excellent chance that hunter success would be lower than in Pennsylvania. Pennsylvania's bear hunt takes place during late fall when leaves have fallen, increasing visibility. It could take 100,000 hunters or more to harvest 1,000 bears in Michigan without bait and dogs.

With bait and hounds being legal hunting methods during 1998 in Michigan and hunter numbers limited by permit, success averaged 25 percent. The longer bear seasons in Michigan contribute to the better success here than in Pennsylvania in addition to the hunting methods used. However, success is far lower than anti-hunters would have you believe, which illustrates that bear hunting with bait and hounds is far from a sure thing. Opponents of bait and hound hunting contend that success with these methods is practically guaranteed.

All of the permittees hunting in Michigan may not see a bear, but they certainly have a much better chance of doing so than in Pennsylvania and the quality of the experience is much better, too. Michigan bear hunters commonly see a number of bears before shooting one and it's not unusual for experienced hunters to end the season with an unfilled tag even though they've had plenty of chances to kill a bruin. The majority of bear hunters who tried their luck in Michigan during 1998 rated their hunt as good

Pennsylvania has far more bear hunters in the field every year than Michigan (100,000 plus versus 7,000), which allows them to harvest more bears during a short season only lasting three days. The most popular bear hunting method in Pennsylvania involves driving the animals from cover by groups of hunters.

to excellent, according to a DNR survey. It's unlikely results of such a survey would be the same in Pennsylvania.

Something the anti-hunters who were trying to ban bear hunting in Michigan really don't want state residents to know is that efforts have also been mounted to ban bear hunting in Pennsylvania. Members of The Fund For Animals have probably been involved in the move to ban bear hunting in Pennsylvania as they were here in Michigan. The Pennsylvania attempts have failed so far, however, due to the fact wildlife

201

biologists there have sound biological data to base the hunt on. Alt said an annual harvest of 1,500 to 1,600 bears is necessary to maintain a steady population of bruins.

Michigan also has sound biological data to base its bear hunt on. Fortunately, that scientific information played an important role in protecting sound bear management practices during '96.

Also worthy of note, is that the potential for shooting too many bears exists with the hunt conducted in Pennsylvania. Alt said it happened in 1989 when 2,220 bruins were shot. An excellent mast crop, good weather and tracking snow contributed to the high harvest that year. The same thing happened during the 1998 hunt when an alltime record 2,579 bears were taken in Pennsylvania during three days of hunting. Years with lousy weather and poor mast crops, resulting in low bear harvests, help balance out the years with high harvests, according to Alt.

By way of comparison, Michigan bear hunters registered 1,512 bears during the 1998 season for a 46-day hunt with the use of bait and hounds. There were 5,652 bear harvest permits issued in Michigan versus 100,000 plus in Pennsylvania. We also have far more bears than Pennsylvania, with a minimum of 13,500 bruins inhabiting the U.P. alone and thousands more in the northern L.P. Pennsylvania's bear population numbers approximately 10,000. The Michigan system obviously does a better job of regulating the bear harvest.

One other major difference between bear hunting in Pennsylvania and Michigan that is just as significant as those mentioned so far is that cubs and females with cubs are legal there and protected here. Alt said 23 percent of the annual bear harvest in Pennsylvania is composed of cubs. Cubs are not protected in Pennsylvania because that state's bears are very productive, according to Alt. Adult females produce lots of cubs.

Pennsylvania cubs also grow faster than those in Michigan because the habitat is more productive and they have longer to grow before bear season is held. Alt said the bear hunt is always held during late November on the three days prior to Thanksgiving. Many cubs weigh 100 pounds or more by then.

Most Michigan bears are in dens by November, especially those in the U.P., and they spend more time in dens than bruins in Pennsylvania, reducing the opportunity for growth each year. Cubs are protected in Michigan because they seldom reach 100 pounds during their first year and most hunters are able to tell the difference between cubs and adults because of the difference in size. Females in the company of cubs are protected to insure an abundance of adults of breeding age for future cub production. Even before a law was established protecting females with cubs, most hunters passed them up anyway. Passing up bears is unheard of during Pennsylvania's hunt because most hunters don't see a single animal.

The fact that most bear hunters in Michigan hunt with bait or hounds makes it possible for them to identify cubs and females with cubs so they can avoid shooting them. Hunters using those techniques usually get a good enough look at bruins to determine those size differences because cubs are most often with their mothers during the fall. Even when cubs are separated from their mothers, their small size is evident to Michigan hunters who use bait and dogs.

The ability of many hunters using bait and hounds to determine the size of the bears they intend on shooting results in a higher harvest of males than females in Michigan, which is important for the future of the state's bears. Higher survival among females will result in greater cub production. Males are larger than females and Michigan hunters frequently choose the largest bear they see. The proportion of males in the harvest over the past five years has ranged from 55 to 64 percent.

One more factor in favor of bear hunting with bait and hounds is that the chances for clean kills are increased because shots are taken at known distances and bears are visible long enough to allow hunters to wait for bruins to be in the best position possible before taking a shot.

Another very important reason that cubs are not protected in Pennsylvania is that with the hunting methods used there, it is difficult to impossible for hunters to determine the size of bear they are shooting. Bruins are often walking or running in thick cover when spotted, sometimes making it impossible to see the entire animal. And animals will frequently be gone from sight quickly, so hunters must shoot fast, if they are going to get a shot at all.

By the same token, if the use of bait and hounds were eliminated as legal hunting methods in Michigan, consideration should be given to removing protection for cubs. Hunters who are not afforded the time to identify the size of their target are bound to mistakenly shoot cubs on occasion. It is far better that those animals be utilized by hunters than abandoned in the woods.

When all of the variables are considered, there's no question that Michigan's current bear hunting situation is better than Pennsylvania's, both for hunters and the hunted. The statewide permit system in effect in Michigan adequately protects the state's bruins from overharvest. The use of bait and hounds insures an adequate annual harvest of the right bears to help control nuisance complaints while still allowing the population to increase. These methods offer hunters the best opportunity to identify their targets so cubs and their mothers can be protected, males can be selectively harvested and the chances for clean kills are improved.

If the use of bait and hounds were banned in Michigan, there would be no need for a permit system. Even if the number of bear hunters in the state increases significantly, it's unlikely that enough bruins could be taken annually to properly manage the animals (prevent a dramatic increase in nuisance complaints). Returning to a bear hunt that coincides with gun deer season when enough hunters are afield to harvest a significant number of bruins without bait and hounds, is also a poor alternative. Most bears are in dens then, which would lead to the killing of many slumbering bruins, including cubs, as it did in the past. There would also be a chance too many bears would be killed then, which is what happened in the L.P. during the 1960s.

Bear hunting in Michigan evolved the way it has because it provides the best protection for the resource at the same time bears can be properly managed. Quality bear hunting recreation is another benefit. There's no good reason for current practices to change and I hope they don't.

Chapter **20**

Trade In Bear Parts
Should Be Legal

Current laws that prohibit the sale of parts from legally taken black bear are largely responsible for the poaching of bears like an adult male killed in Gogebic County during mid-July one year. Inaccurate reporting from some law enforcement officers and the news media about the amount of money poachers stand to make from the sale of bear parts also contributes to the problem. The incentive for poaching bears would be reduced if the true value of a poached bear were publicized and the parts from bruins taken legally could be used to supply the demand in Asian countries.

Where it is illegal to use the parts from legally taken bears, which includes much of North America, most hunters don't bother to salvage those parts, allowing them to go to waste. That cuts off the supply of parts from bears that are already dead. So to secure parts to supply the demand, additional bears are killed illegally.

Only five states where black bears can be legally hunted allow the sale of bear parts. Those states are Idaho, Maine, New York, Pennsylvania and West Virginia. Another six states allow the sale of parts from bears taken elsewhere—Connecticut, Louisiana, New Jersey, North Dakota, Oklahoma and Rhode Island. Another nine states had no regulations on the sale of bear parts when this was written and they are Delaware, Hawaii, Illinois, Indiana, Iowa, Kansas, Kentucky, Vermont and Wyoming.

An estimated 40,000 to 50,000 black bears are legally taken by hunters every year in the United States and Canada. If the parts from most or all of the bruins killed legally could be used to supply the demand, there would be no need for animals to be taken illegally. The solution seems so simple, it's being overlooked.

When it comes to most animals taken by hunters and trappers, they are encouraged to utilize as much of them as possible. The antlers, hides and even hooves of many big game animals are often used to make momentos of the hunt and the meat

(Left) An adult male black bear like this one was reportedly poached in Gogebic County one year for its body parts. If the sale of the parts from legally taken bears were allowed, the incentive for poaching would be dramatically reduced, if not eliminated.

Gall bladder from a legally taken black bear. What better use can the parts of legally harvested bruins have than to save the lives of animals that might otherwise be poached? Current laws in many states and provinces encourage the waste of these parts.

provides plenty of tasty, healthy meals. In fact, hunters are often rightfully criticized if they waste any of the game they bag. Yet, when it comes to bears, the waste of valuable parts of those animals is encouraged, if not mandated by law. It doesn't make any sense.

What better use can the parts of a legally taken animal have other than to save the lives of animals that could otherwise be killed illegally? The use of those parts should be encouraged rather than discouraged. The definition of conservation is the wise use of resources. Allowing parts that are in demand from legal kills to go to waste so that demand can be met from illegal kills is not wise use.

Some estimates of the annual illegal kill of bears are as high as 40,000. Since a higher number of bruins are legally bagged by hunters every year, doesn't it make more sense for those animals to be used to supply the parts trade? Black market prices for items that are in demand are usually higher than those that can be sold legally. However, the black market prices are still not as high as most people realize. The true value of a poached bear is discussed toward the end of this chapter. Legalization of the trade in bear parts from animals taken legally would reduce prices paid for those parts even further, short circuiting incentives for poaching.

There's at least two ways that the parts from legally taken black bears could be incorporated into a plan to reduce bear poaching. The sale of parts could be legalized so licensed hunters could sell them directly to buyers. Trappers already sell the pelts and

*It's currently legal to sell elk and deer antlers like these to the Asian market.
The selling of valued bear parts should also be legal, as long as those parts are
clearly marked and registered as having come from the legal harvest.*

some parts from furbearers they catch, so this concept is nothing new. A scent gland from beavers called castors that are in high demand are commonly sold now.

It's also currently legal to sell elk and deer antlers to supply the oriental medicinal trade. Powdered antler is an ingredient in traditional medicines just as bear parts are. The antlers from elk raised on commercial farms specifically for that purpose now supply much of that demand. Annual antlers are cut from bulls without sacrificing the animals.

The antlers shed by wild elk and deer contribute to the market, too. One of the major fund raising projects conducted by Boy Scouts from Jackson Hole, Wyoming is collecting shed antlers to sell from the large concentration of elk that winter there.

An alternative to allowing hunters to sell bear parts directly, is a plan that would permit state and provincial agencies such as the departments of natural resources, to market the parts to insure adequate controls. Hunters could be asked to donate parts such as gall bladders to the DNR as a means of discouraging bear poaching for those parts. I certainly would be willing to donate parts from any bears I bag to a program to discourage poaching and I know other hunters would, too.

However, some type of incentive would probably encourage more hunters to participate in a "Parts To Reduce Poaching Program." I think refunding the cost of a resident bear license would be an adequate incentive. Plenty of publicity putting the value of a bear gall bladder at $13 would certainly reduce poaching. Marketing of bear parts by state agencies would not only contribute to a reduction in poaching, it would generate much needed revenue to help fund law enforcement, research and/or wildlife management. With shrinking budgets, natural resource agencies should be looking for innovative ways to raise revenue and getting involved in a legal bear parts trade should be given serious consideration.

The DNR Law Division got involved in the fur trade a number of years ago during an undercover operation as a means of identifying the traffic in illegal furs and animal parts. Openly getting involved in the bear parts trade to reduce poaching would be even more worthwhile, in my opinion. And it would be important under such a program for all bear parts from legally taken animals to be sealed or tagged in some way, as otter and bobcat currently are, so there's no way parts from illegally taken bruins could be marketed.

Laws that were enacted prohibiting the sale of bear parts are clearly outdated or are not working and it's time for a change. Michigan's prohibition on the sale of meat and parts from game animals and birds dates back to the Game Law of 1929, according to DNR Sgt. John Wynalda from Lansing. He said the reason for the law was to protect the resource from market hunting, which was certainly justified in view of elimination of the passenger pigeon and major impacts on other species that survived. The rationale behind similar statutes in other states is probably the same.

However, laws prohibiting the sale of bear parts in some states and Canadian provinces have been enacted during recent years with the well-intentioned idea it would help protect black bears in North America and Asia from poaching. Law makers reasoned that if the supply of bear parts could be eliminated, the demand for them would diminish. While that hasn't happened, the supply of parts from legally taken bears was further restricted.

Claims during recent years that the illegal trade in bears parts is increasing are largely due to the fact the practice is now illegal in more places than it used to be, not necessarily due to an increase in poaching. Many violations now involve the attempted sale or transport of parts from legally taken animals where the practice used to be legal.

The reason the demand for bear parts has not diminished and probably never will, is their use is an important part of the oriental culture. The parts from various animals, including bears, have been an important ingredient in Asian medicines for centuries. The use of animal parts for these potions is so deeply ingrained in the culture that they are considered necessities and efforts to change those traditions have met with little, if any, success. Totally banning the trade in rhinoceros and tiger parts, for example, has failed to reduce Asian consumer demand for them and those animals are endangered species.

If anything, laws eliminating the sale of parts from legally taken bears has increased the black market prices paid for those parts, increasing the incentive for poaching, having the opposite effect they are supposed to. And law enforcement efforts have obviously not been adequate to curtail poaching if estimates of as many as 40,000 illegal kills per year is accurate. I think another approach to the problem is overdue.

There is another mechanism designed to control the trade of bear parts and it should be given a chance to work. In the early 1990s, North American black bear were listed under the CITES (Convention on International Trade in Endangered Species) Treaty, not because they are endangered, but because several species of Asian black bears are. The gall bladders from all black bears are similar, so CITES permits have been required for the import or export of bear parts from Canada and the United States to eliminate confusion between parts from North America and Asia.

Hunters from the U.S. who shoot a black bear in Canada, for example, must file a

CITES permits like those being filled out by Tim and Donna Hastings in Manitoba were designed to control the transport and sale of black bears and their parts and they should be used for that purpose rather than outlawing the use of bear parts. Bear hunters from the U.S. who shoot bears in Canada must have a CITES permit to transport the hide and/or carcass across the border.

CITES permit with customs agents to bring any or all of the animal, including the gall bladder, into the U.S. However, in most Canadian provinces, it is currently illegal to even possess a black bear gall bladder, much less export one. Check current local regulations before attempting to salvage a gall bladder from any bear you may legally shoot.

CITES permits are required to export bear parts from either the United States or Canada. Those permits can be used to monitor and control the trade of parts from legally taken black bears. That's what they were designed for and it's time to take advantage of them.

I hope the poachers who killed black bears illegally in Michigan as well as elsewhere, are caught and prosecuted. You can help by reporting any illegal activity you

209

know about to the DNR. A tollfree hotline to report poaching anonymously is 1-800-292-7800. In the meantime, I hope steps are taken to eliminate the incentive for poaching by using the parts from legally taken animals to supply the current demand. If anyone has a better solution to the problem of bear poaching, please let me know.

HOW MUCH IS A POACHED BEAR WORTH?

One of the factors that contributes to the poaching of black bears for their parts besides laws that prohibit the use of parts from legally taken animals is the misconception on the part of poachers that they can make thousands of dollars from the carcass of one illegal kill. The media and some law enforcement personnel help fuel that perception, increasing the potential for more poaching. After parts have been processed and they change hands many times to reach their final destination in Asia, they may fetch thousands of dollars, but poachers will seldom, if ever, earn anywhere near that amount of money.

According to DNR Sgt. John Wynalda from Lansing, the parts from a black bear are only worth $280, not thousands, based on figures obtained by the DNR Law Division in 1992. The gall bladders and paws from black bears are the most valuable in the bear parts trade because of their use in oriental medicines and potions. Wynalda said the market value of gall bladders ranged between $40 and $75 and paws could be sold for $10 to $15 apiece.

Although it is currently illegal to sell individual parts from a legally killed black

The paws of black bears were valued at $10 to $15 each in locations where it is legal to sell the parts.

bear in Michigan, it is legal to sell hides with the paws attached. In 1992, a bear hide was worth up to $25.

A value was also assigned to bear teeth and claws. These items are not in demand in the Asian community, but are used in making jewelry and other trinkets. Wynalda said canine teeth could be sold for $5 to $20 each and claws were worth about $4 apiece.

A final value of $280 was arrived at by assigning the maximum price for each part. Four canine teeth would be valued at $80, for example, 10 claws at $40 and a gall bladder at $75. Prices for bear parts have probably gone up since 1992, but even if they have doubled, that only puts the value of a poached bear in Michigan at $560.

West Virginia is one of the states where the sale of bear parts is legal. Each year, a sealed bid auction is conducted by the state for the sale of bear carcasses in their possession (nuisance animals, road kills, illegal kills that have been seized), excluding gall bladders. According to TRAFFIC USA, the prices paid for entire black bear carcasses during the 1995 auction was $200. Prices paid for bear hides during that auction ranged from $45 to $125. Bear skulls sold for $10-$13 and feet went for $10.

The going price for black bear gall bladders in West Virginia, according to one buyer, was $45 to $50. Considering the highest price paid for each item, a black bear was worth a maximum of $398 in that state during 1995.

TRAFFIC USA's Andrea L. Gaski also presented figures on the prices paid for black bear gall bladders from various states and provinces at the 2nd International Symposium on the Trade of Bear Parts in Seattle, Washington during March of 1997. As expected, the lowest prices paid for these valued parts came from jurisdictions where trade is legal and the highest prices from those where trade is illegal. Refer to the accompanying table for those figures. Even where the highest prices are paid for bear parts, the value of a poached bear would be between $600 to $800.

That's not much incentive when weighed against the risks. If caught, a poacher could lose any and all equipment involved in the violation, including firearms and vehicles. Fines, court costs and restitution for the animal could run as much as $2,000 or more. The poacher could also face up to a year in jail.

PRICES PAID FOR BLACK BEAR GALL BLADDERS

State/Province	Price	Trade Legal	Year
Idaho	$20–25	Yes	1994
Maine	$45–50	Yes	1995
Saskatchewan	$80–100	Yes	1994
Colorado	$40–120	No	1994
Washington	$100–150	No	1994
California	$180–200	No	1994
British Columbia	$150–250	No	1994

Section
4

Anti-Hunting

(Left) Efforts to restrict bear hunting in Michigan began during the mid-1980s with efforts to ban the use of hounds. Since 1990, all bear hunting has been targeted for elimination.

Chapter 21

Hunting Ban Background

Jim Rogers and his wife Beverly from Grand Marais were driving forces behind efforts to ban bear hunting with bait and hounds in Michigan. The couple are not full-time residents of the state. They claim to reside on a large block of land they own south of Grand Marais about seven months out of the year. They usually spend the winter on property they own in Florida, but they also maintain a residence in Indiana.

Their efforts started during the mid-1980s when all of their attention was focused on bear hunting with hounds. They had experienced problems with dog hunters trespassing on their property and sought to ban this hunting method because they said that attempts to solve the problem by contacting law enforcement agencies and DNR conservation officers proved ineffective. They started a petition drive under the name Property Owners Association to drum up support for potential legislation that would eliminate hounding bears.

Although those attempts failed to accomplish what Mr. and Mrs. Rogers hoped to, they set the wheels in motion to begin solving the problem. The attention their efforts focused on trespassing hound hunters brought the issue to the forefront and it became a major topic of conversation among hunters and the DNR Law Division. Hunters became more aware of the importance of their public image and began policing themselves. Most hound hunters respect the rights of private property owners and they resented the fact that the actions of those who didn't could bring an end to an activity they enjoy. Peer pressure can be a powerful force in getting people to modify their behavior.

Intensive law enforcement can also be effective and the DNR Law Division responded by beefing up the ranks of conservation officers in the U.P. during bear

(Left) Attention focused on problems associated with bear hunting resulted in increased law enforcement, which has been successful in eliminating most of the illegal activity. Much of the pressure for banning bear hunting in Michigan is coming from nonresidents and part time residents (DNR PHOTO).

season. There was a major crackdown on bear hunting violations of all types as officers from throughout the state descended on bear hunters across the region. Hunters took notice and many of those who were breaking the law modified their behavior to avoid being ticketed or reticketed. DNR records confirm that trespassing among hound hunters has declined dramatically since the Rogers began their drive to eliminate this hunting method.

That doesn't mean the issue is no longer of concern. It remains a major concern among hunters, the DNR and, most importantly, property owners. Everyone involved wants to continue to control the problem and this can best be done by working together. Organized bear hunters encourage land owners who have problems with trespassing dog hunters to contact them as well as law enforcement officers. Refer to the chapter "Bears and Hounds" for addresses and phone numbers of representatives of the Michigan Bear Hunters Association and U.P. Bear Houndsmen.

I spoke to Jim Rogers a number of times during his campaign to ban bear hunting with hounds and he assured me he and his wife did not have a problem with the use of bait for bear hunting. He told me they did not want to eliminate that hunting method. At the same time, I made it clear that I did not support a ban on dog hunting, but was willing to do what I could to help solve problems associated with the activity. Afterall, a total elimination of bear hunting with hounds is not necessary to correct the behavior of some bad apples. This is true for any hunting method.

The name of the Rogers' organization was eventually changed to Sportsman's & Property Owners' Rights & Tactics Association (SPORT). Unfortunately, the Rogers and members of their group wanted to ban bear hunting with dogs so badly that they began using false information to promote their cause. They claimed that bear dogs frequently chase deer, for example, which is false. It may happen occasionally, but not often because a dog that chases deer simply doesn't make a dependable bear dog. Bear dogs are specifically trained not to chase deer and those that can't be trained to avoid deer are seldom used to follow bear because it's almost impossible for hounds to follow a bear track without encountering the scent of deer.

Claims that dog hunters were responsible for a decline in the bear population were also false. A survey conducted by the DNR during 1986 found that the success ratio among both bait and hound hunters was the same at 17 percent. Since the permit system was started in 1990, success for both groups of hunters has gone up due to the fact there are more bears and fewer people who are able to get harvest tags. And dog hunters only account for about 20 percent of the annual bear kill.

SPORT also circulated stories about bear dogs being abandoned to run wild; another falsehood. Most bear hunters expend every effort possible to recover lost dogs and keep looking until all animals are recovered. I don't know of any bear dogs that have gone unrecovered long enough to revert to the wild. This criticism seems strange in view of the fact SPORT would have liked to make it more difficult for houndmen to find their dogs at the end of the day.

One of the group's goals was to outlaw the use of electronic retrieval collars on bear dogs. Most hound hunters now equip their dogs with these collars so they can locate them after a hunt is concluded. The use of retrieval collars on dogs does not significantly increase the hunters' chances of killing a bear their dogs are chasing, according to a Vermont study, but they do dramatically increase the houndman's chances of quickly recovering his dogs after the hunt is over. Without the use of electronic retrieval collars, there would be more lost dogs, not less.

Despite the progress that had been made in controlling problems associated with

216

hounding bears, Rogers persisted in his efforts to ban the method. In fact, he changed his focus to include all bear hunting by 1990 when his organization joined forces with the Michigan Humane Society. His group lost even more credibility at that point. The Michigan Humane Society is one of the largest, if not the largest, anti-hunting organization in the state. For years Rogers claimed that he didn't have any ties to anti-hunting groups. That was obviously no longer true.

Anyone who believed Jim Rogers when he said he and SPORT were not opposed to bear hunting, just bear hunting with hounds, were in for a surprise on June 13, 1990. He held a news conference in Lansing on that day with Eileen Liska, Michigan Humane Society's Director of Research and Legislation, to express their support for bills introduced in the state legislature to ban all bear hunting in the state.

Rogers and Liska were largely responsible for convincing State Senator John Kelly (D-Detroit) and State Representative Gerald Law (R-Plymouth) to introduce House Bill 5876 and Senate Bill 997. The bills called for a ban on bear hunting while an independent bear population study was conducted by members of the International Bear Biologists Association who are not employed by or in any way connected with the Michigan DNR. Both groups cited concerns for the bear population in supporting the legislation.

There was no need for an independent study of bear numbers or a total closure on bear hunting in the state. State bear hunters and the DNR had already expressed their concern for Michigan's bears and approved a reduction in bear hunting before the legislation was introduced. A statewide permit system limiting the number of bear hunters by two-thirds and the establishment of specific bear management units went into effect during 1990. If Rogers and Liska were really concerned about bear numbers, they would have supported the permit system. They were simply trying to mask their real agenda.

A Humane Society news release issued at the time suggests that Michigan bears were declining due to the fact more young animals were being tagged by hunters, with some of them weighing around 100 pounds. The fact is that the bulk of any big game harvest is composed of young rather than old representatives of a species. An increase in young bears in the kill (those at least 1 3/4 years old) is a sign of excellent reproduction, representing an increasing population rather than one that is declining.

And young bears that are one or two years old are the most vulnerable to hunters because they are often in unfamiliar territory and cover more ground than older animals with established home ranges. Young bears are also the least experienced in understanding the dangers posed by all people, including hunters, and how to avoid them.

It's not unusual for yearling bears of both sexes, which are 1 3/4 years old during their second fall, to have live weights of around 100 pounds or less. One yearling female that was part of Terry DeBruyn's study in Alger County only weighed 25 pounds during March of 1994. As a 2-year-old during March of 1995, she weighed more than three times as much, but was still only 80 pounds. Her weight was probably close to 100 pounds the previous fall. That female's brother weighed 45 pounds as a yearling and 110 as a 2-year-old during March of '95.

Also worthy of note is that small bears weighing around 100 pounds are not always young ones. Some adult female bears may only have field dressed weights around 100 pounds. One adult female live trapped during a study in Alger County had a live weight of 125 pounds. Her dressed weight, had she been taken by a hunter, might have been less than 100 pounds. So there is not always a correlation between age and weight among bears.

Several more sentences from the Humane Society news release indicate that U.P. residents and hunters supported a ban on bear hunting during 1990 because they ". . .

The presence of plenty of young bears in the harvest reflects an increasing population rather than one that's declining.

can see how badly depleted our bear population really is." Those references were not only misleading, they were false. If a majority of U.P. residents supported closing bear season, why did it take legislators from the Detroit area to sponsor the necessary legislation instead of U.P. representatives?

And if the Humane Society or any other group were genuinely concerned about the future of black bears in Michigan, they would be willing to pay for some of the bear studies being conducted in the state to learn more about the animals, so that the animals can be properly managed. Eileen Liska said the Humane Society had not pledged any money for black bears, other than for trying to stop hunting, and it doesn't intend to. In a later conversation with Michigan Humane Society Executive Director Gary Tiscornia, he confirmed that position remained the same. He said the society has a policy against all hunting, not just bear hunting.

The vast majority of the money used to pay for bear research and management in

Michigan is paid by hunters and we're proud of that. Anyone who is serious about the future of the state's bears should do the same.

The legislation introduced during 1990 to ban bear hunting did not pass. There was no need for it and there obviously wasn't enough support for it. In the meantime, the permit system has proven itself as the best way to manage Michigan bears. Limited hunting with bait and hounds have continued under the system while the bear population has increased. There are presently more bears in the state now than there has been for a long time and there's no need to change anything.

Nonetheless, SPORT, the Michigan Humane Society and some new partners—The Fund For Animals, a staunch anti-hunting group based in Washington D.C., and the Great Bear Foundation, a Montana based group opposed to bear hunting with bait and hounds—mounted a new campaign to eliminate the two most popular bear hunting methods in the state. SPORT brought in the big guns that time, enlisting the help of national organizations, but their tactics remained the same. They continued to use false information to generate support for their cause. Refer to the next chapter for details about what they did.

The vast majority of the money used to pay for bear research like that shown here as a bruin is weighed, is paid for by hunters and we're proud of that. We also foot the bill for management and habitat preservation, something anti-hunting groups will never do.

Chapter 22

The New Campaign

The new campaign to ban bear hunting with bait and hounds officially got under-way during May of 1995 under the auspices of a group named CUB, Citizens United for Bears. It was a catchy name obviously chosen to generate support for their cause and to hide their true purpose—to ban hunting methods that currently play an important role in managing black bears in Michigan.

The name was also selected to correspond to the implication that one of the group's goals was to protect black bear cubs from hunters. That was and is unnecessary, of course, because years ago hunters who use bait and hounds to hunt bear agreed that cubs should be protected during hunting season and saw that such a law was passed.

The front of a flyer circulated by CUB has a picture of a bear cub taken by Dr. Lynn Rogers of Ely, Minnesota, showing it standing on its hind legs next to a tree, with its front paws resting on the tree trunk. Bold print on top of the photo asks, "SHOULD-N'T SHE HAVE A CHANCE?"

The answer is "YES" because cubs do have an excellent chance of survival, in the U.P. at least. A nine-year study conducted in Alger County by Bear Researcher Terry DeBruyn (refer to other chapters in this book for more information) has found that al-most all of the cubs born in his 63-square-mile study area survive their first year of life.

On average, one of the cubs born in his study area every year died of natural causes, either as a result of predation or an accident. The one cub that died during 1994, for example, died from injuries resulting from porcupine quills. Five cubs were born to radio collared females that year. Predators were thought to have been

(Left) Cub bears have been protected in Michigan since 1948 due to concern among hunters and the DNR for the future welfare of the state's bears. As a result, cubs have an excellent chance of survival during their first year without any help from C.U.B. (Citizens United for Bears).

responsible for cub losses during other years. It was clear that hunting was NOT RE-SPONSIBLE for cub mortality.

CUB also sent out at least two fund raising letters, one of which included a questionnaire, and they were signed by Jim Rogers. Both letters were full of false information and so was the questionnaire. One of the statements in the form of a question on the questionnaire, for example, was worded this way, "Did you know that dogs are used to track and tree bears; and sometimes cubs are shot out of the tree because the hunter doesn't realize it's a cub?"

The size of treed bears is easiest to determine and dog hunters seldom shoot small animals, even those that are more than a year old and legal to kill. If there's any question about a bear being a cub, it is not killed to avoid making a mistake.

Another statement/question was, "Did you know that out-of-state hunters come to Michigan every year to track and kill bears with bait or dogs because it is illegal in many states?"

Michigan has a permit system that controls the number of bear hunters in the state every year. A maximum of two percent of those permits go to nonresidents annually. It is legal to hunt bear with bait and/or hounds in about half of the states where bear hunting is allowed. The odds of nonresident hunters obtaining a bear license in Michigan are so low because of the permit system, most go elsewhere where they can obtain a license any year they choose.

Nonresidents who do apply for a permit in Michigan do so because the state has an excellent bear population due to proper management. The bear population has been increasing since the permit system started in 1990.

Still one more comment on the questionnaire indicates "a high percentage of the bears tracked and killed in Michigan are chased through private property," which is also false. Most of the bears taken by hunters every year are shot in the U.P. where public land is abundant and many bruins are killed on state and federally owned ground. Some private land owners either hunt bear on their property or allow other hunters to do so.

Both fund raising letters from CUB indicate the U.S. Forest Service supports a ban on bear hunting with bait in Michigan. That claim is false, according to Ottawa National Forest Public Affairs Officer Randy Charles from Ironwood.

CUB literature states that bear bait is set out in buckets, which is illegal. No containers or litter of any type is permitted at bear bait sites and baiting can not begin until 30 days before the season opens.

The propaganda contends that bears that come to feed are shot at point blank range on opening day of hunting season. There's no question that some bears are shot on opening day, but with an average hunting success of 25 percent in the U.P. and 16 percent for the northern L.P., far from every person who hunts over bait manages to shoot a bear. The kill is actually spread out over the entire season, which lasts more than 30 days. If bait hunting is as effective as the members of CUB would have liked you to believe, everyone should have gotten a bear in that amount of time.

And few bears are shot at point blank range. Most shots at bear, even with bow and arrow, are at a distance of at least 20 to 30 feet and more often 60 feet or 20 yards. Gun hunters tend to be farther away. The closer hunters are to baits, the better their chances of being detected by bruins and not getting a shot at all. Bears seldom, if ever, approach a bait when they know a person is present.

In regard to bear hunting with hounds, the CUB letters claim that hunters follow the signal of transmitters in dog collars to treed bears to kill them. The fact is, most dog

Retrieval collars like the one worn by this Walker hound make it easier for hunters to find dogs and properly care for them at the end of a hunt. The collars also increase the opportunity for owners to catch their dogs before they go on private property.

hunters are able to keep tabs on the location of hounds trailing a bear through their baying and most bears chased by dogs do not climb trees, with bruins escaping hunters and hounds most of the time. The retrieval collars worn by bear dogs simply makes it easier for hunters to find the dogs at the end of the day, if contact has been lost with them and/or to recover them from private property.

The use of retrieval collars on hounds reduces the chances of trespassing because dogs can sometimes be stopped before they enter posted land. The collars also make it possible for hunters to locate dogs that have been hurt or killed.

Relaying packs of dogs (putting fresh hounds on the trail of a bear after those that started the chase tire) is illegal in Michigan and pack size is limited to six hounds. Those are self-imposed restrictions by hunters themselves like the regulation that protects cubs.

The CUB literature also characterizes bears being chased by hounds as terrified. I've watched bears being "chased" by hounds that strolled through the woods at a normal walking gait, practically ignoring the yapping dogs around them. Other bruins have successfully fought the dogs off and gone on their way.

In reality, shooting bears over bait or in front of hounds is certainly more humane than the threats bruins face in the wild during most of the year.

Since bait and hound hunters get a good look at the animal they are shooting and have the opportunity to take the best shot possible, kills are quick and humane. It is also essential that hunters have the time to look over the bears they see to avoid shooting cubs and their mothers. If these hunting methods were unsporting, success using them would be much higher than it is.

Who is afraid of who? This walking black bear certainly isn't afraid of the dogs around it. At least one hound is retreating from the bear. Most bears that climb trees ahead of dogs learned to do so as cubs to escape danger and they do so by choice, not because they are forced to.

A letter to generate money to ban bear hunting with bait and hounds in Michigan was also sent out by The Fund For Animals and it was no more accurate than those from CUB. It claimed elimination of these methods was necessary to protect bears from "trophy hunters." Most bear hunters in the state are satisfied with any legal bruin and they utilize the meat from animals they bag. Bear meat provides excellent eating.

The FFA letter also accused baiters of littering the woods with piles of rotting food. This was a contradiction of their implication that bears can't resist bait. If bears are utilizing bait, it doesn't last long enough to rot. If bait is left to rot, bears obviously aren't feeding on it. I wish they would make up their mind.

One of the biggest lies in the FFA letter was that a ban on bear hunting with bait and hounds was necessary to protect Michigan's bruins. As already mentioned, the state's bear population has been and is increasing due to the fact these hunting methods are carefully regulated. Bears are not threatened by hunting due to the permit system, which was adopted jointly by hunters and the DNR.

The FFA tried to imply that they were concerned about the welfare of bears, but they really weren't. I spoke with Heidi Prescott, who was the organization's National Director during 1996, and asked her why they don't spend their efforts in states where bear populations are in trouble such as Louisiana and Florida instead of Michigan where they are healthy and she dodged the question. She did the same thing when I asked about FFA's willingness to fund bear research or habitat preservation. They don't have funds for those worthy causes since their money goes to try to ban all forms of hunting. That's their primary agenda.

If CUB had been successful in achieving their goals, it would not have benefited bears at all. The animals would have become an increasing problem for people living in and visiting bear country. They would currently be viewed as pests, with an increasing number of them killed by home owners and law enforcement personnel as they forage for food in towns and residents' yards because not enough of them would be taken during fall hunting seasons.

The bottom line is that Michigan's black bear population is now increasing. The state DNR and hunters are largely responsible for that through support of the statewide permit system. At the present time, that increase is controlled through an annual harvest of some animals with bait and hounds. Without the use of bait and hounds for hunting, it is unlikely that enough bears could be removed from the population annually to prevent a rapid increase in numbers, with a corresponding increase in problems associated with too many bears.

I guarantee you that SPORT, the Michigan Humane Society and The Fund For Animals would not have been around to help handle or pay for dealing with nuisance bears or console the families of people injured or killed by bears, if their efforts to curtail bear hunting had been successful.

Contrary to what the members of CUB were telling the residents of Michigan, the changes they were striving to achieve would not have benefited black bears at all. The status of bruins would have been reduced instead of elevated, with many of them killed by home owners and law enforcement personnel.

The facts are on the hunters' side in regard to the important role bear hunting currently plays in management. Hunters and nonhunters alike must get involved to counteract the false information being circulated by antihunters as this group of hunters did at an anti-hunting demonstration.

Chapter 23

Bear Symposium

A black bear symposium held at Michigan State University's Management Education Center in Troy on May 13, 1995 marked the official kickoff of a campaign to ban bear hunting with bait and hounds in Michigan. Despite the fact the program was held at a public facility, it was planned to primarily present a one-sided, negative viewpoint of these hunting methods. None of the scheduled speakers were those most informed about the main topics—DNR wildlife biologists or researchers or Michigan bear hunters.

It's no wonder, based on who was involved in the symposium. The Montana-based Great Bear Foundation organized the event, handling registration and selection of speakers. Executive Director Matt Reid was in charge and he wrote a front page article for the spring 1995 issue of the Michigan Humane Society News about how bad bait and hound hunting are. Not surprising, based on the fact the GBF was/is actively trying to ban the use of bait and hounds for bear hunting across North America, the article was filled with fallacies.

Speakers invited to address bear hunting by Reid represented the Michigan Humane Society, the Fund For Animals and Sportsman's & Property Owners' Rights & Tactics Association (SPORT), a state property owners' organization headed by Jim Rogers. Only groups who were obviously opposed to bear hunting with bait and dogs were invited to speak. How could an unbiased presentation be possible with such a stacked deck?

No one from the Humane Society actually spoke during the event, due to a change in the program. Rogers had been trying to ban or limit bear hunting with hounds in Michigan for years and had joined forces with prominent anti-hunting groups by adding baiting to the agenda. Marty Williams, a sporting goods dealer from Cadillac and a board member of the Great Bear Foundation, was another speaker with a strong anti-bait hunting stance.

Colorado Division of Wildlife employee Tom Beck was a major speaker who provided an anti-bait and hound perspective based on the banning of those hunting techniques in his home state.

Retired U.S. Forest Service Wildlife Biologist and black bear expert Dr. Lynn Rogers from Ely, Minnesota was also a major speaker. He presented excellent programs about the biology and life history of black bears and supports bear hunting for management purposes. However, he was also on the dog hunting panel and made comments in opposition to this method, but was not as strong in his opposition as most of the other panelists.

U.S. Forest Service Wildlife Biologist Rex Ennis with the Huron-Manistee National Forest was invited to speak about black bear habitat, but he didn't because no DNR representatives were on the program. However, he was in the audience. The only person on the program with any connection to the DNR who understands the role bait and hounds play in bear hunting in Michigan was former Director of Wildlife Research Carl Bennett, who was then an instructor with Michigan State University.

Fortunately, the program dealing with bait and hounds didn't come off as planned. Prior to the beginning of the symposium, I asked Matt Reid about giving Michigan bear hunters an opportunity to participate and he agreed. I sat on the panel dealing with baiting and Steve Haleen of Pinckney, who is a past President of the Michigan Bear Hunters Association, participated on the panel covering hound hunting.

That time hunters managed to provide some balance to an unbalanced agenda, but I'm sure there were other efforts like that in which the facts about bear hunting with bait and hounds were excluded. So it is extremely important for hunters and non-hunters concerned about bear management in Michigan, to keep an eye and ear open in the future for attempts to do the same thing in the form of newspaper articles and radio and television programs in addition to public presentations. Newspapers, radio and television stations are obligated to present both sides of an issue and so are organizations using public facilities to provide programs. If they don't, requests for equal time can be made.

Such incidents can be dealt with by individuals or local groups, but if you are aware of a biased presentation that you want help with, please notify MUCC headquarters in Lansing or Bill Walker from Bloomfield Hills. Walker is Executive Director of the Michigan Sportsmen Defense Alliance and his telephone number is 810-334-1101. MUCC was and is involved in the effort to protect bear hunting with bait and hounds in Michigan, too, and the phone number for MUCC headquarters is 517-371-1041.

The facts are on the side of hunters, but it is important that those facts get as much play as possible to make sure as many residents of this state as possible understand them. The bottom line is that Michigan's bear population is increasing and the use of bait and hounds for bear hunting plays an important role in managing this big game animal in the state. The statewide permit system started in 1990 allows hunters to harvest some bears annually to help keep nuisance complaints in check while still allowing the number of bears in the state to increase.

Without the use of bait and hounds for hunting, it is unlikely that enough bears could be removed from the population annually to prevent a rapid increase in numbers, with a corresponding increase in problems associated with too many bears. Because cubs and their mothers are protected in Michigan, it is important that hunters be able to clearly identify their target before shooting and the use of bait and hounds is the best means of doing so. These hunting methods also increase the chances for humane kills.

Another factor working in favor of hunters is that they care about the animals they hunt and they back up that concern with thousands of dollars annually used to properly manage and study black bears and to protect the animals' habitat. That's certainly more than The Fund For Animals can claim. I spoke with FFA National Director Heidi Prescott at the symposium about the organization's willingness to fund bear research or habitat preservation. They don't have funds for that since their money goes to try to ban all forms of hunting.

And the FFA also pretends that they care about animals, but they don't. When informed that Michigan bears are increasing and that bear hunting with bait and hounds helps manage the animals, Prescott didn't care. They still spent a significant amount of money to try to ban these bear hunting methods regardless of their positive influence on bear management in Michigan. Fortunately, their efforts didn't pay off.

It was obvious to anyone who was paying attention, that the groups who were claiming to only be interested in specific hunting methods that they considered "unethical," were intentionally trying to mislead the public. While efforts were underway to ban bear hunting in Michigan, for example, the Minnesota Chapter of the Make-A-Wish Foundation granted the dying wish of a 17-year-old boy to go on an Alaskan brown bear hunt with his father. That's when the anti-hunters got involved. They tried to pressure the foundation not to grant the boy's wish for his hunt of a lifetime.

Although this particular controversy primarily involved Minnesota residents and brown bear hunting in Alaska, there were some implications that applied to the controversy surrounding black bear hunting in Michigan. One of the anti-hunting groups that opposed granting the brown bear hunting wish is The Fund For Animals. That group was actively involved in efforts to ban black bear hunting with bait and dogs in Michigan.

They, along with others involved in the Michigan petition drive, proclaimed over and over again that they are not opposed to bear hunting, just those specific hunting methods. Guess what? Brown bear can not be legally hunted with bait or dogs. They are hunted by stalking, the technique they were saying Michigan hunters should use to pursue black bear.

If the anti-hunters were telling the truth in Michigan, they shouldn't be opposed to brown bear hunting in Alaska. But were they telling the truth about their intent for bear hunting in Michigan? They were and are obviously opposed to all bear hunting and would eliminate it, if they could.

Fortunately, the boy's wish was granted and he went on a spring hunt. The Minnesota chapter of the Make-A-Wish Foundation deserves a round of applause, in my opinion, for granting a 17-year-old's dying wish to hunt brown bear in Alaska with his father in the face of pressure against the decision from anti-hunting activists. It was a legitimate wish, one that isn't surprising in view of the fact the young man grew up hunting and fishing with his family.

A brown bear hunt is an adventure that most hunters are not able to participate in due to the time and expense involved. The fact that brown bear hunting is carefully controlled in Alaska and the number of permits issued to hunt them annually is limited, also plays a role in reducing the potential participants. Without the help of the foundation, the young hunter's wish probably would not have become a reality.

That's usually the case regardless of what a dying youngster's wish happens to be, and it's to the foundation's credit for following through on its purpose, as long as a wish is within reason, as this one happened to be. Something the boy, his family, foundation members who granted the wish and most hunters realize, that was ignored in

Some of the same people who said they were not against bear hunting in Michigan, just hunting with bait and dogs, opposed an Alaskan brown bear hunt granted by the Make-A-Wish Foundation even though neither bait or dogs were involved in that hunt. Could they have been trying to mislead people about their true intentions?

press coverage about the controversy, is that the hunt might not end up in the death of a bear.

There's no guarantee on any legitimate hunt that the quarry will be bagged. The young hunter from Minnesota certainly went to Alaska with the intent of killing a bear, if he got the right chance. He knew that chance might or might not come. That's something anti-hunters have a hard time grasping.

They equate hunting with killing, and I assume many nonhunters do, too, but it doesn't always work that way. The truth of the matter is that big game hunters spend most of their time hunting—searching for or waiting for—the game they are after. In many cases, they don't find or see what they are looking for and no shots are fired at all during a hunt. There's also a lot of preparation involved in a hunt of this type that becomes part of the experience.

In other words, big game hunters spend far more time doing other things than killing. Those are the things the boy wanted to share with his father in Alaska. He also wanted to kill a bear, but, as it turned out, he did not succeed.

However, he still felt fulfilled, having shared the hunt of a lifetime with his father. Just as importantly, the boy had a valuable opportunity to take his mind off of his pain, suffering and limited lifespan to do something he so desperately wanted to before he died. It is difficult to put a price tag on the peace of mind and satisfaction that must have come with that.

The money that the Make-A-Wish Foundation provided for the boy's hunting license helped supply funds for future brown bear management in Alaska. Other expenses enriched the Alaskan economy in the same way that revenue from hunting positively impacts the economies of every state where it's legal, including Michigan.

The black bear symposium held at Troy during May of 1995 was video taped, supposedly for educational purposes. Those who participated were told that a copy of the video from the symposium would be available months later. That video was never made available to the public. Several requests for a copy of it went unanswered. I suspect the reason for that was the tape provided too much balance for those who planned on producing it.

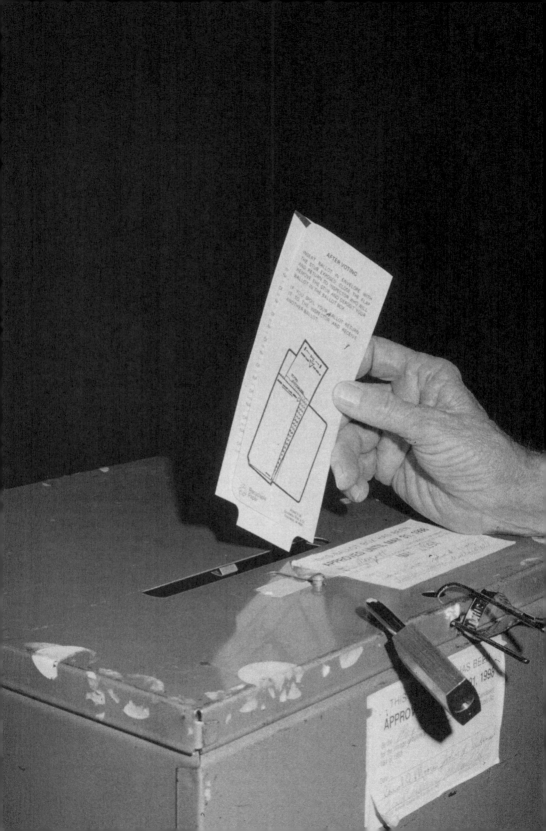

Chapter **24**

Learning From Oregon and Colorado

If you don't think bear hunting with bait and hounds can be eliminated in your state through a ballot initiative, has Roy Hyder from Oregon got news for you. He told members of the Michigan Bear Hunters Association at their annual convention in Gaylord during March of 1995 that Oregon hunters felt the same way, but the practices are now illegal in the state due to a referendum held there during the fall of 1994.

Measure 18, which passed by a four percent margin, outlawed the hunting of mountain lions with hounds in addition to the use of hounds and bait for hunting black bear. Hyder is cochairman of Oregonians for Wildlife Conservation, a group formed to fight Measure 18.

Oregon has healthy populations of both bear (estimated at more than 25,000 and increasing) and mountain lion and hunting with bait and hounds has helped manage those populations, not threatened them in any way. Because hunters knew that, they couldn't accept the fact those forms of hunting could be taken away, according to Hyder.

When the petition drive got underway to gather enough signatures to put the measure on the ballot, hunters didn't think those who supported it would be successful, Hyder said. Once the necessary signatures were obtained and the measure was placed on the ballot, many hunters still didn't believe it would pass because they didn't think enough residents would vote for it. They now know better and the same thing could happen anywhere.

The reason Hyder spoke to members of the state bear hunting organization was so they could learn from the Oregon experience and perhaps prevent the same thing from happening here. The lesson definitely made an impression and

(Left) Bear hunting with bait and dogs were lost at the ballot box in Oregon during 1994 and in Colorado two years earlier. Hunters in Michigan learned from what happened in those states.

certainly played a role in helping to prevent the banning of bear hunting with bait and dogs in Michigan. Roy said Oregonians were still learning from what happened to them during 1994. One of the most important lessons he mentioned is that the campaign against Measure 18 got started too late because the threat wasn't taken seriously.

"Anti-hunters know how to use the uneducated, uninformed people and your laws to their advantage," Hyder said. "Our educational efforts weren't as successful as we would have liked because we found out that urban people don't care about hunting and didn't want to learn.

"We also found out that anti-hunters don't care if they are accurate or truthful in what they say. Most of the film they used in their ads was shot outside Oregon and did not portray Oregon hunting. Their campaign is built around emotional appeal. When you get in a campaign like this, perception is reality regardless of what the facts are."

The question Michigan hunters had to ask themselves was, "Do we want to save hunting as much as they want to outlaw it," Hyder said. "You have a good chance to do right what Oregon did wrong, but it is going to take a lot of dedication and money to win," he concluded.

Rick Story, who is Executive Director of the Ohio based Wildlife Legislative Fund of America (WLFA), took his turn at the podium after Hyder and he reinforced what the Oregon resident said. The WLFA has been involved in battling many anti-hunting/trapping initiatives across the United States.

"The dollars separate the winners from the losers," Story said. "You need a deep, deep, deep war chest to win. A ballot issue campaign is a fund raising campaign. Once the dollars are in place, everything else is easy. If the dollars aren't there, you lose."

Story said $2 million will give Michigan hunters a chance of winning a bear hunting referendum.

"You are playing for stakes much higher than bear hunting," he told the audience. "You have to stand up and protect the fortress represented by sound wildlife management or it will be knocked down one brick at a time."

The loss of bear hunting with bait and hounds in Oregon represents one of those bricks. Another brick was lost in Colorado voting booths during the fall of 1992 when the same hunting methods were banned.

At the time, the question on people's minds was will Michigan be added to that list of states where voters make wildlife management decisions instead of the professionals who are trained to do so? It could have happened on November 5, 1996, but it didn't. Part of the reason it didn't, is Michigan residents who are concerned about proper wildlife management learned from what happened in Oregon and Colorado.

Hunting methods weren't actually the major bear hunting issue that brought about the referendum in Colorado. Spring bear hunting was. Both spring and fall bear hunts were held annually in the state.

Spring bear hunts were timed so that hunters were most likely to see males and lone females. Those are usually the first animals to leave dens in the spring. Females with cubs are normally the last to leave dens. Once sows and cubs leave dens, their movements are often restricted and they tend to avoid areas frequented by males such as bait sites because males prey on cubs.

For those reasons, sows with cubs are least likely to be encountered by hunters during spring seasons. Females in the company of cubs were also protected during hunting seasons in Colorado. Despite the safeguards, and the fact that spring seasons

Dollars separate the winners and losers during challenges to bear hunting like the one in Michigan during 1996. Conservationists were able to raise enough to win at the polls thanks to checks like the one Ottawa Sportsmen's Club President Russ Weisinger is handing over to U.P. Sportsmen's Alliance President Al Heidenreich.

probably offer a better opportunity to increase cub survival rather than reduce it, it didn't matter to those intent on curtailing bear hunting/management options.

How spring hunts increase cub survival is through the harvest of males. Since males are most likely to prey on cubs, spring bear seasons reduce the chances of this type of predation. The best opportunity to harvest males occurs during the spring because those hunts coincide with a portion of the black bear breeding season. Males are most active and, therefore, more vulnerable to hunters, during the breeding season. Spring hunts also provide the opportunity to eliminate potential nuisance animals from the population before they become a problem.

Due to the opposition to spring bear hunts in Colorado, the state Fish and Game Department developed a plan to phase that season out over a period of three years starting in 1992. Under the plan, the state's last spring bear hunt would have been held during 1994, with a limited number of permits available for participants. Bear hunting with hounds would have been eliminated at the same time because that method was only legal during the spring.

That wasn't good enough for anti-hunters. They saw the opportunity to go for even more. Due to the controversy surrounding bear hunting, they knew that hunting with bait was also vulnerable. So they started a petition drive to lump spring, bait and hound hunting together for an initiative on the fall ballot in 1992. They knew that even if the vote didn't go their way at the polls, spring and hound hunts would be out of the picture by 1995 anyway. Anti-hunters hoped to speed up their impact on bear hunting and they were successful in a big way.

Hunters in Colorado were less prepared than they were in Oregon to fight the referendum. In fact, there wasn't much of an organized effort to defeat the measure because a majority of hunters either didn't think it would pass or it would effect them. Some hunters probably even voted in favor of the changes, failing to realize a dangerous precedent was being set. If the public can decide the fate of bear hunting, they can make important decisions about any other form of hunting, ultimately impacting all forms of hunting.

What's so remarkable about what happened in Colorado is that the state Division of Wildlife probably had a hand in passing the referendum. The division contracted a company to survey public attitudes about bear hunting and the statements on the survey were written in such a biased fashion that the responses were easily predictable. Survey statements were written to generate negative responses. Nonhunters unfamiliar with bear hunting who participated in the survey were bound to have a negative attitude when they were done. Amazingly, the results of that survey were used to help set division policy.

The statement on the survey dealing with bait hunting read, "I object to the use of bait as a means of hunting black bears because it gives the hunter an unfair advantage over the bear." The statement regarding hound hunting was worded similarly: "I object to the use of dogs as a way of hunting black bear because it is not a fair way of hunting."

Participants were asked over the telephone if they agreed or disagreed with the statements. They should have been asked if they thought they were true or false because they were based upon false premises. However, participants would have had to be experienced bear hunters to realize that or to disagree with the statements. The statements were worded in such a way to generate overwhelming negative responses and that's exactly what happened.

It's no wonder that many nonhunters and some hunters in Colorado have the perception that bear hunting with bait and hounds is unethical and unsporting. A survey sponsored by the Division of Wildlife says so!

The statement regarding the use of bait should have been worded, "I support the use of bait as a means of hunting black bears because it gives hunters the best opportunity to identify their target and make a humane kill." The statement about hounding bears could have been written in a more positive, accurate way as well. Interestingly, a statement designed to assess public attitudes about the Division of Wildlife was written the way the others should have been: "I believe the Colorado Division of Wildlife carefully and effectively regulates the sport hunting of black bears in the state."

Most participants agreed with that statement, despite the fact that spring hunts, hunting with hounds and bait were being permitted. This accurately reflects that nonhunters and hunters alike trust the state agency empowered with the authority to manage bears to do the best job possible, and that's the way it should be. More importantly, the results from that statement illustrate how meaningless the responses to the other statements were and that how statements are worded can bias results.

The Colorado Division of Wildlife contributed to the elimination of bear hunting with bait and dogs in that state through a poorly worded telephone survey claiming both methods were unfair forms of hunting. The results of the biased survey were used to help set division policy.

Success of the bear hunting referendum in Colorado set the stage for the same thing in Oregon during 1994; Idaho, Washington and Michigan for 1996. The Oregon Department of Fish and Game contributed to the passage of the bear hunting referendum in that state, but it wasn't something they did by choice. Unfortunately, their hands were tied by a misguided state law that prohibits state agencies from taking a position on issues that will be or are on the ballot. The agency was permitted to provide information to parties on both sides of the issue, but couldn't take sides.

Fortunately, Michigan wasn't caught in the same position as the state agencies in Oregon and Colorado when it came to bear hunting. The Natural Resources Commission unanimously adopted a resolution at their January 1996 meeting expressing their support and that of the DNR for current bear management practices, which include bear hunting with bait and dogs.

The resolution started out by stating that scientific wildlife management has been successful in providing abundant populations of wildlife and that hunting is an essential tool in managing some species such as black bear. Then it gets into specifics about bear management in Michigan:

"The Michigan Department of Natural Resources uses sport hunting through a sophisticated zone and quota system to manage the state's bear populations; and 96 percent of the state's bears are taken by sport hunters using hounds or bait; and the efforts of the DNR's wildlife professionals to scientifically manage bear populations would be severely and irreparably damaged if these hunting methods were banned; and unmanaged bear populations would hurt the species because its numbers would become incompatible with carrying capacities and human tolerance levels . . ."

Under the current statewide permit system for bear hunting that has been in effect since 1990, the number of hunters who can hunt bear in each bear management unit is limited. A specific number of harvest tags are issued for each unit and the total permit allocation over the past five years has varied from 5,096 to 7,305, with an annual rate of success among permittees from 23 to 30 percent.

Permit quotas have been increased slightly during recent years because bear populations have been steadily increasing since the permit system started and the number of bruins should continue to go up. However, it is important to prevent bears from increasing too fast to control nuisance complaints from the animals, which have been occurring more frequently during recent years. Current estimates put the bear population in the U.P. alone at a minimum of 11,500 adults.

Annual bear harvests statewide under the permit system have varied from 739 to 1,512, with the highest harvest during the 1998 season with bear numbers at an alltime high.

The final part of the resolution adopted by the NRC reads: "Be it therefore resolved that the Natural Resources Commission and the Michigan Department of Natural Resources reaffirm their commitment to scientific wildlife management and the use of sport hunting as an essential management tool, and that the NRC and DNR express support of and desire to continue the use of all bear hunting methods currently permitted in Michigan, including bait hunting and hound hunting, to scientifically manage bears."

The fact that Michigan does not have spring bear hunting also separates it from the other states where bear hunting has been successfully challenged. The two major stumbling blocks that would determine the outcome of a hunting referendum in this state, however, were hunter apathy and money. Fortunately, those potential problems were overcome in a big way.

COLORADO BEAR HUNTING

Bear hunting and management has undergone major changes in Colorado since spring, bait and hound hunting were eliminated during 1992. Fall hunting remained legal, but the kill declined significantly for a couple of years because hunters were restricted in the methods they could use. Due to the opportunity to see long distances in the mountains, spot and stalk hunting became the most popular method. Some hunters also used predator calls to try to lure bears to them.

By 1995, Colorado hunters had adapted to the change in regulations and the Fish and Game Department increased hunting pressure, to get the bear harvest back to the levels where it had been before the referendum. In the meantime, however, bear numbers increased significantly as a result of reduced hunter harvest of bruins prior to '95. More bears created more problems, causing numerous conflicts with people. There have been a number of bear attacks on people in Colorado since 1992, one of which was a fatality. A bruin killed and ate a person in that case. A total of 12 cases involving aggressive bears were recorded in Colorado during 1997 and there were six during '95.

The state Fish and Game Department developed a more stringent policy for dealing with problem bears due to their increase. Bears used to be killed the third time they got in trouble. Starting in 1993, nuisance animals were eliminated the second time they caused a problem. Problem bears could be identified through ear tags that were attached the first time they got in trouble. A total of 70 bears were killed in the state under the two strikes and you're out policy during 1994. That same year, an additional 42 bears died of nonhunting mortality, including road kills. The more bears there are, the greater the opportunity for them to cause accidents in addition to getting into trouble with people in other ways.

The number of nuisance bears that are known to have been killed in the state increased to 118 during 1995. The total nonhunting mortality of bears in Colorado during '95 was 170. That figure is significant because it equals the number of bears killed legally by hunters during the September bear only season in 1994. Hunters were no longer able to effectively harvest enough bears to manage the population like they were before. State Fish and Game and federal Animal Damage Control employees were/are required to invest much more time than they used to, to manage the state's bears. More land owners were also forced to shoot bears to protect their property.

There were 811 bear nuisance complaints recorded in Colorado during 1994 and that figure went up to a whopping 1,056 in '95. Besides the nonhunting mortality those two years, more bears were live trapped and moved. There were 42 bruins relocated during 1994 and 102 were trapped and transferred for '95. The change in bear hunting and management in the state increased the risk to people from bears. When a spring hunt was held, a significant number of problem animals were eliminated by hunters before they could do any damage.

On top of the increase in time by state employees to deal with nuisance bear activity, the Colorado Department of Fish and Game is also responsible for reimbursing farmers, ranchers and other land owners for damage caused by bears. Payments for bear damage by the state agency have skyrocketed since 1992. The state paid out $94,163.36 for bear damage in '92. By '93 that figure was up to $158,213.24 and it hit $297,682.71 during 1995.

Ironically, the money to pay bear damage complaints in Colorado comes from revenue paid by hunters. Since the public voted for a change in bear hunting and management that is responsible for increased bear damage, the money for those payments should come from public funds. It's interesting how the people and groups who are so vocal in pushing for changes are nowhere to be found when it comes to dealing with repercussions from the changes they help bring about!

Prior to 1993, 80 percent of Colorado's bear harvest occurred during the spring season and the number of hunters who could participate in that hunt was limited by a permit drawing. An unlimited number of bear licenses were available during the fall to hunters during deer and elk seasons. The highest hunter harvest of bears was recorded in 1988 when 623 were tallied.

However, the kill was much lower than that most years. During the last three years spring hunts were in effect, for example, the highest harvest was 475. That occurred during 1992 when 312 bears were registered in the spring and 163 during the fall. In

1991, there were 429 bruins registered; 323, spring and 106, fall. During 1990, only 402 bears were registered by hunters, 347 on the spring hunt and 55 during fall.

Hunters only harvested a total of 274 bears during 1993, when hunting was restricted to the fall. There were 1,000 permits available for a September bear hunt and 154 bruins were bagged during that season. Unlimited bear licenses were still available to correspond with deer and elk seasons and another 124 bears were registered then.

As mentioned earlier, 170 bears were bagged during 1994 by the 1,000 hunters with bear permits. An additional 190 bruins were shot during deer and elk season that year for a total hunter harvest of 360.

Colorado doubled their September bear tags to 2,000 during 1995 to increase the harvest and it worked. There were 281 taken in September. Deer and elk hunters claimed another 251, for a total kill of 532. The number of September bear tags was increased to 3,290 by 1996, but the harvest ended up lower than it had been the year before—521.

Even though the bear harvest in Colorado for 1995 was in the ballpark of what it used to be, there was still an increase in bears killed under damage complaints. And it was necessary for the state to issue an unlimited number of bear licenses to achieve that kill. The increased bear population also made the higher harvest possible. The open habitat in much of the state's bear range makes alternative hunting techniques such as spot and stalking, effective when lots of bears are present.

Spot and stalk hunting would be of little value to Michigan hunters where thick cover common in bear habitat limits visibility. Even if unlimited bear licenses were issued, which would be necessary if the use of bait and hounds was eliminated, it would be impossible for hunters to harvest the 1,300 to 1,500 bruins that have been taken annually under current regulations. Bear numbers have been steadily increasing at those harvest levels. The process of population growth would be speeded up with lower kills.

Also worthy of note in Colorado since spring bear seasons ended is that there are as many, if not more, orphaned cubs as before. Females with cubs are killed by cars and under the stringent nuisance control program. Cub mortality has probably also increased, due to the presence of more adult male bears in the population.

The elimination of bait and dogs for bear hunting has also resulted in an increased harvest of female bears in Colorado. There was a six percent increase in the harvest of females during the four years after the referendum when compared to the four years before the vote. ANTI-HUNTERS WHO CLAIMED THEY WERE PROTECTING CUBS BY ELIMINATING SPRING HUNTING ARE ACTUALLY RESPONSIBLE FOR FEWER CUBS BEING BORN UNDER CURRENT MANAGEMENT. The higher harvest of females means there are fewer of them to have cubs.

THE OREGON STORY

Interestingly, spring bear hunting was not targeted during the Oregon referendum, just the use of bait and hounds. However, the reason for that is probably that spring bear hunting in that state was and is done primarily to control bear damage to trees, according to Wildlife Biologist Don Whittaker. He said spring hunts in Oregon are restricted.

So there was a spring hunt in the state during 1995, but only 62 bears were taken then. Without the use of bait and dogs, the kill declined by 53 percent from 1994. A total of 686 bears were registered by hunters in Oregon during 1995 compared to 1,450 in 1994. Like Colorado, Oregon has a lot of open, mountainous terrain where spot and stalk hunting is possible. Fall bear licenses sold in conjunction with deer and elk seasons are also unlimited.

Despite the alternative hunting methods and an increase in the number of bear tags issued, Oregon's bear harvest by hunters remained below pre-referendum levels after four years. Hunters killed 1,007 bears in the state during 1996, 812 during '97 and 1,053 for '98. Nuisance bears and nonhunting mortality increased, as it did in Colorado, to compensate for the reduced hunter harvest and the presence of more bruins.

Bear damage complaints increased by 64 percent and the number of bears killed during damage control increased by 34 percent between 1994 and '95. Whittaker said there were 327 bear complaints in 1994, resulting in the killing of 151 bruins. There were 537 complaints resulting in the deaths of 205 bears for '95. The number of bear complaints were up to 828 by 1998 and 302 of those animals were killed by land owners, state and federal employees.

Nuisance complaints about bears are sure to escalate even further in the future. Whittaker commented that bear hunting in Oregon was not removing enough animals from the population annually to control their numbers with the use of bait and dogs. Without those methods, bears there are bound to increase even faster.

Since the use of bait and dogs were outlawed in Colorado, the harvest of female bears has increased by six percent. People who claimed they were trying to prevent cubs from being orphaned by eliminating the spring season as well as the use of bait and dogs, are responsible for fewer cubs being born under new management!

241

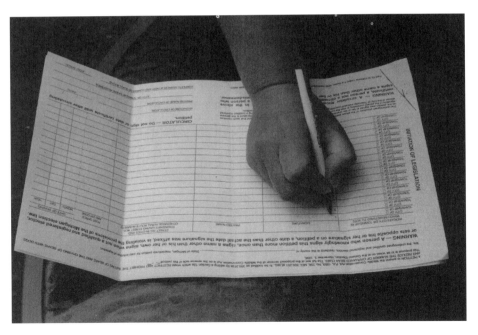

Michigan residents who signed petitions supporting a ban on bear hunting with bait and dogs were misled, both by wording on the petitions and what they were told by those circulating them. If people circulating the petitions had not been paid for gathering signatures, the effort would have been less successful.

Chapter 25

Referendum Process Flaws

Two things are crystal clear to me in view of the fact a measure to ban bear hunting with bait and dogs was approved for the November ballot during 1996. Number one is that money can indeed buy anything. If it weren't for the deep pockets of an individual ramrodding the anti-bear hunting campaign combined with funding from national anti-hunting organizations, there's no way the issue would have endured the lengthy process.

Secondly, there's no common sense in the referendum process. If there were, the proposal would not have made it on the ballot either.

The referendum process is based on lofty ideals. If enough registered voters feel strongly about an issue, it can be put on the ballot through signing petitions, once those signatures are certified by the Board of Canvassers. Considering the fact that hundreds of thousands of valid signatures are required to put something on the ballot (about 250,000 during '96), it's not an easy task.

However, if you've got enough money, and are willing to pay people to gather signatures, getting the necessary number isn't difficult either. The job is also much easier if people are misled and lied to, to convince them to sign the petitions. That's exactly what happened in regard to the bear hunting referendum.

Each and every Citizens United For Bear petition that was circulated had wording in bold type that clearly stated the number of orphaned bear cubs would be reduced by eliminating bear hunting with bait and dogs. The implication is totally false. Female bears with cubs and cubs have been and are protected during bear season, so there's no way that banning those hunting methods will reduce the number of orphaned cubs.

The precise wording on the petitions asks for an amendment to the Wildlife Conservation Act that would ". . . RESTRICT AND PROHIBIT THE BAITING OF BEARS AND THE CHASING OF BEARS WITH DOGS AND REDUCE THE NUMBER OF ORPHANED BEAR CUBS."

Elimination of the targeted hunting methods would have, in fact, increased the opportunity for orphaning cubs. In Pennsylvania, for example, a state where the use of bait and dogs are prohibited for bear hunting, a significant percentage of the annual bear harvest is composed of cubs and adult females that have cubs. The major benefits of hunting with bait and dogs is they allow hunters the best opportunity to identify bears that are seen and select for those that are legal.

Here's some of the other language included in the Michigan initiative: "The lawful taking of bears by any means shall not be permitted during the same time period as the open season for the following animals: deer, bobcat, or raccoon, if the season for such animal allows for hunting with dogs or allows for baiting."

Bow deer season begins on October 1 statewide and so does raccoon hunting in the U.P. Some form of deer hunting remains open until January 1 and all bears are in dens long before then. So the end of September is the latest bears could have been hunted, if the referendum passed.

Other wording of the proposal would prohibit bear hunting before September 1: "It shall be unlawful for any person to take a bear by any means during the period from March 1 through August 31 of any calendar year."

Part of the purpose for that wording was to prohibit bear hunting in Michigan during the spring. A spring bear season was only held in the state during one year— 1953—on an experimental basis. A spring bear hunt is unnecessary under current bear management and there are currently no plans to establish a spring bear hunt in the state.

Hunters who thought that bears could be hunted at the same time as deer, the way they used to be, if bear hunting with bait and dogs were eliminated, were obviously mistaken. At least that wouldn't be possible under regulations that would have been created by passage of the referendum. Had wording included in the referendum become law, the only way bear could have been hunted during the same time frame as deer is if deer hunting with bait were eliminated during part or all of the season.

Of course, that was the purpose of the referendum, to restrict hunting as much as possible. The measure obviously had implications for other forms of hunting besides bear.

Additional initiative language would have made it unlawful to put food out for bears at any time of the year, not just for hunting: "It is unlawful for any person to place bait, or to assist another person in placing bait, for the purpose of attracting bears at any time during any calendar year."

So rural residents who like to feed wildlife, including bear, would have been prohibited from doing so if the referendum passed. Even camp owners who feed deer and birds with food that also attracts bear, would have been prohibited from doing so if this measure would have become the law of the land.

Regardless of the false information contained in the wording on the petitions, the language was approved by whatever state agency or board does such things. That's obviously a major shortcoming in the referendum process that sets the stage for other abuses. There should be a requirement that the wording on all referendum petitions be accurate and factual.

Besides the inaccurate wording on the petitions, I was told by a number of people who were approached by those circulating the anti-bear hunting petitions that additional lies were spoken to encourage voters to sign on as supporters. I'm confident that the necessary signatures would not have been obtained if petitioners had been honest with state residents. However, the bottom line is the opponents of bear hunting did get the necessary number of signatures through deception. In fact, they got almost 100,000 more than they needed—341,000.

If the referendum process works the way it should, the inaccurate wording on the petitions should have been enough to prevent consideration of any of the signatures on them. Unfortunately, that isn't how it works. That's where the lack of common sense comes in.

The Board of Canvassers held a "hearing" in Lansing on July 25, 1996 to make a decision about placing the bear hunting issue on the ballot. I was told they would take public comment before making a decision, so I was there to make sure they understood every person who signed those petitions did so under false pretenses, which should have been enough to render each and every signature invalid.

Wrong! I was told by the board and their attorney that the accuracy of the wording on the petitions has no bearing on their decision to certify signatures. However, at the same time, I was told that if I had notarized affidavits from voters who signed petitions that they were lied to by people circulating petitions, that they would consider those. In other words, it's okay if the petitions themselves are inaccurate, but not the people carrying them.

That doesn't make sense to me. I guess I just don't have a full understanding of how the system works. I was told by the board that the courts are the only place that the petition language could have been challenged, and that would only have been possible after the election. In the meantime, millions of dollars were spent in a major media campaign to present both sides of the issue, an issue that should never have been on the ballot in the first place.

There are undoubtedly some issues handled legitimately by the referendum process and I understand the value of having such an opportunity to get topics before the state's voters, but the way the bear hunting topic came down is a total turnoff. Not only were voters who signed petitions deceived, some of the voters who went to the polls were similarly misled. Fortunately, as it turned out, the majority of the voters who went to the polls were smart enough to sort fact from fiction.

The CUB sponsored hunting initiative that appeared on the ballot had nothing whatsoever to do with protecting cubs or any other bears. It was all about conning people into believing the specified changes would have benefited bears by manipulating the democratic process. Residents who voted for the measure joined the ranks of those who signed petitions in being fooled by CUB's deceptive practices. The reality is that if the changes that CUB sought were enacted by whatever means, bears would have been the losers and so would the residents of Michigan, along with professional wildlife management.

Michigan's voting public were pawns in the game being played by a group composed largely of nonresidents that tried to dictate how black bears should be managed in this state. Their price of admission was substantial, but they were committed to spend whatever they thought it would take to buy your vote. As it turned out, most voters were smart enough to see through the smoke screen being emitted by the members of CUB, proving their vote wasn't for sale.

My biggest fear was that the facts wouldn't matter at the polls anymore than they did during the petition process. Fortunately, I didn't have anything to worry about. Proposal D was not only defeated, it was voted down by a wide margin!

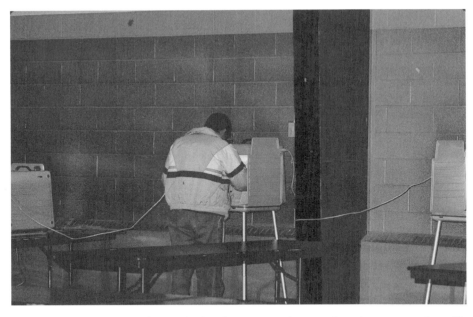

Most Michigan voters understood what they were voting on when they went to the polls during '96. Proposal D was defeated by 62 percent of the vote and G was approved by 69 percent.

Chapter **26**

Referendum Results

During 1996, Michigan joined the list of states in which traditional wildlife management decision making was challenged at the polls. A measure was put on the November ballot that, if passed, would have put wildlife management in the hands of voters and taken it away from the professionals in the Department of Natural Resources who are most qualified to make such decisions. The measure was labeled proposal D. It would have eliminated the use of bait and dogs for bear hunting and shortened bear season.

Similar proposals have passed in a number of other states, but Proposal D did not pass in Michigan. The reason why this happened can be summarized in one sentence. Lots of money, being proactive, thousands of hours of volunteer effort by nonagency personnel and giving voters a choice.

Proposal G also appeared on Michigan's ballot, which vested the authority for making wildlife management decisions in the hands of the Natural Resources Commission. This commission is the policy setting body for the state DNR, with members appointed by the Governor.

G gave the authority to the Natural Resources Commission to make wildlife management decisions, with advice from DNR professionals. Specific wording requires that principals of sound wildlife management be used in making decisions. This measure also clearly provided for the opportunity for public input on wildlife issues before being acted on by the commission. Public input has been possible on wildlife management issues in Michigan for a long time, but many members of the public weren't aware of that opportunity.

It would have been possible for both proposals to be approved, but that did not happen. It appeared as though most voters clearly understood what they were voting for. Sixty-two percent of the people who went to the polls voted against D and G was approved by a 69 percent margin. D was defeated in every county in the state and G was approved in every county.

Anyone who doubts that passage of the bear hunting referendum in Michigan during 1996 would have set a dangerous precedent only has to look at Colorado. Trapping was outlawed there by popular vote a few years after valuable bear hunting methods were voted out. Other forms of wildlife management may follow. (DNR Photo)

If both measures would have passed, the one that had the widest margin of votes was supposed to take precedence.

I'm pleased to have played a role in the defeat of D and passage of G. The fact that there are thousands of others like me in Michigan who are concerned about the proper management of wildlife such as bear, and were willing to get involved, is why it happened. A tremendous team effort on the part of sportsmen and women across the state was responsible for educating voters about the best choices to make on their ballots.

The fact that Michigan has a strong contingent of outdoor organizations was important. The understanding among residents of the state that proposal D was not just about bear hunting was also important. The passage of D would have set a dangerous precedent that could have eventually impacted any and all forms of hunting, trapping, fishing and other methods of management. This realization mobilized a lot of people who otherwise might not have gotten involved.

Colorado is a perfect example of the potential impacts wildlife management referendums can have. That state was one of the first to lose bear hunting with bait and dogs at the polls. Years later, trapping also appeared on the ballot and another wildlife management opportunity was lost.

Wildlife research by state or federal agencies and universities can also be negatively impacted by ballot initiatives as Massachusetts found out during 1996. A proposal on that state's ballot that outlawed the use of hounds and snares for hunting and trapping also eliminated their use for research purposes. Bear dogs used to play an important role in bear research in that state, but that's no longer possible.

Michigan residents who are concerned about wildlife management also learned valuable lessons from what happened in Colorado and Oregon. Many hunters in those states did not believe that bear hunting proposals would make it on the ballot, much less be approved by voters. The threat wasn't taken seriously, if at all, until too late in those states.

That did not happen in Michigan. Our state's referendum was anticipated by at least two years by those of us who were paying attention. On a personal level, I had been planning on writing a book about Michigan black bear and the pending referendum gave me the incentive to do it, with the idea of using it as an educational tool. I had been closely following bear research and management in the state for many years as a hunter, writer and photographer, spending a lot of time with state researchers.

My wife and I published the first edition of *Understanding Michigan Black Bear* in the fall of 1995. We crammed as much information as possible about bears in the book, which ended up being 192 pages. Thanks to the support of a dedicated group of bear hunters—the Upper Peninsula Bear Houndsmen—copies of the above book were sent to all state legislators and I would like to think the information on its pages helped in the passage of proposal G and defeat of D.

You're holding the second edition of the book in your hands. This edition has far more information than the first. The information it includes is designed to help reduce the chances of another challenge to bear hunting besides educating the public about bears and bear management.

Also during 1995, a coalition of hunting organizations formed the Citizens for Professional Wildlife Management, which was the main group that campaigned against D and for G. Ron Lundberg from Davison did a superb job of heading up this essential coalition. One of the most important members of CPWM was the Michigan United Conservation Clubs. This conglomeration of sporting groups that already existed provided staff members and their office for fund raising and educational efforts. Michigan Chapters of Safari Club International also played a prominent role, as did many active hunting organizations in the state and one of Michigan's most prominent hunters—Ted Nugent.

Fund raising was the backbone for the successful campaign for G and against D. Like any political campaign, and that's what this was, the amount of money in the war chest often separates winners from losers. The Upper Peninsula Sportsmens Alliance, one of the member groups of CPWM, came up with the best fund raising idea that helped lead to victory.

The alliance conducted a raffle that raised over $1 million ($1,010,000). The grand prize is what set this raffle apart from others. Forty acres of recreational land with a log cabin kit to put on it, was the grand prize. The 17 other prizes in the raffle included valuable outdoor equipment. Tickets sold extremely well.

More than 200,000 tickets were sold in the raffle all across the country. So many tickets were sold, in fact, that a larger drum had to be constructed to hold them all, days before the drawing was held. Dave and Jean Marko from Flint sold the most tickets—an amazing 50,000. UPSA officials Jim Dabb and Al Heidenreich and their wives put in a tremendous amount of effort coordinating the sale of those tickets. The couples spent countless hours processing sales, sending out tickets and keeping track of the

A number of influential people and organizations played important roles in protecting professional wildlife management in Michigan such as rock-n-roller Ted Nugent shown here during a practice session with bow and arrow. MUCC, Safari Club International, Michigan Bear Hunters Association, U.P. Bear Houndsmen and UPSA were some of the many organizations that did their part.

income. The Heidenreich's daughter—Kathy Clawson—did a lot of the bookkeeping. They deserve credit for the many hours of volunteer effort devoted to this all important task.

Appropriately enough, the raffle drawing was held on September 28, 1996 at the Sagola Township Sportsmen's Club near Channing. It was National Hunting & Fishing Day. In fact, it was the 25th anniversary of the celebration of that day.

The money raised in the raffle, auctions, banquets and from pledges made it possible to buy critical television time and ad space in newspapers to get the message to voters before the election. Long before proposal D was officially on the ballot, bear hunting organizations were collecting pledges. A total of $1.8 million dollars was raised and most of it was used in the fight to protect professional wildlife management.

So many tickets were sold for the UPSA raffle that a larger drum had to be constructed to hold them all days before the drawing was held on the 25th anniversary of National Hunting & Fishing Day.

The ticket drawn for the grand prize proved to be one of 1,000 purchased by the Ottawa Sportsmen's Club in Baraga. Club President Russ Weisinger commented that they didn't buy that quantity of tickets with winning in mind. The club did so to help protect Michigan's hunting heritage.

Reserving television time early is critical during an election year. If CPWM had waited until signatures were certified to put the measure on the ballot, it might have been too late to purchase the necessary TV time. Successful fund raising efforts made it possible to get the necessary time.

Besides ad time and space, proposals D and G generated a lot of news coverage. Members of CPWM met with the editorial boards of many major newspapers in the state and got the support of all but one of them. To the credit of the Detroit News, one of Michigan's largest newspapers, their editorial writer took the time to go on bear hunts with bait and dogs, to find out for herself what they were like.

A Seattle, Washington based crew from CNN (the Cable News Network) did the same thing. I took the editorial writer and CNN crew on bait hunts and the Michigan Bear Hunters Association hosted them on hound hunts.

Michigan has its share of outdoor writers and outdoor television shows, most of which devoted space and time to the ballot proposals. On a personal note, I wrote more newspaper and magazine articles about black bear during 1996 than ever before, in an effort to get the truth out about bear hunting and management. I actually spent a lot of time countering false information distributed by the proponents of D.

Most of the campaign by the proponents of D was designed to deceive the public

The grand prize winning ticket in the UPSA Raffle was drawn jointly by (left to right) UPSA President Al Heidenreich, DNR Director K. L. Cool, UPSA Officer Jim Dabb and the late MUCC Executive Director Rick Jameson. All four men played key roles in the battle to save bear hunting. The winning ticket was one of 1,000 purchased by the Ottawa Sportsmen's Club.

and we didn't let them get away with it. They maintained that eliminating bear hunting with bait and dogs would protect cubs. Cubs have been protected in Michigan since 1948. Sows in the company of cubs are also protected.

They claimed that both hunting methods are unsporting, unethical and inhumane. Both hunting methods that were being challenged increase the opportunity for humane kills rather than decrease it. They also offer hunters the best means of clearly identifying protected versus unprotected bears. I've always understood that two of the most important responsibilities of an ethical hunter are to identify their target and make clean kills. I've also been told that nonhunters support hunting that meets that criteria.

In terms of rates of success, approximately 25 percent of bait and dog hunters in Michigan manage to shoot a bear. Any method that only results in one out of four hunters filling a tag does not qualify as unsporting.

Proponents of D also claimed that bait and dog hunting was hurting the state's bear population, another falsehood. The bear population has been increasing annually under a permit system started in 1990. Our permit system is similar to those in Minnesota and Wisconsin, limiting hunter numbers in specific management units, offering the best protection for bear numbers. Passage of D would have eliminated Michigan's very successful bear management system.

Those who supported D also told voters they weren't against bear hunting, just the use of bait and dogs. Then the Make-A-Wish Foundation sent a youngster from Minnesota, who had a brain tumor, on an Alaskan brown bear hunt. That hunt, which involved neither bait or dogs, was strongly opposed by The Fund For Animals, one of the groups seeking passage of D in Michigan.

The support of Governor John Engler and DNR Director K. L. Cool, who accepted the directorship about the time the referendum was heating up, also played a role in the defeat of D and passage of G. Director Cool appeared in commercials supporting proposal G and he was able to do that because he is not classified as a civil servant. And no public funds were used to make the commercials.

As far as advice for other states who may face a referendum on wildlife management in the future, I would suggest the formation of fund raising efforts by coalitions of sporting groups like CPWM as soon as possible. The more time they have to raise as much money as possible, the better. I would also suggest making an attempt to have measures like proposal G passed in states before other hunting measures make it on the ballot.

I didn't mention that Michigan's proposal G was passed by the state legislature. Proposal D got on the ballot through the collection of voter signatures. People who circulated petitions to get D on the ballot were paid up to $2 per signature. And there's no requirement that petition language be accurate to get a measure on the ballot. Wording on the Michigan petitions claimed that a ban on bear hunting with bait and dogs would protect cubs, which is false, but it helped them get the signatures they needed. The petition language could only have been challenged after the election.

Another thing I think may help in the effort to protect professional wildlife management is solid research on the hunting methods that are being questioned. To my knowledge, not enough research effort has been spent gathering specific data on bear hunting with bait and dogs. In my opinion, it's time for that to change.

We do know basic information about how many bears are bagged by hunters using these methods, that hunters select for males, the opportunity for humane kills is maximized and success rates are much lower than most people realize. What we don't know is how many bears visit bait sites and benefit from this supplemental food source versus the number shot by hunters. Nor do we know how many of those bears only visit them nocturnally or how much human contact is required at baits to cause bears to change their habits such as reverting to nocturnal feeding or abandoning the sites altogether.

And there's no specific information that I'm aware of to quantify the black bears' preference for natural foods over bait. I know the use of baits is much lower during years of natural food abundance and the harvest with this method undergoes a corresponding decline, but how much lower? There is evidence that the use of bait for bear hunting can reduce nuisance complaints from bears, especially during years with poor natural food supplies, but how do you prove or disprove this is true? There's also evidence that bear hunting with bait does not create nuisance animals. I suspect that enough information is available to verify that from the hundreds of radio collared bruins that have been monitored, if the data is examined with that in mind.

Research can be designed to answer pressing questions about bear hunting with hounds, too. In many cases, scientific studies would be helpful to verify and quantity some of the things that hunters already know or think they know. Everyone benefits from information generated through research, even if the results are different than expected.

The Michigan United Conservation Clubs can provide additional advice for anyone who may face a referendum similar to Michigan's in the future. The telephone number for MUCC is 517-371-1041. The address is P.O. Box 30235, Lansing, MI 48909. I would also be willing to help in any way I can.

Books by Richard P. Smith

Understanding Michigan Black Bear—2nd Edition—Learn all about Michigan black bears; their habits, life history and behavior in addition to how to avoid problems from them when in bear country. One of the chapters is a history of bear attacks. The text also provides valuable insights into bear research and management in the state. (256 pages; more than100 photos)
    Price: $19.50 postpaid

Great Michigan Deer Tales, Book 1—Learn How, Where and When some of the state's Biggest Bucks were bagged, including a Boone & Crockett bow kill taken by **Mitch Rompola** from Traverse City. Read about whitetails with the largest ANTLERS as well as those that were the HEAVIEST and OLDEST. If you are interested in bagging a BOOK BUCK in Michigan, studying this collection of success stories will help make it happen. There's no better way to learn than from those who have already accomplished the feat. (128 pages; 40 photos)
    Price: $15.50 postpaid

Great Michigan Deer Tales, Book 2—More Great Deer Tales from Michigan. Read about the highest scoring typical ever recorded for Michigan through 1997 seasons. Find out about the biggest bucks bagged by **women** in the state. Learn about trophy bucks with **locked antlers**. Read about a trophy rack recovered after almost 40 years and the end of a 70-year mystery surrounding a B&C nontypical. If you haven't gotten the first book yet, you will want to get both.
    Price: $16.50 postpaid; Set of Book 1 & 2—$28 (save $4)

Stand Hunting for Whitetails—Learn the best places to hunt, most productive times, dressing for -20 F, how to hunt safely above the ground and how to avoid being detected by deer from ground and elevated stands. Read about Boone and Crockett bucks and a hunt with baseball great **Wade Boggs**. Stand hunting is the most popular and effective whitetail hunting method. **Learn how to do it more effectively!** (256 pages)
    Price: $18.50 postpaid

Tracking Wounded Deer—2nd Edition—Learn how to recover all of the deer you shoot by reading blood sign, tracking after dark and in the snow and using a string tracker. Decide when to begin tracking, determine type of hit and distinguish between tracks of wounded and healthy deer. This book is must reading for bowhunters since trailing arrowed deer is part of every successful hunt. Eight pages of color photos show blood and hair sign. (160 pages; 72 photos)
    Price: $19.50 postpaid

Deer Hunting—2nd Edition—This best selling book was so popular it was updated to include even more information and photographs. Learn all you need to know to successfully hunt whitetails and mule deer. There are bonus chapters on deer biology and management, hunting ethics and more. For beginners or experienced veterans like the author. (260 pages; 139 photos)

   Price: $18.00 postpaid

MICHIGAN BIG GAME RECORDS (1ST-3RD EDITIONS)—The 3rd edition is a bigger and better reference for Michigan hunters with the addition of turkey records. This 272-page volume continues the tradition of providing the best and latest information about trophy deer, bear and elk hunting in the state. The who, how, where and when of trophy kills from 1989–1992 are covered in the 3rd edition. Those taken from 1986–'88 are discussed in the 256-page 2nd edition and trophies taken through 1985 are covered in the 1st edition (216 pages). Each edition of the record book has different chapters about big game hunting in Michigan, with emphasis on deer, and hundreds of photos. You will want to own a set of all three books to become one of the state's most knowledgeable big game hunters. **We are sold out of the 4th edition.**

   All three editions remaining are offered in both hard(HC) and soft(SC) cover versions.

   Price: Set of 3(SC) $55, 2nd &3rd Editions(SC) $21 each, 1st Edition $18
   Set of 3(HC) $113, 1st,2nd,& 3rd Editions(HC) $39 each

Reduced

Hunting Rabbits & Hares—The first complete book written on the subject that tells all there is to know about hunting all species of North American rabbits and hares with shotgun, rifle, handgun, black powder arms and archery equipment. Additional chapters cover population cycles, tularemia and detailed photos show how to butcher these small game animals without cutting the body cavity open. (153 pages; 130 photos)

   Price: $13 postpaid (SPECIAL PRICE, $3 OFF)

Animal Tracks & Signs Of North America—It's the first guide book including actual photos of wildlife tracks and sign rather than sketches. Bonus chapters cover aging tracks, tracking wildlife and much more. (271 pages; 200 photos)

   Price: $20 postpaid.

Hunting Trophy Black Bear—A 328-page hard cover volume with 157 photos. Information on this book's fact-filled pages tells the reader all about hunting this controversial big game animal, covering all of the bases as far as hunting techniques, guns and bows. Record book bears, hiring a guide, bear biology, management and the future for black bear and more are also covered in the text.

   Price: $23 postpaid.

Book Order Form

Quantity   Price

_____   **Understanding Michigan Black Bear ($19.50)**   _____

_____   **Great Michigan Deer Tales, Book 1 ($15.50)**   _____

_____   **Great Michigan Deer Tales, Book 2 ($16.50);**   _____

_____   **Set of Book 1 & 2—($28)**   _____

_____   **Stand Hunting for Whitetails ($18.50)**   _____

_____   **Tracking Wounded Deer—2nd Edition ($19.50)**   _____

_____   **Deer Hunting—2nd Edition ($18.00)**   _____

_____   **Michigan Big Game Records (Specify edition)**   _____

_____   **Hunting Rabbits & Hares ($13)**   _____

_____   **Animal Tracks & Signs Of North America ($20)**   _____

_____   **Hunting Trophy Black Bear ($23)**   _____

Total Payment Enclosed   _____

Prices include postage and handling. Make checks payable to:

Smith Publications

Please send U.S. funds.
Canadian orders add $1/book(Parcel Post) or $3/book(Air Mail).

Name_____

Address_____

City _____   **State/Zip** _____

Phone# _____

Circle card type:

MC/Visa #_____

Expiration Date _____

Signature _____

Send orders to: Smith Publications
814 Clark St.
Marquette, MI 49855